David Munrow

Foreword by André Previn

Instruments
of the Middle Ages and Renaissance

Oxford University Press
Music Department
44 Conduit Street London W1

Foreword

First published 1976. Twice reprinted 1976

ISBN 0 19 321321 4

Published by Oxford University Press
Music Department
44 Conduit Street, London W I R ODE

Designed by Alan Bartram
Photographs by Godfrey Macdomnic
Printed in Great Britain
by Shenval Press Limited, Harlow

I admire David Munrow enormously, for a variety of reasons. He is, without question, a formidable virtuoso; to hear him play any of the dozens of instruments which have almost become his private domain, is to listen to a consummate artist. He is also the undisputed expert in the field of medieval and renaissance music, and his Early Music Consort of London is a shining light in the vast field of British music and musicians. He is possessed of an acerbic wit, is a popular broadcaster, tells a great anecdote, has with it all the face of a slightly immoral schoolboy, and finally, is shorter than I am, a statistic I cherish.

In this book, you and I will at last be able to find out all about the music and the instruments which David and his musicians have done so much to revive. My personal work involves me with all the instruments of the modern symphony orchestra. In my ignorance, I always thought of that field as a fairly all-encompassing one. Therefore, it is amazing and entertaining and valuable to find out, through this volume, that the ancestry of all these modern instruments is a lifetime's study. I don't mean to imply that this book is just a scholarly research trip into the past. What makes it so readable is the way it brings to life conditions under which the musicians of bygone days had to work, just what the day-to-day routine of a minstrel or town bandsman or member of the royal household was like. And it is made abundantly clear that being a professional shawm- or rommelpot-player was not always a bed of roses.

No one is better qualified to write on this subject than David Munrow. His practical experience and theoretical knowledge have produced a book which will appeal to the specialist and general reader alike. His ability to mix scholarly detail with amusing stories should make this volume find a place on thousands of bookshelves.

Andre Previn

A note on pitch

It should be remembered that, during the Middle Ages and Renaissance, pitch was far from standardized. In this book, where specific pitches are referred to, the following system of pitch notation has been used:

In giving the ranges of wind instruments the following conventions have been observed: the basic compass is given in white notes, with a line indicating the fully chromatic range. Black notes are used for extensions to the basic compass (*eg* low pedal notes on the sackbut, high overblown notes on the cornett or flute), described by Praetorius as 'falsetto' notes, obtainable only by skilled players.

With wind instruments there is also a problem of terminology in order to distinguish clearly different sizes of the same family. Renaissance musicians were far from consistent in this matter and even today there is still a certain amount of confusion. Some makers refer to the bass recorder (lowest note f) or the bass rackett (lowest note F) as *bassett* instruments, and there are further complications through the common English habit of designating the soprano recorder (lowest note c″ or d″) *descant* and the alto (lowest note f′ or g′) *treble*. In this book the following names have been used: great bass, quint bass or quart bass, bass, tenor, alto, soprano, sopranino.

The performers

The following performers appear in photographs in this book: unless otherwise stated in the captions, the instruments shown are from their own collections.

Contents

Preface

In ten years of giving concerts of early music there is one question which I have been asked with predictable regularity: please will you explain the instruments? This book is a response to the hundreds of people who have asked me that question and to my own gradual awareness that I was certain of very few of the answers. For me, writing the book has been the same sort of process of discovery that I hope it will be for those who read it. For the general reader I have tried to provide a balanced introduction to early instruments by summarizing, and in some cases no doubt over-simplifying, the vast amount of research which has been done in recent years. For the specialist who wishes to follow up certain instruments in greater detail the extensive footnotes should provide fruitful sources of further reading. Wherever possible references have been given to the works which have been consulted, including books and periodicals (in English only) as well as modern editions and facsimiles. I have endeavoured to give as much information as possible about the social and historical background, since without it an understanding of the function of early instruments must remain incomplete. The division of the book into two parts (before and after *c.*1400) is intended to show which instruments properly belong to the Middle Ages and which to the Renaissance, a fundamental point that, through the enthusiasm of early music performers (including myself), has sometimes been overlooked. Chapter 5 deals with both medieval and renaissance percussion instruments and acts as a bridge between the two parts. It should be noted that Part Two describes the instruments which *developed* after 1400, and where a medieval instrument continued in use more or less unaltered during renaissance times, it is fully dealt with in Part One. Thus, details of the following are to be found in Part One only: pipe and tabor, gemshorn, portative organ, clavichord, psaltery, dulcimer, and tromba marina.

In order not to cram the book with information which would be superfluous for many readers, I have assumed a working knowledge of modern orchestral instruments and some acquaintance with the history of music before 1600. Readers who do require guidance on the latter point are referred to Gustave Reese's two books, *Music in the Middle Ages* (Norton, New York 1940), and *Music in the Renaissance* (Norton, New York 1954), or to the earlier chapters by Alec Harman in *Man and his Music* (Barrie and Rockliff, London 1962). Inevitably, since new discoveries are still being made and new evidence is still coming to light, this book will be out of date in some respects before it is published. Even as I write, the appearance of Sybil Marcuse's *A Survey of Musical Instruments* (David and Charles, London 1975) makes available much fascinating new information too late to be included here. Readers who are eager to keep abreast of all the latest developments are strongly advised to subscribe to the periodicals regularly mentioned in the footnotes. They will find especially valuable the journal *Early Music* (published quarterly by the Oxford University Press) which contains the most up-to-date information available about makers of early instruments and details of where replicas may be obtained.

Any fresh attempt to contribute to the study of musical instruments must inevitably draw on the work of other writers in this field. My debts are too numerous to acknowledge in detail here: a full account of the sources of information I have used is given in the footnotes, whilst the authors to whom I am most indebted are mentioned in the text itself. Special tribute must be paid to the work of the Galpin Society: through its annual journal and the individual publications of its members a vast amount of important research has appeared in print. I would particularly like to acknowledge the influence of the writings of Anthony Baines. It was the publication of his *Woodwind Instruments and their History* (Faber, London 1957) which first stimulated my interest in early instruments; in writing this book I have found myself constantly referring to his *European and American Musical Instruments* (Batsford, London 1966) for information about instrument construction and the clarification of distinctions between different instrumental types. His lucid, concise, and informative style has been my model.

In writing this book I have benefited from the practical help and co-operation of a number of people. To James Blades, John Caldwell, Christopher Hogwood, Edgar Hunt, Christopher Monk, Mary Remnant, and James Tyler my thanks are due for reading various chapters and giving me their advice and comments. Between them they spotted an alarming number of errors and inconsistencies, though for any that may remain I of course take full responsibility. I am also grateful for the assistance I have received from Clifford Bartlett, Donald Gill, Ian Harwood, Robert Spencer, and John Thomson. To the Librarian of the University of Leicester my thanks are due for allowing me to borrow, for an extended period, a large number of books greatly exceeding my allotted quota. Over the years I have learnt a great deal from my friends and colleagues in the Early Music Consort of London, many of whom appear in the illustrations of this book. It is from their study and skills that much of my practical knowledge has been derived. To James Tyler I owe a special debt of gratitude. In endless conversations over the last few years he has constantly stimulated my imagination and regularly challenged pre-conceived ideas and woolly thinking. He has also placed all the fr of his own research at my disposal, and, with equal generosity, allowed me to borrow free from his extensive collection of books and articles. Many museums, libraries, and publishers have kindly given permission to reproduce illustrations; full acknowledgeme will be found in the captions.

To the Oxford University Press my thank are due for the patience and courtesy by whi I was allowed to over-run a whole series of deadlines. Without the help and encourage of Anthony Mulgan and Sally Wright I dou if this book would ever have been complete I am most grateful to Sally Wright for all the assistance she has given me, particularly with the time-consuming task of organizing the illustrations. Without the support of my wif Gill, however, this book would never have been started, let alone finished. Gill has man to discreetly remind me of my promise to w it at the moments when I was most inclined forget, encouraged me to carry on at the moments when I was most liable to give up, and always been ready to discuss things whe got stuck or sit down at any hour of the day night and type out a new section as soon as it was written. I think she is now the only pers left who can actually read my handwriting. From the first draft to the final proof-readin her help has been invaluable.

DAVID MUNROW
November 1975

tory of musical instruments is almost as
s that of mankind: the beginnings lie
ided in pre-history and the process of
ition has been a gradual one, amazingly
in the early stages. Music itself was a slow
oper amongst the other arts: the introduc-
o Europe of many medieval instruments
ided with the first attempts at writing
ared part-music, a fundamental process of
osition which might be compared to
ng to paint in colour, to write in verse, or
nstruct a stone archway. Yet when Léonin
érotin produced the earliest monuments
yphony it was in the shadow of the great
dral of Notre Dame (started in the year
when Europe had finally emerged from
ark Ages and men were looking back for
ation to the art, architecture, and literature
Greek and Roman civilizations. The
lled 'Renaissance of the twelfth century'
n witnessed such important musical develop-
s also saw the establishment of universities
is, Montpellier, Oxford, Bologna, and
10, a new learning and literature in Latin,
e flowering of troubadour poetry and the
a of the medieval church. Amongst these
arts music was something of a beginner,
e instruments of music were still at an
stage in their development. However,
cal ideas and ideals, as interpreted by the
eval theorists, were to exercise a profound
on their use, representation, and subsequent
tion.
olution is perhaps a dangerous word to
ince it is a mistake to view the history of
cal instruments in terms of the survival of
ttest. The extinction of a particular species
enerally been the result of changing taste
hion rather than inherent weakness; the
cians of the Middle Ages and Renaissance
ame any shortcomings or limitations
n might seem apparent from a twentieth-
ry viewpoint. Their instruments perfectly
ed the musical requirements of the society
nich they belonged and few of them can be
issed as primitive or regarded merely as
otypes. The majority of them played a vital
n musical life, their natural habitat was the
y civilized *milieu* of the European courts,
heir repertoire included some of the most
sticated art-music of the times. Nor should
ill and artistry of the performers be under-
ated; whilst we shall never know precisely
Dufay sang or Dowland played we may
re that in both technique and interpretation
were amongst the supreme masters of any
The professional musicians then combined
ility with virtuosity just as modern folk
cians still do now in countries such as
e, Turkey, the Balkans, and the Middle
mpared to the instruments of the modern

symphony orchestra (the product of man's
conscious selection) those in use before 1600 are
clearly limited in many respects. The wind
instruments especially demonstrate severe
restrictions of compass, tonal range, and volume
which, although compatible with their original
function, prevented their continued use in later
ages. Yet to some extent all modern orchestral
instruments represent a compromise in terms of
sound in order to facilitate greater technical
control and dexterity. Whilst the brass and
woodwind departments provide a vivid example
of man's scientific ingenuity, there is a debit
side to all the mechanical improvements and
innovations of the nineteenth century. There is
no orchestral instrument as strident as the shawm,
as sweet as the gemshorn, or as hollow as the
panpipes, nothing to compare with the nasal
edginess of the rebec or the biting rattle of the
tromba marina, nothing to match the vocal
timbre of the cornett or the rich buzz of the
crumhorn and regal. And with plucked instruments the renewal of interest in music before
1600 has brought back into being a bewildering
panoply of subtle and exotic sounds previously
lost to European musical life outside folk music.
The people of the Middle Ages and Renaissance
liked gorgeous colours in their clothes, sharp
contrasts in their paintings, and highly spiced
dishes at their table. The characteristics of their
musical instruments were equally individual
and uncompromising.

The revival of interest in early instruments
began during the last century with the work of
(amongst others) François Joseph Fétis (1784–
1871) whose collection of seventy-eight instruments provided the nucleus for that of the
Brussels Conservatoire (now known as the
Brussels Museum of Musical Instruments).
Through the enthusiastic direction of Victor
Mahillon (1841–1924) the collection swelled to
over 1,500 items including a number of renaissance replicas which Mahillon commissioned.
The best-known pioneers were both English
and, curiously enough, born in the same year:
Arnold Dolmetsch (1858–1940)[1] and Francis W.
Galpin (1858–1945).[2] Since their day detailed
research has multiplied, amassing an enormous
body of material about the history, construction, and use of early instruments. The
nature of the evidence is so varied that it may
be helpful to summarize the main sources of
information, bearing in mind that evidence is
often conflicting or misleading and not always
to be accepted at face value.

1. ORIGINAL INSTRUMENTS
Instruments from before *c.*1600 which have
been preserved in good (and unaltered) condition
are relatively rare. Many museums confidently
exhibit instruments which have been drastically
'improved' in later centuries and surviving

instruments usually require restoration or at
least the replacement of strings, reeds, crooks,
keys, or mouthpieces. Whilst stringed instruments, like good wine, mature with age, wind
instruments can eventually fall into a decline
since wooden bores warp easily and metal tends
to become brittle with age. Informed opinion
now favours the principle of preserving intact
what original instruments remain, avoiding any
radical form of renovation. Otherwise future
generations will be left without any true originals
to study or copy.

Medieval survivals in any state of preservation
are naturally scarce and dispersed in collections
all over the world. For a survey of them readers
are referred to Frederick Crane's *Extant Medieval
Musical Instruments* (University of Iowa Press,
Iowa City 1972). With renaissance instruments,
many more examples still exist and three European collections are especially valuable – those
of the Brussels Museum of Musical Instruments,
the Staatliches Institut für Musikforschung,
West Berlin, and the Kunsthistorisches Museum,
Vienna. Some of the finest specimens from
these, and other important collections, are
included in Anthony Baines' *European and
American Musical Instruments* (Batsford, London
1966).

2. FOLK INSTRUMENTS
The dearth of original medieval instruments is
more than compensated for by the existence of
countless folk-music survivals. In many countries
folk music has preserved medieval traditions of
making and playing and quite a number of
instrumental types have lived on, virtually
unchanged, since the Middle Ages. They provide
a fascinating link with the live sounds of the
past, missing in all other forms of evidence.
Our knowledge of medieval music-making is
immeasurably richer through the continued
existence of the Arab lute, the fiddles of the
Balkans, the shawms of Turkey and the Middle
East, and the many other survivals mentioned
or illustrated in this book.

3. ICONOGRAPHICAL EVIDENCE
Medieval and renaissance artists have preserved
a wealth of information about musicians and
their instruments in countless carvings, statues,
paintings, manuscript illuminations, and
woodcuts. Such evidence must be treated with
great care. The stylization of medieval art often
obscures playing techniques and details of size
and construction, whilst throughout the Middle
Ages and Renaissance conventions of classical
and religious symbolism governed the work of
all artists to a considerable degree. The most
obvious instance is the dazzling variety of
musical instruments shown in the hands of
angels by religious painters of the fourteenth
and fifteenth centuries. Such angel concerts

belong not to this world but to paradise and they
bear little relation to contemporary church-
music practice, where the emphasis was on
a cappella singing. For an illuminating study of
this subject the reader is referred to Emanuel
Winternitz's *Musical Instruments and their
Symbolism in Western Art* (Faber, London 1967).

4. LITERARY EVIDENCE
Whilst literary references to musical instruments
are numerous, writers, like artists, were affected
by prevailing conventions. In French pastoral
poems of the Middle Ages, for example, the
classical association between shepherds and their
pipes leads to an extraordinary emphasis on
wind instruments, quite at variance with the
dominance of stringed instruments in the real
musical life of the time. In one study of 184
poems,[3] only three out of 104 instrumental
references are to stringed instruments.

5. ACCOUNTS OF PERFORMERS AND PERFORMANCES
Eye-witness accounts of music-making are
regrettably rare before the sixteenth century: if
only there had been a medieval equivalent of
Dr Burney how enlightened our knowledge of
performance practice would be! A fascinating
amount of information has been assembled by
Werner Bachmann in chapter IV of *The Origins
of Bowing* (Oxford University Press, London
1969) and it reveals that versatility was taken
for granted. The medieval minstrel of *Les deux
Bordéors ribaus* says: 'I shall tell you what I can
do: I am a fiddler, I play the bagpipe and flute,
harp, chifonie and giga, psaltery and rote, and I
can sing a song as well.'[4] The ability to sing and
double on instruments of such different types
may surprise us today but it is echoed by William
Kemp's praise of the Norwich Waits in 1600:
'Who, besides their excellency in wind instruments, their cunning on the viol, and violin:
their voices be admirable, every one of them
able to serve in any cathedral church in all
Christendom for quiristers.'[5]

Although concerts of early music today
tend to feature fairly small combinations of
performers, special occasions evidently demanded
forces of orchestral proportions. At the celebrations at Westminster in 1306 over sixty
instrumentalists are listed as taking part[6] and the
magnificent banquet known as the Feast of the
Pheasant[7] held at Lille in 1454 featured a wide
variety of colourful ensembles including
twenty-eight musicians inside a huge pastry
castle. During the Renaissance such court
extravaganzas became more common and are
regularly chronicled.

6. THEORETICAL WORKS AND TUTORS
Medieval theorists, following Greek practice,
were more concerned with the academic and
philosophical aspects of music than with prac-

tical details, and references to instruments and their use are tantalizingly scarce. The first substantial account comes in the treatise *De Inventione et Usu Musicae* written in about 1487 by Johannes Tinctoris (1445–1511). Even he includes only those contemporary fifteenth-century instruments which he could confidently derive from classical antiquity.

Information is more plentiful when we reach the sixteenth century. *Musica getutscht* (Basel 1511) by Sebastian Virdung is the first known instrumental tutor, dealing especially with keyboard instruments, the lute, and the recorder. Martin Agricola re-worked Virdung's material in his *Musica instrumentalis deudtsch* (Wittenberg 1528) and more specialized tutors followed, such as those by Sylvestro Ganassi for recorder and viol. The most informative and practical of renaissance writers on instruments is the German composer Michael Praetorius (1571–1621). The second volume of his treatise *Syntagma Musicum* (Wolfenbüttel 1618–19) is entitled *De Organographia* and deals in fascinating detail with all the instruments of the day. The third volume of *Syntagma Musicum* contains a mine of information about contemporary instrumental practice. Finally, Marin Mersenne (1588–1648) devotes a substantial part of his *Harmonie Universelle* (Paris 1636) to instruments, and although he clearly lacked much of Praetorius' practical knowledge, his treatment is encyclopedic.

7. PAYMENTS AND INVENTORIES

Besides giving precise information as to who played what, where, and when, accounts of payments to musicians make absorbing reading, underlying the menial status of much of the profession and its inherent insecurity. Even musicians on a municipal or royal pay-roll often found their wages in arrears, whilst freelance itinerants were regularly classed with rogues and vagabonds. For a study in depth of one particular period, the reader is referred to Walter L. Woodfill's *Musicians in English Society from Elizabeth to Charles I* (Princeton University Press, 1953; reprinted Da Capo, New York 1969), and for lists of musicians employed in the English royal household to Henry Cart de Lafontaine's *The King's Musick* (Novello, London 1909; reprinted Da Capo, New York 1973).

A number of important inventories exist from the sixteenth century onwards, listing instruments belonging to various courts and households. Amongst the most valuable are the Henry VIII Inventory[8] and the Cassel Inventories.[9]

8. THE MUSIC ITSELF

In the days when composers wrote for the present rather than posterity and musicians performed what was, stylistically speaking, a very narrow range of music, it was unnecessary to write down everything relating to perform-ance. Consequently, pieces with specific instrumentation are rare before 1600, though some unusual examples will be quoted during the course of the book. The only instruments which acquired an extensive repertoire of their own were the keyboard and lute families, and to a lesser extent the viol. This was the result of the use of tablature, a type of notation specifically designed for the instrument concerned.

Apart from the earliest keyboard tablatures, virtually the only purely instrumental music to have been preserved from the Middle Ages is monophonic dance music: the surviving *estampies* and *saltarelli* must represent a tiny part of a vigorous but largely unwritten tradition, governed by memory and improvisation. The principal role of instruments in art music was an accompanying one: to support the human voice in the song forms of the day – the ballade, virelai, and rondeau – though instrumental arrangements of these forms must surely have been made too. The restricted compass of medieval music made many different sizes of the same instrumental type unnecessary, and most instruments seem to have existed as a single basic size, with many variants. The independent lines of medieval polyphony suggest the use of contrasting instrumental types in an ensemble, rather than a uniform sonority, and much of the evidence already cited supports this.

With the Renaissance came the development of instrumental polyphony and the 'consort' principle. To cope with the demands of a new musical style, makers produced instruments in soprano-to-bass sets following the different categories of the human voice which composers began to distinguish clearly during the fifteenth century. But whilst the typical 'consort' of the Renaissance was a family unit, heterogeneous ensembles were popular too. The development of instrumental music greatly benefited from the start of music printing, pioneered by Petrucci in 1501 and followed by Attaingnant, Susato, Ballard and Le Roy, and many others. The quantity of instrumental music published during the first century of music printing is staggering: readers are referred here to Howard Mayer Brown's exhaustive survey *Instrumental Music printed before 1600* (Harvard University Press, Cambridge, Mass. 1965). A comparison of its contents with those of the inventories mentioned above reveals an apparent anomaly. The vast majority of music published is for strings (mostly lute) and keyboard, yet in the inventories it is the wind instruments which predominate. The explanation is a social one. Wind players were mainly professionals whilst for commercial success music publishing needed to appeal to the amateur market. And amateurs, both courtly and middle class, generally preferred strings. Playing the lute or virginals was an infinitely more decorous pastime than blowing a crumhorn or rackett and the gentle sounds of renaissance stringed instruments were ideally suited to domestic music-making.

It might be argued that this book omits what was the most important instrument of all in medieval and renaissance times: the human voice. Amongst theorists, composers, performers, and listeners its supremacy was unquestioned, and its influence on the development of man-made musical instruments was profound. Whether they were accompanying singers, doubling voice parts, or even replacing them entirely, instruments were measured against the human voice. Wide though it is, the spectrum of sound provided by early instruments can be seen as being made up of different facets of vocal timbre. And there was no doubt that the instrumentalist's job was to imitate the human voice as best he could. In the preface to the first recorder tutor, the *Fontegara* published in 1535, Sylvestro Ganassi shows clearly where his priorities lie. His opening remarks may be quoted by way of a *caveat* to this whole book:

'Be it known that all musical instruments, in comparison to the human voice, are inferior to it. For this reason, we should endeavour to learn from it and to imitate it . . . just as a gifted painter can reproduce all the creations of nature by varying his colours, you can imitate the expression of the human voice on a wind or stringed instrument . . . I have heard that it is possible with some players to perceive, as it were, words to their music; thus one may truly say that . . . only the form of the human body is absent, just as in a fine picture, only the breath is lacking.'[10]

1 For an account of Dolmetsch see Margaret Campbell, *Dolmetsch: the Man and his Work* (Hamish Hamilton, London 1975).
2 Galpin's principal writings are: *A Textbook of European Musical Instruments* (London 1937) and *Old English Instruments of Music*, fourth edition revised by Thurston Dart (Methuen, London 1965).
3 See Gerald Hayes, 'Musical Instruments', *New Oxford History of Music*, III (Oxford University Press, London 1960) p.479.
4 Werner Bachmann, *The Origins of Bowing*, translated by Norma Deane (Oxford University Press, London 1969) p.119.
5 Walter L. Woodfill, *Musicians in English Society*, (Princeton University Press, 1953; reprinted Da Capo, New York 1969) pp.86–7.
6 Bachmann, op. cit., pp. 128–9.
7 For an account of this event see Edmund A. Bowles, 'Instruments at the Court of Burgundy', *Galpin Society Journal*, VI (1953) pp.41–3.
8 Printed in Francis W. Galpin, *Old English Instruments of Music*, fourth edition revised by Thurston Dart (Methuen, London 1965) pp.215–22.
9 See Anthony Baines, 'Two Cassel Inventories', *Galpin Society Journal*, IV (1951) pp. 30–8.
10 Sylvestro Ganassi, *Opera Intitulata Fontegara* (Venice 1535; ed. Hildemarie Peter, Robert Lienau, Berlin 1956; English translation by Dorothy Swainson) p.9.

Medieval woodwind instruments offer a clear example of the 'soft' and 'loud' categories of music which Europe inherited from the East. Most of the reed instruments were loud and used mainly out of doors, whilst the intimate sound of the flute types was more appropriate indoors. The rules were not hard and fast, however. We know shawms were occasionally used in church, bagpipes found their way into soft ensembles, and the pipe and tabor and the military fife were regularly used in the open air.

Over details of pitch and range, it is impossible to be precise and in any case there was no standard type of each instrument but rather a whole series of regional variations. But it seems fairly safe to assume that most of the woodwind instruments on which overblowing was possible (all except panpipes, bladder pipes, and some bagpipes) had a range of roughly a diatonic octave and a half. Some chromatic notes, though certainly not all, could be obtained by cross fingering, but the bagpipes, bladder pipes, double pipes, and tabor pipes must have been very limited in this respect.

Reed instruments

The shawm

It is surprising just how *different* medieval instruments can be from any of their modern descendants. The shawm, derived from the Latin word *calamus* meaning a reed (hence also the French *chalemie* and *chalemele* and the Spanish *chirimia*), was the chief double-reed instrument until the seventeenth century. Yet who would suspect, listening to the intimate and seductive tone of the orchestral oboe today, that it was the offspring of such an aggressive outdoor parent? Of all medieval instruments the shawm is the wildest and most extrovert. Judging by survivals as far apart as Morocco and China, its tone was brilliant, piercing, often deafening. In folk music it is still used with other loud outdoor instruments such as trumpets and drums, and this was the case in the Middle Ages too. Even today in countries such as Turkey it is still possible to earn your living as an itinerant shawm player. In Istanbul it is a regular occurrence to hear a shawm and drum playing in the streets. The shawm player walks slowly in front, cheeks puffed out, blowing incessantly without pausing for breath. He is using the same technique as that employed by glass-blowers: the pressure from his cheeks helps him to blow *out* through his mouth whilst breathing *in* through his nose at the same time. Behind him comes the drummer playing on a *davul*, which is rather like a small bass drum. The player uses two sticks: a big spoon-shaped one for the basic

beat and a thin double-ended stick for elaborate cross-rhythms. And at the same time he manages to pick up the money which people throw as they pass by.

It is fortunate that there are so many folk survivals of the shawm since they can teach us much about the instrument's history. Ensembles of shawms, trumpets, and drums formed the typical Saracen military band during the time of the Crusades. The noise must have been shattering, particularly when it assailed the ears of the early crusaders to whom such instruments were something of a novelty. The shawm is probably a Mohammedan invention and is said to have been developed in Baghdad during the time of the Calif Harun-al-Rashid (763–809).[1] Whilst the scholar Curt Sachs put the invention at least some 600 years earlier, in the second century AD,[2] it seems fairly certain that the shawm spread into Europe from the east, as a result of the Crusades, the trade through Constantinople, and the Moorish occupation of Spain.

The typical oriental shawm is a keyless instrument a foot or so long with seven finger-holes and a thumb-hole. Its essential features are its double reed and expanding conical bore. Although the wide flared bell is the instrument's

Traditional shawms from (left to right) Egypt, Turkey, Morocco, and Turkey. (Author's collection)

most recognizable feature it makes compar tively little contribution to the tone or volume. Whilst the length and shape of the bore govern the pitch, it is the small *reed* an the way it is used which account for the sha amazing carrying power, helped in perform by the way many folk players blow the instrument upwards in the manner of a jazz trumpeter. A cylindrical section of softish r such as maize, is flattened out and squeezed a waisted shape. It is mounted on a metal st and is not controlled by the lips at all, but j by breath pressure. The player presses his li against a metal disc at the base of the staple,

Enlargement of oriental shawm reed mounte its staple. The 'waist' of the reed is bound wi wire.

taking the entire reed inside his mouth.

The earliest medieval shawms in Europe v presumably very similar to their Eastern counterparts. From the twelfth century onw the shawm starts to appear regularly in illust tions and carvings and we may assume that i continued to fulfil the same sorts of function it had done in the east: playing a principal pa in military and ceremonial music, procession and dance music. A typical literary reference comes in the fourteenth-century English romance *Sir Degrevant*, linking the shawm w trumpet and drum:

With the trompe and with nakere
And the scalmuse clere.[3]

s time the European shawm had emerged
her different form from that of its
l parent. The disc had been replaced by a
tte and the nature of the reed and
chure had changed (see chapter 6,
). Larger sizes were developing too.
as the earlier type of small shawm
d in the upper part of the treble stave
ding to somewhere near F above middle
larger type of shawm went an octave or
ower. During the fourteenth century it
d the separate name of *bombard* or
d (French *bombarde*, German *Pumhart*,
rious other corruptions) from the Latin
, meaning drone or buzz. The word was
ntly taken over from an artillery piece of
ne name, and first occurs in the sense of
cal instrument in 1342.[4] In 1376 *grosses
des* were described as 'new', and in 1453
d a *chalemie appelée bombarde* (a shawm
oombard).[4] In his *Confessio Amantis* (1393)

iconographical and literary evidence do suggest
a wide and varied use of the instrument. It is
particularly interesting that shawms were
certainly used on occasions in church, not only
ceremonially as when in 1235 the Abbot of
St Albans was received 'with the minstrelsy of
shawms', but also to double the voices of the
choir.[7]

Reed pipes and hornpipes
Whether it was playing martial music, dances,
church music, or chansons, the sound of the
shawm must always have been an intoxicating
one. It belongs to the orgiastic tradition of reed
instruments which begins with the Greek *aulos*,
used to accompany the dithyramb in the wild
rites of Dionysus, and continues with the jazz
saxophone and clarinet of our own day.[8]

The precursor of all these is the simple
reed pipe in which reed, mouthpiece, and
finger-holes are all fashioned out of the same

RIGHT
Primitive reed pipes: hornpipe from Finland,
single reed pipe from Greece, double reed pipe
from Ibiza. (Author's collection)

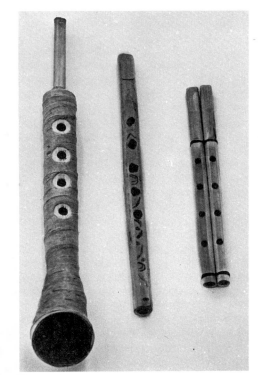

Middle Ages. A Saxon vocabulary of the eighth
century mentions one made of bone – the
swegelhorn.[9] Double hornpipes were probably
more common than the single variety, often
minus one of the horns. All in all, single-reed
instruments seem to have occupied a more
important place in medieval music-making
than they are generally given credit for. Nor
was their use necessarily restricted to popular
music if the Beauchamp window in St Mary's
Church, Warwick, is anything to go by. The
beautiful stained glass panels (designed in 1447)
show an angelic consort in which single and
double hornpipes are mixed with instruments
of serious music-making such as the cornett,
harpsichord, organ, and clavichord.[10]

Bagpipes and bladder pipes
Features of all the instruments described so far
are to be found in the widely differing forms of
bagpipe. No other medieval instrument can

Welsh pibcorn (Welsh Folk Museum, St Fagans,
Cardiff) and, *bottom*, Basque double hornpipe
(Horniman Museum, London)

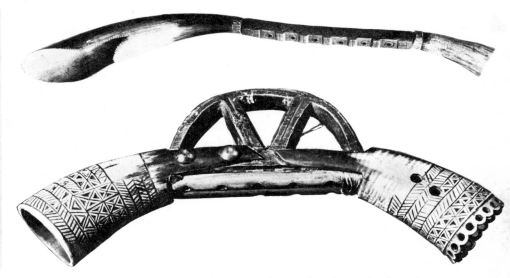

al shawm from Hong Kong, showing how
are pressed against the metal disc. The
inside the mouth.

c actually distinguished the two types:
unde of bumbarde and of clarionne with
nuse and shalmele . . .'[5]
manuscript of about the same date,
ning music by Hermann, Monk of
rg,[6] there are simple polyphonic
ositions in which the lowest part is
d *der pumhart*, a rare medieval instance
cified instrumentation. At a time when
was rather a shortage of sustaining
nents of tenor pitch, the bombard must
een very useful for coping with the tenor
n the chansons and motets of Machaut,
ni, and their contemporaries. Although
n diverges on this point – the participation
shawm in polyphonic music – both

short length of cane. In most parts of the world
where suitable cane is grown, these reed pipes
are still common. Greek, Spanish, and Arab
shepherds alike while away their time by making
and playing these most primitive of reed
instruments. A section of cane is cut leaving a
knot at one end. Four or five evenly spaced
finger-holes are burned out with a hot wire or
nail, and the single reed is made by slicing out a
small tongue, shaving it down but still leaving
the base attached to the knot. And so it must
have been throughout the Middle Ages and
long before.

This straightforward instrument has developed
many variants including double pipes and the
more sophisticated hornpipe. As a single

instrument, this survived in Wales until the
eighteenth century as the pibcorn (literally
'pipe horn'). The handsome example now
preserved in the Welsh Folk Museum, St
Fagans, near Cardiff, shows the three-sectional
construction. The central section is of wood
and two horns are attached to it, the larger one
at the lower and acting as a bell, the other as a
mouthpiece enclosing the detachable single
reed which is inserted in the top of the pipe.
Hornpipes of this kind thus qualify as the
earliest type of reed-cap instrument, though the
horn makes a much less satisfactory and less
comfortable cap than that later devised for the
crumhorn and its relatives. Hornpipes must
have been fairly common in Europe in the early

claim such widespread and continuous use
since the Middle Ages: Scotland, Ireland,
France, Spain, Italy, Bulgaria, Czechoslovakia,
Hungary, Poland, and Egypt are some of the
countries in which distinctive varieties of
bagpipe are still flourishing. Information about
the instrument is voluminous and readers who
would like more detail than the scope of this
book permits should consult the authoritative
works on the subject by Anthony Baines and
Francis Collinson.[11]

Although the origins of the bagpipe are
unknown, its history goes back long before the
Middle Ages and it must have started life as a
rustic instrument. What more natural than for
a herdsman who tended sheep or goats and

Traditional bagpipes from Spain and Bulgaria.

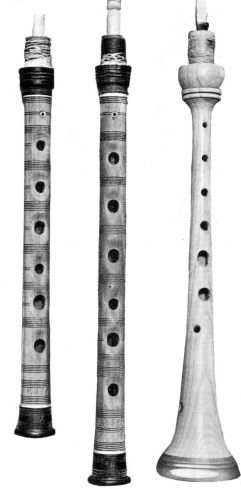

Alternative Bulgarian chanters (cylindrical bore) and Spanish chanter (conical bore). During the Middle Ages the conical chanter became the standard European form.

Bagpipe reeds (*l* to *r*) Spanish drone (single) and chanter (double), Bulgarian drone (single) and chanter (single).

Platerſpil

Bladder pipe from Virdung's *Musica getutsch* (1511).

played a reed pipe to think of combining the two? Yet the earliest mention of the bagpipe is in the hand of an emperor. The Roman historian Suetonius relates how the Emperor Nero 'towards the end of his life . . . had publicly vowed that if he retained power he would at the games in celebration of his victory give a performance on the water-organ, the *choraulam*, and *utricularium*'.[12] The *tibia utricularis* is mentioned elsewhere, and the Greek Dio Chrysostom is specific. He says that Nero 'knew how to play the pipe with his mouth and the bag thrust under his arms'.[12] This royal association should not altogether surprise us, even though Nero's vow must have been in the nature of a penance. Throughout the Middle Ages the bagpipe was far from being a mere peasant instrument: it was heard and appreciated at all levels of society.

The reason for the bagpipe's development and enormous popularity is not hard to understand. The nature of any solo wind music, particularly medieval or folk dance music, makes a continuous sound desirable: yet this is impossible to achieve without the oriental breathing technique previously mentioned. The bag of the bagpipe solves the problem: the player can keep up the flow of air by squeezing the bag with his arm whilst he takes a breath to renew the air supply. The most common material still used for making the bag is the complete skin of some suitable animal such as a sheep or goat. Its neck and front leg-holes are useful for attaching the instrument's various pipes, though the joints are reinforced with *stocks*. These are wooden sockets fitted into the holes and secured by binding the skin tightly round them.

Besides the bag and stocks, the only other features common to all medieval bagpipes were the mouthpipe and the chanter. The mouthpipe contains a simple device which allows the player to breathe. A round piece of leather hinged on to the bag end of the mouthpipe acts like a non-return valve. When the player blows air in, it opens; when he stops blowing, the pressure in the bag forces the flap shut. The chanter usually has seven finger-holes and a thumb-hole giving a basic octave-and-a-note scale plus a tuning hole or two at the bottom end. The medieval bagpipe chanter existed in two different forms, either cylindrical bore plus single reed – adapting the reed-pipe idea – or conical bore plus double reed, following the principle of the shawm. Horns were sometimes added to the end of the cylindrical chanter after the manner of the hornpipe. Overblowing is only possible on pipes with conical chanters: modern Spanish players increase the pressure on the bag to extend the range two or three notes up into the second octave, but how far back this practice goes is uncertain.

It may seem surprising that the drone – to us the most characteristic feature of the bagpipe's sound – was not ubiquitous in the Middle Ages. Although drones were certainly in common use from the thirteenth century onwards, they were by no means universal. It is likely that the earliest forms of the instrument were droneless, like the simple bagpipe to be heard in the nightclubs of Cairo to this day. The drone pipe is always cylindrical[13] and sounded with a single reed. In order to permit accurate tuning with the chanter (normally two octaves below the chanter's key note) the drone is made in two or more sections, so that the player can sharpen or flatten it by adjusting the length. The miniatures in the thirteenth-century *Cantigas de Santa*

María[14] manuscript include bagpipes with drones but this seems to have been unusual until renaissance times.

The bagpipe made an ideal instrument f[or] solo dances and monophonic music, but it seems to have taken part in polyphonic m[usic] too. Guillaume de Machaut (*c.*1300–77) in[cludes] bagpipes in a rare and rather baffling clue [to] instrumentation of his own music. In *Le L[ivre] du Voir Dit* he suggests that his three-part ballade *Nès que on porroit*[15] may be played [on] the organ, bagpipes, or other instruments [and] that 'this is its very nature'.[16] If only Mach[aut] had been more specific! Only the tenor pa[rt of] the piece, with a range of a diatonic octave[,] seems at all negotiable on the bagpipe and [even] here the rests present a bit of a problem. W[ith] its limited compass the use of the bagpipe [in] polyphonic music remains quite a mystery[.] The existence of a drone removes the poss[ibility] of any change of keynote, and even witho[ut a] drone there is the problem of articulation. [One] cannot tongue a note on the bagpipe becau[se] the air reservoir in the bag acts as a barrier between tongue and chanter. Instead the e[ffect] of articulation is achieved by some kind of 'gracing': at its simplest this means soundi[ng] another note with a quick flick of the fing[er] which has the effect of a very short acciac[catura.] We simply do not know what sort of grac[ing] medieval bagpipers used, but it may have sometimes been quite elaborate, as in High[land] bagpipe music today, where gracing has b[ecome] an art as subtle and varied as the ornament[ation] of the French *clavecin* composers such as Rameau and Couperin.

Although it is frequently pictured or list[ed in] the company of other instruments (includi[ng the] ensemble of twenty-eight at the Burgundi[an] *Feast of the Pheasant*[17]) it is difficult to see h[ow] the bagpipe could have ever been a satisfa[ctory] instrument for polyphonic music. As so of[ten] the medieval theorists give us no practical [help.] The bagpipe is 'above all other instrument[s,]' says Jerome of Moravia (*c.*1250) echoing w[hat] John Cotton said a century before.[18] Yet th[e] existence of the *bladder pipe* from the thirte[enth] century onwards suggests that whatever th[e] bagpipe's status, players may have been tr[ying] to solve some of the problems just mention[ed.] In essence, the bladder pipe seems to have

n attempt to have it both ways: to
ne the bagpipe's continuous air flow with
rument which could stop and start more
and on which some kind of tonguing and
ation may have been possible. Instead of
animal skin which requires arm pressure
e it work, the bladder pipe employs an
animal bladder which will expel a certain
t of air down the pipe just by its own
ty. The air reservoir is much smaller than
bagpipe, so the player would have had to
a quick breath when necessary as opposed
more leisurely breathing possible on the
e. The bladder pipe continued in use up
sixteenth century, even after the crumhorn
come popular. Virdung includes it in his
getutscht (1511) under the name *Platerspil*.
strument had already taken various
the *Cantigas de Santa María* manuscript
a curved single bladder pipe and a
t double one. Although the curved
ment, like Virdung's, is apparently made
a solid piece of wood in the manner of a
orn, the shape must have come in the
ace from a horn bell added to a straight
on the hornpipe. This feature is preserved
re Polish shepherd's instrument,
ntly the only real modern survival of the
r pipe.[19] It is curious that whilst the
e has gone from strength to strength,
dder pipe has almost entirely died out.

ouçaine

the reed instruments so far described
xist both folk music survivals to tell us
hey sounded like, and medieval pictures
ings to tell us what they looked like.
ch help is forthcoming for the *douçaine*,
st mysterious of all medieval instruments.
gularly mentioned in European literature
thirteenth, fourteenth, and fifteenth
ies in various spellings including *dulçema*
sh) and *douchaine* (Low German). Machaut
ons the *douceinne* in the *Remède de Fortune*,
the fourteenth-century poem *Les Échecs
ux*, *douchaines* are described along with
s being very soft and very pleasant.[20]
g together the scanty information
le has led different scholars to varying
sions:
e soft oboe' (Sachs)[21]
st a suspicion that it might have been a
flute' (Hayes)[22]
e cannot altogether rule out another
le answer, namely that the instrument
kind of shawm' (Baines)[23]
most specific information comes in the
entione et usu musicae (c.1487), one of the
tical works of Tinctoris, who classes the
as a type of *tibia* (reed instrument). He
guishes it from the shawm (*celimela*) which
fect instrument on which any kind of

composition can be played. 'On the other hand
that *tibia* called the *dulcina*, on account of the
softness of its sound, has seven holes in front
and one behind, like a *fistula* (recorder). Since
not every kind of piece can be played on it, it is
considered to be imperfect.'[24]

In other words the douçaine has the restricted
compass characteristic of cylindrical bore reed
instruments. It was certainly soft – the adjective
is several times applied to it – and it certainly
had a reed according to Tinctoris. If its bore was
cylindrical, the douçaine must very probably
have operated at tenor rather than treble pitch.
Pitch, compass, and volume would have thus
made it ideal for medieval tenor parts which are
often limited to an octave and a note in range.
What is unclear is the nature of the reed (single
or double) and the technique used for playing it
(direct contact or some kind of reed cap), and
unless more evidence comes to light, it seems
extremely unlikely that the mystery will be
satisfactorily solved.

The flutes

Medieval instruments of the flute type
employed two quite different methods of
sound production:
1. blowing across a round mouth-hole, as on
the panpipes or transverse flute,
2. blowing into a whistle mouthpiece, as on the
recorder or flageolet.

It is clear that the word *flute* and its variants
were used indiscriminately for both types:
Machaut distinguishes the *flaustes traversaines*
(transverse flutes) from the *flaustes dont droit
joues quand tu flaustes* (flutes that you hold
straight when you play).[25] Confusion over flute
nomenclature persists to this day: there is still a
surprising number of people, including
conductors, who are not aware that during the
baroque period flute or *flauto* specifically meant
recorder and *not* transverse flute. But whereas
baroque composers were precise about their
terminology, medieval composers and writers
were not. Machaut also mentions the *Flauste
brehaingne*[26] (literally 'sterile flute'), the *floiot de
saus*[26] (osier flute), and the *ele*[27] (perhaps a
shortened form of *frestel*). Other literary sources
mention the *flajol, flajolet, floyle, frestel,
fletsella, muse d'ausay,* and *estiva* which different
authorities have all identified as flutes of some
kind.

It is doubtful if we shall ever succeed in
sorting out all the various names into specific
flute types nor is it likely that many of the
names had a single specific meaning. In any case
their number is slight compared to the number
of flute types which existed in the Middle Ages,
each subject to almost infinite regional variation.

Traditional panpipes from Ecuador (*below*), and
two sets from Portugal. (Author's collection)

Flutes were exceedingly popular and ranged
from simple peasant instruments to those of
highly sophisticated courtly society. Especially
with the whistle types the same situation applies
today: there is scarcely a country in the world
which cannot boast its own whistle instrument
of some kind.

Panpipes and transverse flutes

Although these two instruments are linked by
their method of sound production, their history,
appearance, and playing technique could
scarcely be more different. The origin of both
is a simple bamboo tube stopped at one end,
open at the other. But whilst several pipes of
different length were bound together and
sounded vertically to make the panpipes, a
single tube held horizontally became a transverse
flute when finger-holes were added, together
with a mouth-hole near the stopped end. The
transverse flute may well be regarded as a
rationalization of the panpipe principle, and
therefore a later development. Both instruments
have a history stretching back long before the
Middle Ages. Panpipes are most familiar to us
from illustrations and literary references in
classical times: the name comes from the
association of the instrument with the mythological god Pan. Greek and Roman artists show
the orthodox form of the instrument as seven

lengths of cane bound together. Similar
representations were common in Europe
throughout the Middle Ages, Renaissance, and
Baroque, but this should not lead us to suppose
that the panpipes played an equally significant
part in music-making during all this time.
Even in Greek times the panpipes were
unimportant compared to the *aulos* or the
kithara and for much of the post-classical period
they existed as rustic or popular instruments
only. When we find the panpipes played side
by side with the *real* instruments of music in
late medieval or renaissance art their presence
is usually of purely allegorical or symbolic
significance.[28]

As an instrument of practical music-making
the heyday of the panpipes was the time of the
troubadours and trouvères (eleventh to
thirteenth centuries). During this period the
instrument is represented in a variety of forms
which differ considerably from the orthodox
classical type, both in the number of pipes and
the method of construction. A twelfth-century
manuscript, now in St John's College,
Cambridge,[29] illustrates the solid type of
construction in which the pipes are drilled
out of a flat piece of wood. Solid pottery
construction was used too: all the surviving
medieval panpipes are ceramic with the
number of pipes varying from five to eleven.[30]

Canon Galpin also mentions 'trustworthy examples' of the panpipes constructed in semicircular shape from medieval manuscripts and instances one of the early eleventh century.[31] This curved shape encourages greater fluency on the instrument and is found on the most sophisticated modern survivals, such as the Romanian *naiu* with twenty-six pipes. Virtuosi such as Gheorghe Zamfir have achieved a technical and expressive mastery of

Traditional panpipes from Hungary. (Author's collection)

the instrument which any woodwind player must envy. His repertoire of solos, often borrowed from the violin, includes brilliant display pieces demanding phenomenal agility, staggering breath control, and double and triple tonguing of great rapidity. Equally impressive are the slow mournful pieces in which the panpipes can produce every nuance of feeling by varied tone colours, vibrato control, and a characteristic 'droop' in pitch – sometimes by as much as a semitone – achieved by altering the angle of embouchure.

The style of medieval panpipe playing must have been simpler and less sophisticated, perhaps resembling that used by the South American Indians today. The number of pipes was more limited, giving a short diatonic range ideal for dance music or the more straightforward troubadour and trouvère melodies. This simple *chanson à refrain* could be played on a six-pipe instrument.

Anonymous thirteenth-century chanson à refrain.

Six-holed transverse flute from the Andes, Bolivia. (Author's collection)

But once the development of polyphonic music demanded the use of accidentals outside the basic mode, the panpipes' usefulness was on the wane.

The rise of the transverse flute seems more or less to correspond with the decline of the panpipes. To regard one as a direct replacement of the other in music-making would be an over-simplification, but it is true that, whilst maintaining some of the panpipes' hollow tone-quality, the cylindrical six-holed flute can manage most of the important chromatic notes by cross fingering or occasionally half-holing. Added to that, the flute must have been capable of a good two-octave range, though whether medieval players used it all we don't know. The use of the keyless flute in the classical music of China and India testifies to the wide range and advanced technique which are possible on the instrument.

Besides a history in the Far East which extends to remote antiquity, the flute was also known to the Etruscans, the Egyptians, and the Greeks. It was through Byzantine influence that the flute finally made its way into central Europe in the twelfth century. Important evidence comes from the encyclopedia *Hortus Deliciarum* (late twelfth century) where the flute is given the German name *swegel*.[32] The instrument became something of a German speciality and the expression *German* flute is found off and on for the next 800 years as a means of distinguishing the *transverse* flute from whistle types.

The Germans developed two distinct uses for the flute: courtly and martial. It was evidently a popular instrument amongst the Minnesänger (the German equivalent of the troubadours) and we find the flute depicted alongside other courtly instruments such as the fiddle and harp. From the thirteenth century onwards it also

becomes associated with the drum as a military band instrument, although it was not until the following century that the flute, in either role, became common outside Germany.

Six-holed pipe and double pipes

More examples of whistle flutes have survived from the Middle Ages and earlier times than of any other kind of instrument. Frederick Crane[33] lists no less than 140 of them in a great variety of forms as well as numerous simpler whistle types without finger-holes. Their method of sound production is familiar from the modern recorder and penny whistle, and their essential features are:
the lip cut near the top of the tube,
the fipple (usually a block of wood) inserted in the mouthpiece,
the windway: a narrow channel above the fipple through which the breath is directed against the edge of the lip to produce the sound.

The whistle mouthpiece seems an ingenious idea compared to the other flute types. It is easy to see how primitive man could have stumbled on the principle of the panpipes by idly blowing across a stopped piece of cane, but it is more difficult to imagine how the whistle mouthpiece developed by chance. Yet the history of the whistle mouthpiece seems to go back almost as far as that of *homo sapiens*: the earliest whistle instrument so far discovered dates from the Upper Paleolithic period.[34]

The variety of whistle flutes in medieval times is matched by the many forms found today. The most common material is still cane or bamboo, used for rustic instruments, which are as easily fashioned as the reed pipes. It is presumably what Machaut meant by his *floiot de saus* (osier flute) and in a typical pastoral poem of the thirteenth century the trouvère

Colin Muset describes the making of the instrument.

L'autr'ier en mai, un matinet,
M'esveillerent li oiselet,
S'alai cuillir un saucelet,
Si en ai fait un flajolet.[35]
(The other day on a May morning I was w
up by the little birds. I went out to cut a r
and have it made into a *flajolet*.)

The number of finger-holes no doubt vari
but six holes (*ie* no thumb-hole or little-
finger-hole) seems to be a common standa
today.

Although Colin Muset and others used word *flajolet* we should perhaps avoid tran
it literally as *flageolet,* or using the word at
as an umbrella term for whistle-flutes. The
special characteristic of the flageolet prope
two thumb-holes, and the instrument was
standardized until the end of the sixteenth
century when the French flageolet was
'invented' by Le Sieur Juvigny.[36] Besides f
finger-holes and two thumb-holes, the late
seventeenth-century design of the flageole
incorporated a mouthpiece cap containing
sponge to absorb the moisture from the pl
breath. This instrument remained popular
largely as an amateur instrument, until the
nineteenth century. Unfortunately Englis
makers such as Bainbridge and Potter then
developed a new instrument, retaining the
special mouthpiece and the name 'flageole
dropping the flageolet's special feature, the
thumbholes. Since then, confusion has mul
over what is, or is not, a flageolet and even
penny whistles are now sold under that na
If inflation has made the name 'penny whi
obsolete, we should return to Mersenne's
definition *la flute à six trous*[37] or the six-hol
pipe.

Double pipes were popular too, presum
because a solo on them could make more
impact than on a single pipe, though the c
tradition of double *auloi* may have encour
an excessive number of representations in
and sculpture. Certainly double pipes do c
up in some rather unlikely playing positio
The Pied Piper figure in Simone Martini's
fresco *L'investitura di San Martino* looks in

Detail from *L'investitura di San Martino* by
Simone Martini (1284–1344). (Basilica di S
Francesco, Assisi)

lties: he seems to have more finger-holes
e can cope with and some balance
ms too, since the right-hand little finger
g used to support the instrument. It would
much easier if the pipes were *parallel* and
d together. Folk instruments confirm
is must have usually been the case, and
s to distinguish two basic types of double
e-flute. In both the two pipes are to some
unequal. On one type there is a melody
us a drone pipe; it is easy to see how the
e encouraged this sort of thing. The
lav *dvojnice* is a more sophisticated
ment carved out of wood, elaborately
ted and designed so that the two pipes
ay together mostly in thirds.[38] Medieval
e pipes of this kind were more likely to
een designed for playing in consecutive
s or fifths. A wooden example excavated

at Christ Church, Oxford,[39] has a thumb-hole
and four finger-holes in each pipe. The lowest
note of the right-hand pipe is c″, that of the
left g″. Such an arrangement makes possible
the playing of simple part music.

Pipe and tabor
An even more common addition than a second
pipe was some kind of percussion instrument:
pipe and tabor, pipe and tambourin (stringed
drum), even pipe and triangle were all used,
though the pipe and tabor was by far the most
popular. When Jehan Erars wrote:

Guis dou tabor au flahutel
Leur fait ceste estampie[40]
(Guy with his tabor and pipe plays them this
estampie)

he was describing a one-man-band which is

ideal for dance music: the drum giving the beat
and the pipe playing the melody. The technique
required of the player is rather specialized,
involving three distinct skills which must be
co-ordinated, yet independent.

Modern folk players always *lead* with the
drum, holding the stick loosely in the right hand
and often allowing it to beat quite intricately
decorated rhythms. The tabor itself (a kind of
snare drum: for more details see chapter 5,
page 32) is slung in various ways on the
left-hand side of the body: it can be secured to
the waist, slung over the left arm, or even, in
the case of a very small tabor, suspended from
the little finger. The left hand holds the tabor
pipe: a long slender cylindrical pipe with holes
for two fingers and thumb. The narrow bore is
important because it enables the player to
overblow easily and obtain not only the second

harmonic (overblowing at the octave) but the
third, fourth, and fifth harmonics (overblowing
at the 12th, 15th, and 17th respectively).
Whereas the basic scale of all the instruments so
far described consists of their *fundamental* notes,
the fundamentals of the tabor pipe are very
weak and not used at all. Instead the basic scale
starts with the second harmonics, enabling a
mere three holes to produce a complete diatonic
scale. The following chart makes clear how

Compass and fingering chart of tabor pipe.

led pipes from (*l* to *r*) Turkey, Hungary,
cco, Bulgaria, Peru, Thailand. (Author's
ion)

Dvojnice from Yugoslavia, with two melody
pipes, and double pipes from the Andes, Bolivia,
with a drone pipe and melody pipe. (Author's
collection)

Woodcut from the title page of William Kemp's
Nine Daies Wonder (1600). Notice the large tabor
pipe and the way the tabor is slung over the left
arm by a strap.

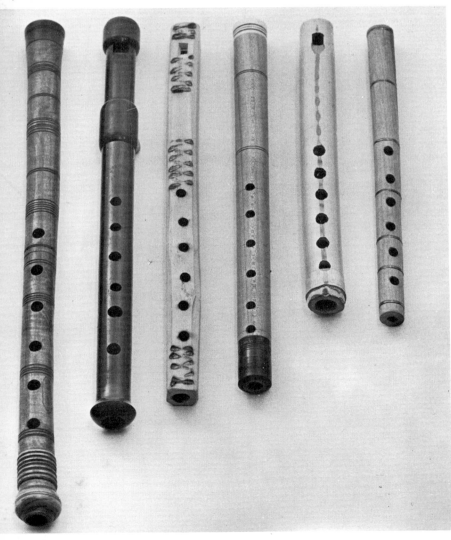

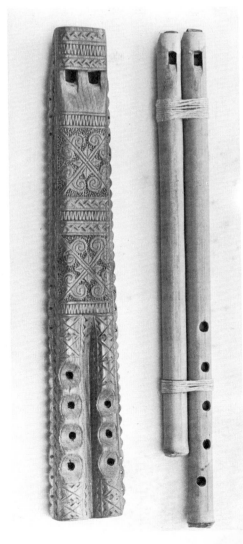

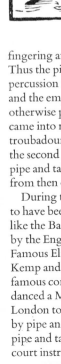

fingering and breath pressure are combined.
Thus the pipe and tabor combines single-stick
percussion technique, woodwind fingering,
and the employment of the harmonic series
otherwise peculiar to brass instruments. It
came into regular use during the time of the
troubadours: a Polish tabor pipe survives from
the second half of the eleventh century[39] and
pipe and tabor players are regularly illustrated
from then onwards.

During the Renaissance the tabor pipe seems
to have been quite a large and sturdy instrument
like the Basque *chistu* or the 'alto' pipe supplied
by the English Folk Dance and Song Society.
Famous Elizabethan players included William
Kemp and Richard Tarleton, two of the most
famous comedians of the day. In 1599 Kemp
danced a Morris dance all the way from
London to Norwich, apparently accompanied
by pipe and tabor as he went. By this time the
pipe and tabor had fallen in social status from a
court instrument to an instrument of the
common people. Literary references link it
with rustic merry-making and the maypole.

Small pipe, stick, and tabor (English Folk Song and Dance Society)

Thomas Weelkes's ayre beginning:

Strike it up, Tabor,
And pipe us a favour[41]

is a typical example. As a folk instrument, the English pipe and tabor just survived into this century, and with the revival of interest in our folk music and the work of the English Folk Dance and Song Society it is now once again a regular thing to see pipe and tabor players playing for Morris dancing, as they did in Elizabethan times. Abroad in France and Spain the Provençal *galoubet* and the Basque *chistu* continue a tradition which has flourished for 900 years.

The recorder
Amongst the variety of medieval whistle instruments the recorder only gradually emerged as the most useful and versatile type. Its tremendous popularity in later ages has tended to over-emphasize its place in medieval times, when its status was at best *primus inter pares* with the other instruments discussed in this section. In any case it is difficult to chronicle the early history of the recorder because of the problem of positively identifying what is and what is not a recorder in medieval art and sculpture. The essential features of the recorder are its beak-shaped mouthpiece and the number of its finger-holes: seven finger-holes plus a thumb-hole. But since its playing position is similar to that of so many other wind instruments it is often impossible to be sure whether a particular illustration depicts a recorder, another whistle type, or some kind of reed-pipe or shawm. The earliest portrayal which has been accepted as being of a recorder comes in a twelfth-century Psalter in the library of Glasgow University.[42] This is two hundred years before the word 'recorder' appears: the earliest reference to come to light so far occurs

in the household accounts of Henry, Earl of Derby (later King Henry IV), for 1388 noting payment for a *fistula nomine Ricordo* (a pipe called a keepsake).[43] During the fifteenth century the word 'recorder' seems to have come into use in England, whilst on the continent the more general (and confusing) name 'flute' continued to be employed.

By this stage the recorder had developed a variety of sizes just as the shawm had. Whereas most early medieval whistle-flutes were probably fairly small and high-pitched like the surviving bone specimens,[34] by the fourteenth century there were almost certainly instruments which could go as low as middle C (the bottom note of the modern tenor recorder). The existence of a variety of sizes of late medieval recorder made them the most useful flute type when an ensemble was required. In 1385, at the marriage of the Duke of Burgundy with Margaret of Bavaria at Cambrai, the music for the Mass was performed by *molt brafs contres et flusteurs musicals* (excellent singers and flute players).[44] The likelihood is that the *flusteurs* were recorder players, who could cope with the different ranges of voice parts, doubling them an octave higher.

The gemshorn
All the instruments so far mentioned in this section possess a basically cylindrical bore. The only medieval flute type with a sharply tapering

conical bore was the *gemshorn* (the German name means chamois horn) where the taper unavoidable because of the natural shape of animal horn. This gives the gemshorn a swe watery tone colour somewhere between a s recorder and an ocarina. The history of the gemshorn is rather a puzzle. A large numbe antler whistles have been found from the Bronze Age onwards, though their nature i disputed.[45] Yet the first clear illustration of instrument is not found until Virdung's *Mu getutscht* (1511) where the horn is apparently cow or ox rather than chamois. The only surviving instrument, discovered by Curt S is generally similar though made of goat's h and with six finger-holes instead of Virdung four, together with a vent hole near the tip. Agricola includes the gemshorn in the first edition of his *Musica instrumentalis deudtsch* (but omits it from the final edition of 1549, suggesting that the instrument had by then fallen out of use. Praetorius (1619) and Mersenne (1635) mention the gemshorn onl as an organ stop. *Lieblich* (lovely) is Praetori description of the sound.[47]

Since organ builders were already imitati the gemshorn by the mid-fifteenth century instrument must have been quite common then.[47] What is missing is some connection between the primitive medieval antler whis and the more sophisticated gemshorn types the early sixteenth century.

Traditional recorders, (*l* to *r*) two from Turkey, and one from Norway.
(Author's collection)

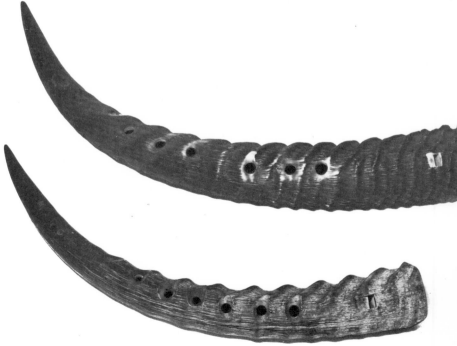

Two gemshorns by Rainer Weber, Bayerbach, following the pattern of the instrument described by Curt Sachs. (Author's collection)

Keyboard

...ugh it would be misleading to describe all ...val instruments as 'crude' or 'primitive' ...as their *playing* techniques are concerned, ...ue that the techniques involved in their ...uction are mostly straightforward. The ...ce of woodwind keys, brass valves, or the ...plicity of parts involved in violin-making ...racteristic of the days when most players ...also the makers of their own instruments. ...e whole, musical instruments in the ...e Ages were not the masterpieces of ...anical ingenuity that many of them are ... So the extent to which keyboard ...ments developed before the fifteenth ...ry may seem surprising, since in order to ...ion at all a keyboard instrument requires a ...anical action, a whole series of sound ...cers – either strings or pipes – and a degree ...chanization quite foreign to other types of ...ment.

...early medieval organ

...l keyboard instruments the organ is much ...dest. As with so many aspects of art and ...e the Greeks can claim credit for its ...tion and initial development. It was ...bios, a Greek engineer living in Alexandria, ...built the first organ in history during the ...century BC. Pliny the Elder described the ...tion as one of the wonders of the world[1] ...s reputation has grown since, partly ...gh a misunderstanding of its name ...ulis (from the Greek *hydor,* water, and ...pipe). 'Water-organ' is the usual transla-...a rather unfortunate one since it conjures ...fantastic vision of plumbing with water ...ing through the pipes: during the Middle ...it was actually thought that the hydraulis ...mployed boiling water or even steam! ...t, water was simply used in order to ...ide stabilization of wind pressure. Nor does ...ound appear to have been as loud and pene-...g as has often been stated. Cicero describes ...ound as a sensation which is as agreeable ...e ear as the tastiest fish is to the palate.[2] ...oth the Greeks and the Romans the ...aulis was an instrument of private rather ...public entertainment and the outdoor ...iments which accompanied gladiator ...s and acrobatic shows seem to have been ...xception rather than the rule. Most ...rtant of all, the hydraulis established the ...ciple of the keyboard – a series of levers, ...equipped with a return mechanism, which ...pressed down by the fingers to obtain the ...ired series of notes.

...uring the fourth century AD the hydraulic ...hanism was superseded by the introduction ...llows and the hydraulis gave way to the ...matic organ. From this time onwards ...iptions of the bellows' action are regularly ...led with accounts of the organ's devastat-ingly loud noise. 'It emits a strong sound through twelve bronze pipes so that it can be clearly heard everywhere within a thousand paces'[3] says one account of a fourth-century organ, worked by no less than fifteen 'smith's bellows'. The famous *Utrecht Psalter* of about AD 860 vividly illustrates the amount of elbow-grease required, although the instrument depicted is, in fact, a fanciful version of the ancient hydraulis. Four men are straining away on the long beams connected to the huge wind chests, beneath a rather diminutive array of pipes, whilst two monks encourage the men to even greater efforts. From England we have copious information about a gigantic organ installed at Winchester towards the end of the tenth century. According to the poetic account of the monk Wulstan there were four hundred pipes and twenty-six bellows requiring the efforts of seventy strong men who were:

Labouring with their arms, running with sweat,
Each urging his companions to force the wind up
With all his strength filling
The wind chest's vast cavity that it may rumble . . .
Like thunder, the strident voice assails the ear,
Shutting out all sound other than its own;
Such are its reverberations, echoing here and there,
That each man lifts his hands to stop his ears,
Unable as he draws near to tolerate the roaring
Of so many different and noisy combinations.[4]

Even allowing for poetic licence, Wulstan's long and detailed description is very informative and makes clear several important features of the large medieval church organ. Taking into account various sources of evidence, pictorial and literary, the nature of the large medieval church organ before the thirteenth century may be conveniently summarized as follows:
1. The pipes were of the 'flute' type, *ie* voiced with a lip like the recorder.
2. Instead of the keyboard developed on the hydraulis there were a series of *linguae* (tongues) or sliders which had to be pulled out and pushed in manually.
3. Because of this clumsy mode of operation, two players were often required, seated at the same manual and dividing the overall compass between them.
4. There were often more pipes than sliders (on the Winchester organ the proportion was ten to one).
5. When this was the case each note was produced by a simultaneous 'mixture' of different pipes, producing a variety not only of timbre but also of pitch. There were 'unisons' (sounding at the basic pitch), 'octaves' (sounding an octave higher), and 'quints' (sounding one or more octaves plus a fifth higher).
6. When a medieval organ had a number of different ranks of pipes, it still had only one basic sound, since there were no draw-stops to change the combination of pipes. These were not developed until the fifteenth century.
7. The spectrum of sound from top to bottom of the register was a changing one, since according to many illustrations all the pipes were of the same diameter. On later organs the diameter is proportionate to the length, so that the shortest pipes are narrow and the largest much broader.

However limited their musical scope the sound of these large organs was clearly impressive, but their precise function in church music is still a matter of debate. With all its secular associations from Greek and Roman times the organ was not entirely welcomed by the early Christian Church and its use was regularly questioned. 'Whence hath the Church

Hydraulic organ from the Utrecht Psalter (AD 860).

so many Organs and Musicall Instruments? To what purpose, I pray you, is that terrible blowing of Belloes, expressing rather the Crakes of Thunder, than the sweet-nesse of a voyce?' So wrote Aelred, Abbot of Rievaulx in Yorkshire during the twelfth century (the translation is from William Prynne's *Histrio-mastix* published in 1633).[5] Yet there was a very obvious purpose to which organs could have been put during the twelfth century and that is doubling the voices of the choir or even replacing them entirely in the long sustained tenor parts which occur in the works by composers of the Notre Dame School. The huge *organa* of Léonin and especially Pérotin cry out for some kind of instrumental support[6] and it has been suggested that the whole practice of organum came from the organ in the first place. It must be remembered, however, that the Latin word *organum* meant any kind of instrument, not just the organ, and it cannot be established with any certainty that the cathedral of Notre Dame actually possessed an organ during the time of Léonin and Pérotin.[7]

Portative organ and positive organ

During the thirteenth and fourteenth centuries the trend in organ-building seems to have moved from the monstrous to the miniature. All the important developments took place on much smaller types of instrument on which it was possible to restore the delicate keyboard of antiquity, and it was for them that the earliest surviving examples of keyboard music were designed. The old custom of labelling the sliders with letters for each note of the scale led to the development of alphabetical organ tablature. It is not clear precisely when the clumsy slider movement was abandoned in favour of the keyboard, permitting an infinitely

King David seated at an organ; on his right is an organ blower and on his left a hurdy-gurdy player. Thirteenth-century Psalter. (Belvoir Castle)

more sensitive finger technique, but the Belvoir Castle Psalter and other sources prove that the organ keyboard was well established by the thirteenth century, as was the practice of playing with both hands.

The change in emphasis in organ-building was certainly bound up with the changing role of the Church in political and social life. The image of the Church was becoming mercenary and corrupt, its authority was on the wane, and the process of decline culminated in the rivalry of the Papal Schism (1378–1417), during which two Popes vied for the position of God's highest representative on earth. Composers turned their attention to the court rather than the Church and there was a tremendous surge of interest in the composition of secular music. It is no accident that the earliest collections of keyboard music contain a high proportion of secular pieces: the dances in the Robertsbridge fragment[8] (*c.*1320) and the many settings of ballades, madrigals, and ballate in the Faenza Codex[9] (late fourteenth century). When Guillaume de Machaut referred to the organ as the 'king of instruments'[10] he was surely paying tribute to its versatility as well as its virtuosity and to its ability to enhance every realm of music-making.

Virtuoso the organ certainly had become by the fourteenth century. The Robertsbridge and Faenza collections demand some nimble finger-work, especially from the right hand. Organ-playing was even becoming competitive. At a contest held in Venice, probably in 1364, the organ playing of Francesco Landini (*c.*1325-97) is said to have earned him a laurel wreath from the King of Cyprus, and although this has been disputed[11] Landini's skill as an organist is beyond doubt. One of the most charming compliments comes in a *novella* by Giovanni da Prato. 'After this story, the sun was coming up and beginning to get warm; a thousand birds were singing. Francesco was ordered to play on his organetto to see if the singing of the birds would lessen or increase with his playing. As soon as he began to play, many birds at first became silent, then they redoubled their singing and, strange to say, one nightingale came and perched on a branch over his head.'[12]

The *organetto*, usually known today as the portative organ, was one of the most popular instruments, regularly illustrated from the thirteenth to the sixteenth centuries. There are usually two rows of pipes giving a range of up to two octaves (one pipe to a note) and judging by the size of the pipes the lowest note must have been round about middle C. Some medieval illustrations (like the picture of Landini on this page) show a couple of much longer pipes at one end, perhaps to provide some kind of drone. The portative was of light construction and when supported by a sling could easily be carried about or played in procession. Its unique feature was the way the player provided his own air supply, using the right hand on the keyboard and the left hand for the bellows. And that was not the limit of the player's dexterity. According to the thirteenth-century *Roman de la Rose*:

Orgues i r'a bien maniables,
A une sole main portable,
Ou il-meismes soufle et touche
Et chante avec a plaine bouche
Motes, ou treble ou teneure . . .
(There are easily manageable organs that can be carried in the hand, the same person simul-taneously pumping (the bellows), playing (the instrument), and singing aloud motets, either soprano or tenor . . .)[13]

Unlike the other types of organ, the portative was a monophonic instrument, suited to playing a solo dance or a single part in a chanson or instrumental piece. As with the larger organs, its keyboard was diatonic to start with, though by the end of the fourteenth century it had probably become more or less fully chromatic.

Medallion from the Squarcialupi Codex (Cod. Pal. 87) showing Landini playing the organetto or portative organ.

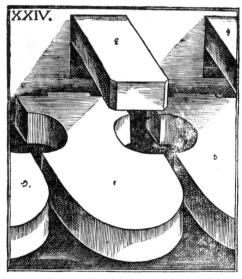

Detail showing the keys of the Halberstadt organ, from Praetorius' *Syntagma Musicum* (1619).

Although the 'great' church organ replaced its old slider mechanism with a version of the new keyboard it remained an unwieldy, clumsy instrument. During the fourteenth century additional keyboards were added to offer some variety of tone. On the organ completed in 1361 at Halberstadt Cathedral in Germany there were three manuals and a pedal keyboard, though this must have been unusual for the time. But in spite of the existence of twenty bellows worked by ten men, the compass was only twenty-two notes with fourteen 'naturals' and eight 'sharps'. The instrument was renova-ted in 1495, and Praetorius (1619) gives us a description of it and illustrates its keyboards.

The clumsiness of the keys is clear enough: Praetorius even suggests that the lowest of the three manuals could be played with the knees. As for the sound:

'All was of a coarse mixture. This is evident from the . . . size of the clavier, which did not extend high enough for beauty, but produced a deep, coarse roar and a fearful growling to which the mixture pipes added an extraordinary loud noise, a terrible scream.'[14]

Such an instrument could demand strenuous physical effort from the player. When the wind pressure was enormous it might need the full muscular force of the arm to keep a key down. The playing technique was similar to that still used on the carillon today where each key is struck with the closed hand. With the clumsy action of some medieval instruments players must have occasionally resorted to a strong blow from the fist. The carillons – sets of bells played by means of one or more keyboards – were built in the Low Countries at the end of the Middle Ages, and their development is related to that of the large organ. In the four-teenth century in the Netherlands carillons were played with the feet as well as the hands,[15] no doubt because the player could exert more strength with his feet, and the existence of this technique may have encouraged the develop-ment of the organ pedal keyboard. What the Dutch writer Fischer said about carillon players

Modern portative organ by Noel Mander. The pipes are graded in diameter, as on the renaissance portatives which have been preserved.

in 1738 certainly applies to medieval organ too: 'A musician requires nothing more th thorough knowledge of music, good hand feet, and no gout.'[15]

Whilst the 'great' organ remained in the Church's domain and the portative was use primarily for courtly entertainment, the 'positive', lying between the two types in s was suitable for both Church and chamber music. It was larger than the portative, re-quiring two or three sets of bellows and an assistant to operate them; this enabled the to use both hands at the keyboard. Longer extended the compass downwards, and the typical positive had a basic 'mixture' sound several pipes to one note. Although it was 'portative' in the sense the organetto was, the positive could be moved about fairly ea Larger instruments stood on the floor while smaller ones are often shown standing on a table. Of the three types of organ, the posit was the most versatile and though it surviv an independent instrument in its own right also became incorporated in the 'great' chu organ. Hence the names 'positive' and 'grea used since the Renaissance to describe two o the organ's manuals. In England the positiv became known as the 'chair' organ, which gradually become corrupted to 'choir' orga

The hurdy-gurdy

The first stringed instrument to which the keyboard principle was applied was the hu gurdy, variously known as the *organistrum*, *symphonia* or *chifonie*, *organica lyra*, *armonie*, *vielle à roue*. This last name (literally 'wheel-fiddle') explains one of the two processes of mechanization involved. The bowing actio the fiddle is replaced by a wheel cranked by handle. The wheel, the outer rim of which coated with resin, makes all the strings reso at once, whether drone or melody strings, a provides a continuous sound. In the same w that the bag of the bagpipe avoids stopping breath so the wheel of the hurdy-gurdy avo changes of bowing. In addition the process fingering is mechanized too, the same string being stopped at different points to produce required scale.

The earliest evidence for the hurdy-gurdy Europe dates from the first part of the twelf century though, like the art of bowing, the principle may have been inherited from earl experiments in the East.[17] By the time of the Notre Dame School (late twelfth century) t instrument was both widely used and highl regarded. From the thirteenth century onw both construction and playing technique changed considerably. There are several in-teresting parallels with the development of organ and broadly speaking two distinct hu gurdy types may be chronicled as follows.

the thirteenth century

earliest hurdy-gurdies were large two-man ments, one person being needed to crank andle and the other to operate the key- . This division of labour was necessary not through the size of the instrument but se of the key action. The 'keys' are best bed as revolving bridges each requiring a twisting movement to bring them into ct with the strings. The action might be ared to turning a series of front-door keys: ayer clearly needed both hands for the job

After the thirteenth century

Like the organ, the hurdy-gurdy developed a more compact form during the thirteenth century and much improved its key mechanism. Two players became superfluous since the same person could manage both handle and keyboard. The revolving bridges were replaced by keys operating sliding tangents (Latin *tangere*, to touch) which had to be pressed up against the string and then allowed to fall back into position. The keyboard resembled that of the portative organ and the finger action required was

strings were added and by the fourteenth century there were as many as five or six. The keyboard increased in range too: from a simple diatonic octave it gradually progressed to a fully chromatic two octaves. Mersenne mentions as many as forty-nine keys.[19] It is worth mentioning that the typical waisted or figure-of-8 shape of the hurdy-gurdy, linking it with the fiddle, is found in all periods. The oblong box shape sometimes found illustrated does not represent the prototype, only a variation on the basic form. The hurdy-gurdy continued to

flourish during later ages, and it still survives, in countries such as France and Belgium, as a folk instrument.[20]

Monochord and clavichord

The principle of the early hurdy-gurdy – stopping a string by means of a series of movable bridges – is related to that of the *monochord*. And for the origins of this instrument we must once again turn to Ancient Greece. First described by the mathematician Euclid in about 300 BC, the monochord dates from the time of

apocalyptic elders with large hurdy-gurdy
unknown twelfth-century master.

(Cathedral of Santiago de Compostela, Spain)

Traditional French hurdy-gurdy (early nineteenth century). (Collection of Oliver Brookes)

even so speed must have been very re- ed. Because of the key cover which pro- the mechanical 'keyboard', details are hard ake out in medieval illustrations of the y-gurdy. One source however[18] clearly s that the bridges press against all three gs. Although details of tuning are uncertain, does suggest some kind of 'mixture' gement. If the tuning was in fifths and ves, for instance, the hurdy-gurdy would played in a kind of strict parallel organum some of the names given to the instrument – istrum, *symphonia,* and *armonie* – do suggest sociation with early polyphony.

similar except that each key had to be pressed upwards instead of downwards. The tangents were arranged so as to be selective: they touched only the melody string, leaving the others to sound a permanent drone. Thus the whole character of the hurdy-gurdy changed: from a slow-moving instrument capable of playing in consecutive fourths, fifths, or octaves it became an ideal instrument for dance music with an agile keyboard for the melody and a fixed drone for the accompaniment. To start with three strings seem to have been the norm: a tuning of G and d for the drone strings and c for the melody strings would correspond with one of the regular tunings of the fiddle. More

A hurdy-gurdy (called *lyra*), from Virdung's *Musica getutscht* (1511).

Pythagoras three hundred years earlier. According to Aristides Quintilianus: 'as he prepared to leave this earthly life Pythagoras besought his disciples to play the monochord.'[21] Be that as it may, the Greeks developed the monochord as a piece of laboratory apparatus for defining and demonstrating the basic laws of harmonics and teaching scales and intervals. It consists of a simple oblong sound box equipped with two bridges and a string stretched over them, hence the name monochord (*monos* meaning one, *chordè* meaning string). The string is attached at one end and held in position by a weight or peg at the other. Besides the fixed bridges there is a movable bridge used to divide the string at different points. The monochord was eagerly adopted by the medieval theorists. According to an anonymous scholar of the tenth century: 'Just as the teacher first shows the letters in a table, so the music teacher can show all the notes of the chart with the help of the monochord.'[22] Using some kind of plectrum to sound the string, the teacher would have begun his lesson by demonstrating the simplest ratios between two sections of vibrating string. If the bridge was placed so as to divide the string in the ratio 1:2 the interval was an octave (*diapason*); if the ratio was 2:3 the interval was a fifth (*diapente*); if the ratio was 3:4 the interval was a fourth (*diatessaron*); and so on.

In spite of its name, the monochord seems to

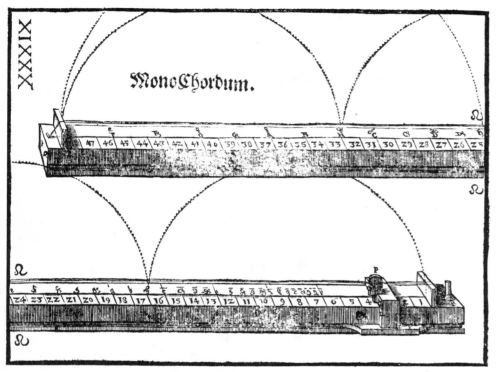

Calibrated monochord from Praetorius' *Syntagma Musicum* (1619). The movable bridge is shown at the bottom right-hand end.

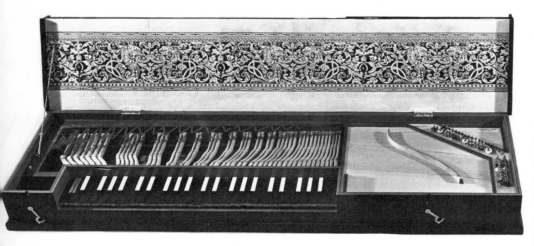

Copy by Christopher Nobbs of a fretted clavichord with Flemish decoration in the Museum of Musical Instruments, Brussels. There are thirty-three pairs of brass strings, giving a range of four octaves.

have acquired more than one string, probably to demonstrate the effect of sounding several notes at once.[23] But whilst the Greeks restricted its use to a piece of scientific equipment, at some point during the Middle Ages the monochord became a musical instrument in its own right. As a *monacorde*, or the corrupted *manichord* or *manicordio*, it is mentioned in French romances and courtly epics and depicted in miniatures from the time of the troubadours. Whilst this aspect of the monochord's career was fairly short-lived, as a measuring apparatus it continued in use right up to the nineteenth century and is mentioned by such authorities as Zarlino (1588), Kircher (1650), Mattheson (1739), and Paul (1868).[24]

As it stood at the end of the Middle Ages the monochord was of greater potential than practical use. Having to move the bridges to obtain different notes exercised the same sort of restraint as having to turn the keys on the early hurdy-gurdy. The solution lay once again in the application of the keyboard principle, though unfortunately we do not know the precise date or whereabouts of the clavichord's invention. As Sebastian Virdung says in his *Musica getutscht* (1511): 'But who it was that may have invented it or thought it out, that made a key for every point according to the same division of the string, that strikes the string exactly at that position or point, and then produces that sound only and no other than seems to have been given it by nature at that point of division, that I cannot tell; nor do I know who dubbed or named the instrument clavichord, after those same keys.'[25]

The trouble is that to start with the instrument was not always dubbed *clavichord* but sometimes *clarichord* or *manichord*, a name which stuck throughout the renaissance and baroque periods and causes confusion between clavichord and monochord. To make matters worse, there are a number of fourteenth-century references to an instrument called the *eschiquier, exaquier, chekker,* and other variants. Edward III gave one to John of France in 1360, Machaut refers to the *eschaquier d'Engleterre* in his poem *La Prise d'Alexandrie* (c.1367), and King John of Aragon mentions an *exaquier* several times in letters written between 1387 and 1388, on one occasion describing it as *sturment semblant dorguens que sona ab cordes* (an instrument resembling the organ but sounded by strings).[26] Various theories have been put forward as to the indentity of this mysterious instrument, ranging from the clavicytherium or upright harpsichord to a hypothetical instrument which has disappeared altogether. Thanks to the researches of Edwin Ripin[26] it now seems certain that the *chekker* was in fact a clavichord, and we can safely assign the development of the clavichord to the mid-fourteenth century,

though there must in all probability have be a period of experiment with different kinds keyed monochord first.

The clavichord's name is self-explanatory the application of a key (Latin *clavis*) to the string, but, perhaps less obvious is what the instrument inherited from the old. Like the monochord, the early clavichord used the sa string to produce several notes (two, three, even four) by stopping the string at differen points along its length. Instead of one mova bridge for each string, there was now a brid for each note, brought into contact with the string by pressing a key on the keyboard. A instead of having a separate plectrum to sou the string, the bridge did that job too, produ ing a very soft attack. You could compare th sound to that obtained by pressing down a string on the fingerboard of the guitar with left hand, *ie* without plucking. Because of th process of stopping the string which it share with the guitar and lute families, the early clavichord became known as *gebunden*, or th 'fretted' clavichord. There were of course, certain notes which you could not play simu taneously because they both employed the s string. On the oldest surviving clavichord[27] there are forty-five keys to twenty-two dou sets of strings. But whereas the lowest notes fret-free, in the upper register several strings have to produce four different notes, for example, f', f♯', g', g♯'. This was rather a restriction if you wanted to play suspensions although as Praetorius pointed out it certain saved time in tuning the instrument. Gradua the proportion of strings to keys increased, though throughout the seventeenth century certain adjacent semitones continued to share the same string. It was not until the early eighteenth century that the richer musical vocabulary demanded complete flexibility a some clavichords became fret-free.[28]

From the outset the clavichord must have been an instrument of private practice and recreation. Even though it is sometimes illus ted in consort with other instruments, its sof voice was too small for any kind of competit and is principally designed to delight the ear the player. It was, and still is, an ideal practic instrument for organists, enabling them to play at home instead of in a cold church. Mu organ music sounds well on the clavichord, f instance many of the pieces in the famous Buxheim Organ Book[29] (c.1470), which the late Thurston Dart suggested may in fact ha been intended for the clavichord.[30] Specific repertory for the clavichord does not occur until the seventeenth century and it was not until the baroque period that makers were encouraged to increase the range and volum beyond the tiny sound of the small fretted clavichord of the Renaissance.

Brass

dieval ancestors of the modern trumpet,
nd trombone were not always made of
Many different materials were used for
nstruction, including other metals, ivory,
rn, so strictly speaking we should call
up mouthpiece' instruments rather than
struments. In common with the modern
ral brass, medieval trumpets and horns
unded by blowing into a cup-shaped
piece. The player used different lip
es to obtain different notes: slack
e for low notes, tighter pressure for high
he mouthpiece (often an integral part of
rument rather than a separate unit)
considerably in shape and often restricted
yer to one or two notes rather than
aging the development of a wide range.

rumpet

ly trumpets, without slides, valves, or
holes, were in any case restricted to the
l' notes obtainable from an open tube,
he notes of the harmonic series. The
f the notes is dependent upon the length
ube, but the intervals between the notes
ays the same. An instrument eight feet
roduces a fundamental note of approxi-
C below the bass stave, and a rising
f 'open' notes belonging to the common
of C.

2   3   4   5   6
(fundamental)

ems unlikely that medieval trumpeters
red much further up the harmonic series
nis. Like modern buglers, they must have
ensated for any lack of musical variety by
lume and brilliance of their tone. The
nature of medieval trumpet calls will
s remain something of a mystery, since
s virtually no written evidence before the
nth century. But the Burgundian com-
Guillaume Dufay gives us a fascinating
se of what medieval fanfares may have
ike in his Gloria ad modum tubae written
ut the year 1420.[1] As the title *in the
r of a trumpet* suggests, the two instrument-
ts of the Gloria consist of fanfares playable
edieval trumpets pitched in C. Only four
are used in each part: g c' e' g', that is,
onics 3 to 6 as shown above.
torial evidence confirms that the typical
val straight trumpet was an imposing
ment over six feet long. It was usually
in jointed metal sections, often with a
bell, and was commonly known as the
e, a corruption of the latin *buccina*.
er trumpets of two or three feet in length
distinguished by the name *claro*, or
. The word trumpet – a diminutive of

trump or trompe – seems to have been used
rather indiscriminately to cover many different
types. The claro was particularly suited to
military use. It was easier to carry about than
the more cumbersome buisine, and its high-
pitched signals could be clearly heard even in the
heat of battle. In *La Prise d'Alexandre*, Machaut
mentions all three names: 'Trompes, buzines

ABOVE
Pair of traditional long wooden trumpets from
Sweden. (Author's collection)

et trompettes' and elsewhere he distinguishes
between the *Trompe* and the *Trompe petite*.[2]

The long trumpets were ideal for ceremonial
music: a dozen or more buisine players with
standards flying from their instruments made a
splendid impression on the eye as well as the
ear, a fact which kings and princes were quick
to appreciate. Trumpets became the prerogative
of the nobility; trumpeters together with their
attendant drummers were an essential part of
every royal household. They acted as heralds on
all public occasions, travelled in the royal
retinue, and occupied a more elevated social
position than most other professional musicians.
As early as 1087, at the siege of Rochester,
William II took possession of the town with a
royal blaze of trumpets,[2] and the instrument's
popularity was subsequently encouraged by the

Crusades. The pomp and splendour of the
Saracen bands of shawms, trumpets, and drums
impressed the crusaders and encouraged them
to form similar bands of their own. An alternative French name for the buisine was *cor
sarrazinois* (*Saracen* horn).

There are various survivals of the medieval
trumpet. The post horn retained the clarion's

BELOW
Nineteenth-century French post horn and
traditional trumpet from Morocco with large
flared bell. The wide mouthpiece of the latter
favours the production of the fundamental.
(Author's collection)

function as a signalling instrument right up to
the end of the nineteenth century. The traditional birchbark trumpet, still made and used by
Swedish shepherds, offers a living example of
the clear ringing tones which the buisine must
surely have had. The Moroccan trumpet still
retains its old ceremonial associations and a place
in the outdoor band along with shawms and
drums. In Marrakesh such a band can still be
heard playing for wedding processions, with the
trumpets supplying a continuous low drone.
The Moroccan trumpeter is very much a one-
note man, quite content with a supporting role
in the ensemble. It is likely that this sort of
performance practice spread to Europe from
the East during the Middle Ages, particularly
for dance music.

Cow horn and oliphant

In one sense the medieval trumpet's musical
limitations were its virtue: it was isolated from
all other instruments. But as far back as late
Saxon times men had already begun to look for
some way of filling in the gaps between the
natural notes of the harmonic series. The whole
history of early brass instruments consists of the
the different attempts which were made to cope
with this problem. The first attempt combined
techniques of brass and woodwind. Cow and
goat horns had already been used as signalling
instruments for many centuries. With the tip
removed to enable a mouthpiece to be carved
into the narrow end of the instrument, a couple
of useful and fairly booming notes could be
produced, a fourth or fifth apart. By the tenth
century finger-holes were added, making possible a series of consecutive notes so that the
horn could be used for simple melodies. Cow
horns with three finger-holes are still made by
Scandinavian shepherds: by skilful use of a

Shepherds with simple, hole-less cow horns, from
Velislav's Bible (1340). (University Library,
Prague)

Cow horn with three fingerholes. (Collection of Alan Lumsden)

couple of hand-stopped notes they can produce a useful range of a sixth. Because the bore of the horn is conical, as opposed to the trumpet's basically cylindrical bore plus bell, the tone is plaintive rather than aggressive.

Long after the development of the finger-hole horn, hole-less instruments continued to be used. The most splendid variety was the *oliphant* (from the French *cor d'olifant*, elephant's horn). These ivory instruments reached the West from Byzantium during the Middle Ages and were highly prized. Although their musical use was as restricted as the simplest cow horns they were often richly carved and became the symbol of royalty.[4] The oliphant crops up regularly in medieval French literature and the instrument continued to be made throughout the Renaissance and into the seventeenth century. In the treasury of St Guy's Cathedral, Prague, is the famous hunting horn thought to have been sounded by Roland, nephew of Charlemagne. Legend has it that the sound of this horn carried for an amazing distance. When Roland lay wounded in the Pyrenees in the year 778 he blew the horn to summon help. The story goes that Charlemagne heard him from many miles away, but Roland blew so hard that he burst an artery in his neck and cracked the horn.[5]

The medieval cornett

Scandinavia is also the home of another interesting medieval survival, the Finnish *tuohitorvi*. This represents an interim stage between the fairly primitive cow horn and the sophisticated cornett (literally 'little horn') of the renaissance. The finger-hole horn was an extremely limited instrument. There was normally room for no more than three finger-holes, the overall pitch was entirely dependent on the dimensions of the animal horn, and the maker had very little control over the sort of instrument he could make. So at some stage towards the end of the Middle Ages, makers changed from horn to wood. The tuohitorvi provides us with a typical cornett prototype. It is made in two halves hollowed out lengthwise and then glued together and bound with bark. The

Finnish *tuohitorvi*. (Collection of Christopher Monk)

shallow cup mouthpiece is carved at the narrow end of the conical bore and a piece of horn is inserted at the other by way of a bell, a reminder of the tuohitorvi's animal horn ancestry. There are five finger-holes and thumb-hole, and the instrument speaks well over a diatonic range of an octave and a half, the lowest note being approximately the A below middle C.

The development of the medieval cornett may well have taken place in Germany and Austria. Amongst the instruments listed at the Feast of the Pheasant in Lille in 1454 is a *German* cornett,[6] and a manuscript containing the songs of Hermann, monk of Salzburg (late fourteenth century),[7] provides evidence of interest in wind playing in the Alpine regions. Many of the songs are based on popular Alpine melodies and three are described as *gut zu blasen* (good for blowing). The titles *das nachthorn* (the night-horn), *das taghorn* (the day-horn), and *das kchühorn* (the cow-horn), suggest the use of an instrument of the finger-hole horn or cornett type, and the fairly crude part-writing seems to reflect a popular instrumental rather than vocal style. It is hardly surprising that cowhorns and cornetts developed in mountainous regions where the raw materials were readily available and where their carrying power would be useful. It is in just such regions of Scandinavia and elsewhere that folk survivals are found today.

The slide trumpet

A fourth piece by the Monk of Salzburg is entitled *der trumpet*, and if by this Hermann intended the trumpet to participate in the performance he must have meant some kind of *slide* trumpet, since the range of the parts excludes any instrument relying purely on the harmonic series. The date at which the slide trumpet first appeared is uncertain, though it may be as early as the fourteenth century, when the Spanish word *sacabuche* (literally 'draw-pipe') was in use.[8] It developed from the *buisine*, which towards the end of the Middle Ages was lengthened, and to avoid an instrument of inordinate length was re-formed into a flattened S shape. The fact that the tube was cylindrical made possible a telescopic mouthpipe: the player could steady the mouthpiece against the lips with one hand and slide the whole instrument in and out along the mouthpipe with the other. So whilst the cornett had *shortened* the sounding length of the tube with a series of finger-holes, the slide trumpet *lengthened* the sounding length with a series of extended slide positions. The theory behind this invention was brilliant, but in practice the slide trumpet must have proved tricky to handle. Since the mouthpipe is a single tube, not a double one, each slide position is roughly twice as long as that of the modern tenor trombone. This in itself makes fast passages a problem, but the difficulties are

increased by the basic imbalance of the instrument. The moving section is so much heavier than the slender mouthpipe that an over-hard return to first position can knock the player's teeth out.

Other names for the slide trumpet include *draw trumpet*, *Zugtrompete*, and *trompette des ménestrels* (minstrels' trumpet). Modern reconstructions based on surviving illustrations suggest that the slide trumpet would probably have been pitched in C or D with a comfortable range of f to a' or g to b'. It is several times depicted playing with shawms for the *basse danse*, the most popular court dance of the fifteenth century. The slide trumpet would have been ideal for the slow-moving tenor part on which the dance was always based. A handful of fifteenth-century works appear to have been written with the slide trumpet in mind.[9] They range from Mass sections, such as the Gloria Arnoldus de Latins with a contratenor marked *Tuba sub fuga*, to the *rondeau J'ayme bien* by Pierre Fontaine with its contratenor *Trompette* added almost certainly by Guillaume Dufay in 1434 or 1435.[10] As it stands the two-octave range of the latter part (D–d') lies far too low for any kind of slide trumpet. Yet according to the composer Adam of Fulda a feature of Dufay's compositions was the way he added several notes in the bass register in order to accommodate instruments.[11] One cannot help wondering if this part was designed for another type of sackbut on which the U-shaped slide could cope with the low notes (see chapter 5, page 68). By the early sixteenth century the slide trumpet had been largely superseded by the sackbut, though the instrument continued to be used in Germany well into the eighteenth.

An angel playing the slide trumpet, from *Angel Musicians* by Hans Memling (c.1435–94). (Triptych of Najera (left panel), Musée Royal des Beaux Arts, Antwerp)

4 Strings

y. The *tromba da tirarsi* required in seven
...'s cantatas is a slide trumpet, though
...glish slide trumpet of the baroque period
...nts a quite different line of development

involving a *backward*-operating *double* slide.
The *flat trumpets* which Purcell calls for in his
funeral music for Queen Mary (1695) are of
this latter type.

Because of their antiquity and their diverse and
widespread forms, stringed instruments present
a complex problem for the historian. Tracing
and documenting their development in Europe
during the Middle Ages is a far from easy task,
made particularly difficult by the stylized
representations of medieval art and the
ambiguous and confusing way in which names
were used by contemporary writers. The word
vielle, for instance, described instruments as
different as the medieval fiddle and the
hurdy-gurdy. Before the tenth century *lyra*
signified lyre, during the later Middle Ages it
was applied to the rebec, harp, or even lute,
whilst during the Renaissance it meant *lira da
braccio* as well as being used for the hurdy-gurdy
and a style of viol playing. The word *chrotta*
and its variants (*rotta, crot, rote,* etc.) seem to have
been applied at various stages to the harp, lyre,
crwth, and hurdy-gurdy. Modern research has
not yet managed to sort out all the problems
and occasionally has even compounded the
confusion. Mistakes have been made over
dating, translation, and (especially) the
interpretation of iconographical evidence.
Tuning keys have been identified as plectra,
plectra have been identified as bows, and in the
case of a famous drawing in the Utrecht
Psalter (AD 860) a long pole has been variously
defined as a bow, a sword, and a measuring
rod.[1] Because of the restricted scope of this
book, what follows will inevitably involve
some degree of over-simplification.

Instruments with open strings only

The harp and lyre represent two of the most
ancient types of stringed instrument. Each
played an important part in various pre-
Christian civilizations and both still survive all
over the world in many primitive forms.
Relatively sophisticated forms of harp and lyre
have been in existence for five thousand years
and were amongst the most valued instruments
in the Babylonian and Egyptian civilizations.
Although obviously different in construction,
shape, and playing technique, they are linked
with the psaltery and dulcimer by their
exclusive use of open strings. Because none of
the strings is stopped with the fingers, as on
the violin or guitar, each string will produce
only one note, and the range of the instrument
is therefore entirely dependent on the number
of strings.

In the Middle Ages strings were made
principally from twisted animal gut (usually
sheep gut), though horse hair and even silk were
occasionally used.[2] From the thirteenth century
onwards metal came increasingly into use, and
wire strings were made of copper, steel, and
even silver. Metal was found particularly
serviceable on instruments which were struck,
such as the dulcimer, or plucked with a
plectrum, such as the psaltery. The tone was
louder and more brilliant and the strings
themselves were less liable to break. Harps too
were strung with metal as well as gut, in spite
of normally being plucked with the fingers or
finger nails.

The instruments in this section are also
linked by their method of tuning. Each string
was attached to a wooden peg or metal pin and
the string tension was normally adjusted with a
tuning key. The system of tuning was diatonic,
never chromatic, and restricted the instrument
to one mode or basic scale at a time. Thus an
instrument tuned in the Dorian mode would
only be able to play the following notes:

Yet a piece written in the Dorian mode was
quite likely to demand an occasional B♭ or C♯,
and just how the players coped with such
accidentals is rather a puzzle. There seems to be
no evidence for any quick-change device like
the little metal flaps fitted on the modern Arab
qānūn which enable the players to alter the pitch
of a course of strings with an adroit flick of the
fingers. Equally the levers found on the
traditional Irish harp placed below the tuning
pins to raise the pitch of each string by a
semitone are a fairly recent development.
Just what medieval players did do to obtain

...cal fifteenth-century basse-danse ensemble
... shawms and slide trumpet. From *The
...he Court of King Yon of Gascony before the*

Betrothal of his daughter Clarissa; miniature by
Loyset Liedet or his workshop, between 1468
and 1470. (Musée de l'Arsenal, Paris)

...nics
...rmonic notes need sharpening.

...struction by Philip Bate of a fifteenth-
...y slide trumpet, based on Hans Memling's
...ng.

ABOVE
Chart by Alan Lumsden showing range and
positions of a slide trumpet in C.

Tuning key in action. Velislav's Bible (1340).
(University Library, Prague)

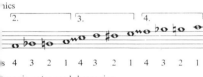

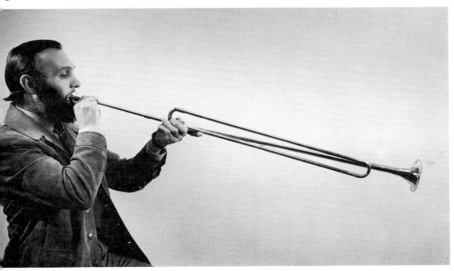

Reconstruction by Alan Crumpler of an early medieval harp, based on an illustration in an English psalter, *c*.1050.

proper things for any man to have in his house were 'a virtuous wife, his cushion on his chair, and his harp in tune'.[3] According to Guillaume de Machaut the harp was the best of all the soft instruments[4] and the survival of 'Harper' as a common English surname is an indication of the popularity of the instrument. If only medieval harpers had developed their own system of notation,[5] as organists and lutenists did, we should be a great deal wiser about exactly how the harp was used. It would be fascinating to know just how it accompanied the monophonic songs of the troubadours, or what the free preludes were like which apparently prefaced singing and recitation on formal occasions. The harp must have developed quite an extensive solo repertory during the Middle Ages, including some kinds of part music, but performers must have relied primarily upon memory and improvisation.[6]

Two Burgundian composers: Guillaume Dufay with a portative organ and Gilles Binchois holding a typical 'Gothic' harp. A miniature illustrating Martin le Franc's poem *Le Champion des dames* (1451). (Bibliothèque Nationale, Paris)

accidentals remains unclear. Perhaps they had their own rules of *musica ficta* by which they altered the difficult notes or even left some of them out altogether. A surprising number of medieval illustrations do show tuning keys ready to hand, particularly with harps and psalteries. So it may be that certain notes were re-tuned during performance, even though this involved playing with one hand only.

The harp
The question of accidentals is especially perplexing with regard to the harp, whose high standing and importance in medieval music-making are unquestioned. According to the twelfth-century *Laws of Wales* the three things indispensable to a gentleman were 'his harp, his cloak, and his chessboard' whilst the three

There can be no doubt that the harp was customarily played with great expressiveness and brilliance. The latter effect was sometimes obtained by plucking with the fingernails rather than the tips of the fingers. There are several references like that which occurs in the thirteenth-century *Kyng Horn*: 'Teach him to harpe with his nayles scharpe.'[7] In 1183 Giraldus de Barri, court chaplain to Henry II, commented on the technical facility of the Irish harpers: 'Their style is not, as on the British instruments to which we are accustomed, deliberate and solemn but quick and lively . . . It is remarkable that, with such rapid fingerwork, the musical rhythm is maintained and that, by unfailingly disciplined art, the integrity of the tune is fully preserved throughout the ornate rhythms and the profusely intricate polyphony . . . They

introduce and leave rhythmic motifs so subtly, they play the tinkling sounds on the thinner strings above the sustained sound of the thicker string so freely, they take such secret delight and caress [the strings] so sensuously, that the greatest part of their art seems to lie in veiling it . . .'[8]

Such technical facility is certainly the hallmark of South American players today, who still use the lineal descendant of the sixteenth-century Spanish harp. Their astonishing agility in repeated broken-chord patterns or scales of consecutive thirds or octaves is a reminder that the diatonic harp can be a virtuoso's instrument and their sharp aggressive attack is a far cry from the delicate rippling effect we associate with the orchestral harp today. During the Middle Ages harpers must have displayed a mastery of different playing styles but there certainly seems to have been a penchant for hard rather than gentle tone. For instance, a 'buzzing' or 'rattling' effect could be produced by setting the 'bray' pins so that the strings rattled against them. This practice, particularly effective on wire-strung harps, is mentioned as late as 1619 by Praetorius: 'On the [common] harp . . . the strings also rattle and crackle if they come into contact with the pegs with which they are fastened into the frame of the instrument, at the bottom. This rattling is usually referred to as *harfenierend* or a harp-like sound.'[9] (See harp with 'bray' pins on p. 74.)

The principal feature which distinguishes the harp of medieval Europe from its predecessors in the ancient civilizations of the East is its three-sectional construction. Whereas the ancient harp had relied on a soundbox and a peg arm only to support the strings, the addition of a fore pillar completed the triangular frame and produced a firm sturdy structure. Tradition gives Ireland the credit for this development, but although the frame harp certainly flourished in Celtic lands its origins remain obscure. It is regularly illustrated from the ninth century onwards and shapes and sizes seem to have varied enormously.[10] Some illustrations show as few as six or seven strings, but the twelfth-century troubadour Guiraut de Calanson recommends seventeen strings and in the fourteenth century Guillaume de Machaut compares the twenty-five virtues of his lady to the twenty-five strings of his harp.[11] The harp acquired an equal variety of names. The word harp itself probably derives from an Indo-European root meaning 'to pluck'. Regional names included the Irish *cruit*, the Scottish *clarsach*, and the Welsh *telyn*, whilst the medieval theorists used *lyra, harpa, chrotta,* and *cythara*. As late as 1511 Sebastian Virdung complained: 'What one man calls a harp, another calls a lyre.'[12]

The harp played an important part in legend

Copy of a typical nineteenth-century Irish h[arp] by Keith Theobald.

and folklore. Not only was it traditionally [King] David's instrument but popular superstiti[on] credited the harp with supernatural power[s] which could 'destroy the feynde's myght'. In the tenth century St Dunstan, Archbish[op of] Canterbury, was charged with sorcery bec[ause] he left his harp where the wind could blow through the strings, producing magical an[d] mysterious music.[14] Other stories include t[he] of Alfred the Great who entered the Danis[h] camp disguised as a harper (*c.* AD 878) and [the] famous Irish legend of the curse of St Ruad[] (AD 560) immortalized in the ballad 'The H[] that once through Tara's Halls'.[15] At this e[] date, however, it is more likely to have be[en a] lyre, rather than a harp, which remained [] for evermore.

The lyre
Europe inherited the lyre from classical ant[iquity] and preserved its function as an accompan[ying] instrument. Anglo-Saxon minstrels used t[he] lyre for support during the recitation of a g[] epic or romance, though musically the sup[port] must have been of a very simple kind, whe[ther] melodic or chordal. The typical early med[ieval] lyre had six or seven strings running from tuning pegs over a bridge to a tailpiece fas[tened] at the base. Unlike the classical yoke-plus-[] design the instrument was of solid constru[ction] with a slightly waisted shape. The body w[]

ed out for some distance into the arms
exposed area covered with a sound-

Greek times onwards the lyre occupied
in mythology as well as real life, and this
se to accounts of miraculous skill in
nance. Galpin cites an old Gaelic legend
h a Druid chieftain invokes his magic
aning lyre) during a battle which
edly took place in the year 1800 BC.

fect of the Druid's performance was
onderful: the story tells how, in order
over the fate of a favourite musician, he
o comrades had penetrated into the camp
nemy, where they found the lyre
g in the banqueting hall. At the voice of
id it leaped from the wall and came to
once, killing nine persons on its way.
e played the three great musical strains
ation: at the sound of the first tears filled

struction of an early eighth-century lyre
ristopher Wright. (Collection of Oliver
es)

s; with the second he overcame them
ncontrollable laughter; and finally, with
rd, he sent the entire host to sleep, during
the three champions made good their
with the magic Crot.'[17]

ing the later Middle Ages the lyre was
eded by two instruments of greater
l capability: the harp and the *crowd,* or
l lyre. During the Renaissance the
pment of the cittern was a conscious
t to revive the *kithara,* the lyre of classical

times. Yet because of its classical associations
and its symbolical significance, the lyre
continued to be illustrated long after it had
fallen out of practical use.

Psaltery and dulcimer
These two instruments may conveniently be
dealt with together since they represent different
facets of the same basic instrumental type, one
plucked, the other struck. Both consist of a
sound box above which the strings run from
side to side over one or two sets of bridges.
The tuning pins are often set on alternate sides
and both instruments eventually adopted the
idea of courses rather than single strings. A
course of two or more strings to each note has
several advantages. Besides producing better
tone and carrying power, it provides some
insurance against breaking strings and,
particularly on the dulcimer, gives the player
more to aim at than a single thin strand.

The psaltery developed in the Near East and
filtered into Europe during the Crusades. It is
regularly illustrated from the twelfth century
onwards and chiefly goes by two names of
Greek origin: psaltery (from *psalterion*) and
canon or *canale* (from *kanon*). The Arabic *qānūn*
today is a large psaltery played with great
virtuosity in Middle Eastern orchestras, and is a
direct descendant of the forerunner of the
European psaltery. Other important survivals
are the Finnish *kantele,* and the zither of the
Austrian Tyrol.[18] The shape varied enormously:
triangular, trapezoidal, square, oblong, even
semicircular instruments are illustrated. The
most characteristic form was trapezoidal but
with incurved sides, and it is clearly this
snout-like shape which inspired the Italian
name mentioned by Praetorius in 1619,
istrumento di porco (pig's instrument). The
psaltery was played either resting on the lap or
leaning up against the chest, and fingers as well
as quill plectra seem to have been used. There
are many literary references to the psaltery,
often listing it in mixed ensembles of various
kinds, but evidently it was also satisfactory as a
solo instrument. In Chaucer's *Canterbury Tales*
the scholar Nicholas diverts himself with the
'gay sautrie' and the romance of *Eger and Grime*
provides us with a charming account of a lady
psaltery player:

the Ladye lovesome of hew and hyde
sett her downe by his bed side,
shee layd a sowter upon her knee,
and theron shee playd full love somlye.[19]

The dulcimer is basically a psaltery struck
with hammers and its arrival in Europe can be
chronicled only with difficulty. Since there is
very little structural difference between the
two instruments, identification in pictorial
representations depends on being able to

distinguish between plectra and hammers, not
always an easy matter. Some authorities have
identified dulcimers as early as the twelfth
century, others not until the fourteenth. The
word dulcimer (*dowsemere, dulcoemel,* etc, later
dulce melos) first occurs in the fourteenth century
and implies that the instrument was endowed
with sweetness of tone. The striking action gave
rise to the name *tympanon,* variants of which
occur in Celtic, French, and Italian. The
German name *Hackbrett,* meaning a butcher's
board for chopping meat, may have been
suggested by the action and the shape of the
instrument. Dulcimers were normally
trapezoidal and played resting on the lap or on a
table. Itinerant musicians of later ages regularly
fastened the instrument round their neck with
a sling.

Praetorius actually describes the psaltery as a
Hackbrett played with the fingers, whereas the

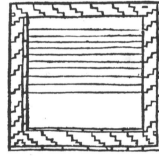
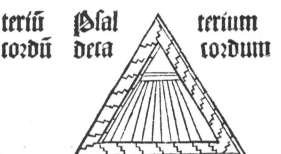

Italians called the dulcimer *salterio tedesco* –
German psaltery. Such evidence confirms the
close link between the two instruments, and it
is quite likely that during the Middle Ages long
plectra were used both to pluck and to strike
the same instrument. In the East the psaltery
and dulcimer had evolved their separate
identities before their introduction to Europe.
The home of the dulcimer seems to have been
Persia, where as the *santur* (derived from the
Greek *psalterion*) it is still played with great
brilliance today. Survivals of its migration
westward include the Greek *santouri* and
especially the Hungarian *cimbalom,* a large
concert instrument which has occasionally
found its way into the modern orchestra (as in
Kodály's suite *Háry János*).[20] The dulcimer
spread eastwards too. As late as 1800 it reached
China where it is still referred to as *yang ch'in,*
the *foreign* zither.

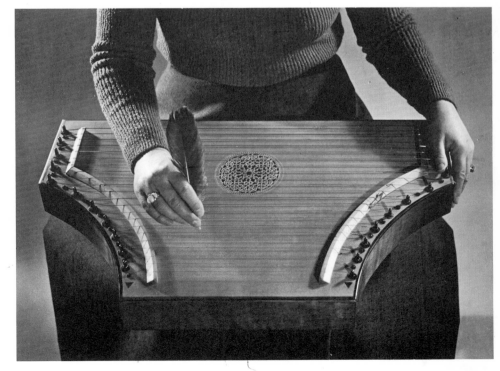

TOP
Square and triangular psalteries from Virdung's
Musica getutscht (1511).

BOTTOM
Reconstruction by Alan Crumpler of a typical
medieval snout-shaped psaltery.

TOP
Allegory of Music: illustration from a late fifteenth-century manuscript of the poem *Les Échecs amoureux*. The lady seated on the two swans is playing the dulcimer: in the background (*l* to *r*) we see pipe and tabor, shawm, bagpipes, and a group of singers. (Bibliothèque Nationale, Paris)

BOTTOM
Chinese dulcimer from Hong Kong.

Although the tuning of both psaltery and dulcimer was invariably diatonic during the Middle Ages, the compass and number of strings varied enormously. Large instruments are illustrated, with sufficient string length for quite deep bass notes. In 1528, Agricola describes a psaltery with a compass of over three octaves descending to F. Even if this was unusually low, some medieval dulcimers and psalteries would have been large enough to cope with tenor and contratenor parts in chansons, *musica ficta* permitting. But judging from surviving folk music practice, the chief glory of the dulcimer and psaltery was their treble register, from about middle C upwards. This would have made them ideal for solo dance music or for decorated versions of chanson treble parts.

Both instruments were ultimately superseded by the development of the keyboard: the psaltery by the virginals and harpsichord with their 'plucked' action, the dulcimer by the piano with its mechanical hammers. After the fifteenth century, the psaltery fell out of regular use, though the dulcimer continued to flourish in the realm of popular music. On 14 May 1662 Samuel Pepys heard one in the band playing for the puppet play at Covent Garden. 'Here, among the fiddles, I first saw a dulcimer played on with sticks, knocking of the strings, and is very pretty.'[21] In the early eighteenth century the German Pantaleon Hebenstreit became an international touring virtuoso on the dulcimer. In 1717 Gottlieb Schröter, one of the 'inventors' of the piano, claimed that Hebenstreit's playing had given him the idea for the piano's hammer mechanism.[22] It is curious to reflect that the essential details of piano mechanism were worked out as early as the middle of the fifteenth century. A manuscript compiled by Henri Arnault of Zwolle, physician to the Duke of Burgundy, describes a special type of *dulce melos* in which the strings are hit by a rebounding tangent which is jerked upwards by a checked key.[23] A *dulcemel para tañer* (=keyboard type of dulce melos) is also listed in an inventory of 1503 as belonging to Queen Isabella of Spain.[23]

The fretted instruments

Whilst the plucked instruments so far discussed all emerged as fairly distinct types during the Middle Ages, it is rather harder to sort out those which involved stopping the strings against a fingerboard, marked off by means of a series of frets. The principle of the lute and its relatives is a very ancient one. The earliest 'lute-like' instruments appear in Mesopotamia in about 2000 BC:[24] they had small bodies, long necks with many frets, and two strings which were

played with a plectrum. Since then the lut[e] occupied a place of honour in many differ[ent] civilizations ranging from Islam to China, though nowhere outside Europe has it dev[eloped] such a bewildering number of relatives, a[ll] employing a similar plucking action and f[retted] fingerboard. Bearing in mind the inconsis[tency] of much medieval evidence, iconographic[al] and literary, it may be as well to start by establishing what are important difference[s of] construction and what are just variable de[tails]. The fundamental distinctions would seem [to be] based on the following points:

1. Strings: whether they are made of meta[l] or gut.
2. Frets: whether they are made of gut tie[d] round the fingerboard and therefore easily movable or glued-on pieces of wood or m[etal] and therefore fixed.
3. Bridge: whether or not the strings pass [over] a movable bridge.
4. Back: whether the back of the instrume[nt is] flat (as on the guitar) or rounded (as on the [lute]).
5. Shape: whether the body is waisted (as [on] the guitar) or pear-shaped (as on the lute a[nd] cittern).

Of course, individual instruments displa[y] other important characteristics, but these [points] help to distinguish the three lines of develo[pment] which in the Renaissance produced three individual types of plucked, fretted instrum[ent]. In order to help distinguish their ancestry [they] are summarized here.

a. *The lute,* with gut strings, gut frets, no movable bridge, a round back, and a pear-shaped body.
b. *The guitar,* with gut strings, gut frets, n[o] movable bridge, a flat back, and a waisted [body].
c. *The cittern,* with metal strings, fixed fret[s,] movable bridge, a flat back, and a pear-sha[ped] body.

During the sixteenth century these thre[e] types all possessed their own idiomatic syst[em] of tuning. Unfortunately next to nothing i[s] known about the tuning of their medieval ancestors. Some authorities, notably Curt Sachs,[26] have attached great importance to [the] position of the pegs (frontal, rear, or latera[l) in] distinguishing types of stringed instrumen[ts,] bowed as well as plucked. Yet although th[e] nature of the peg box was important, espe[cially] with the distinctive shape which develope[d in] the mandora, there seems to have been suc[h a] variety of forms in the Middle Ages (just as [with] folk instruments today) that it is not until t[he] more standardized types of the Renaissanc[e that] the details of the peg box regularly confor[m] with other details of construction. Much th[e] same can be said about the shape and placin[g of] the sound-holes.

From the five distinguishing points liste[d] above, it is obvious that iconographical sou[rces]

e no help for 1 and 2: you cannot *see*
her strings are metal or gut or whether
are fixed or movable, and if the right
is in a playing position you can often not
e of the existence of a movable bridge
. So we are obliged to rely on literary
nce, which from the Middle Ages is very
y. There is one point, however, which is
d dispute and which links all the
ments in this section: their playing
ique. The strings were plucked not by the
s but with a plectrum, and although lutes
uitars seem so obviously *chordal* to us,
medieval ancestors were used primarily as
y instruments. The plectrum – usually a
quill – produces a hard attack and bright
ideal for a clearly etched single line. But its
evitably restricts the possibilities of chord
t playing: it is rather like playing the
with one finger. You can aim for one
at a time or use a strumming action to
all the strings at once, but what you
t do, if readers will pardon the pun, is to
nd choose. If, for example, you want to
chord involving top and bottom strings
issing out the rest, you have to abandon
ectrum and pluck with your fingers
d, which is exactly what lutenists did
g the course of the later fifteenth century.

ute

te and its playing technique filtered
gh to Europe from the East, as a result of
oorish occupation of Spain and the
des. We borrowed the Arab name *al 'ūd*
r words *lute, luth* (French), *Laute*
an), and *lauto* (Italian). In the Middle
oday you can still buy the most exquisitely
lutes, particularly in Damascus which is
led as the Mecca of lute making. The old
g traditions survive too, giving us a good
f what the monophonic style of the
e Ages was like. Listening to Arab players
makes one realize that there is almost as
difference between the sound of the lute
Machaut knew and that of Dowland's time
ween the psaltery and the harpsichord or
lcimer and the piano. And the repertory
ually distinct too: the medieval lute was
rily an ensemble instrument, not a solo
polyphonic music it would have played
e line, perhaps doubling a sustained
d adding, impromptu, some of its own
atic embroidery.[27] Here is Tinctoris
g in about 1487 and giving us the clearest
ption we have of the medieval style of
aying:

yre which is called the lute, we use at
dances and public and private
ainments, and in this, many Germans are
lingly renowned. Thus some teams will
e treble of any piece you care to give

TOP
Ud, made in Damascus *c.*1900. For the purposes of
playing medieval music this instrument has been
fretted although frets seem to have dropped out
of use on the Arabic lute during the eighteenth
century.

them and improvise marvellously upon it with
such taste that the performance cannot be
rivalled. Among such, Pietro Bono (Avogari)
lutenist to Ercole, Duke of Ferrara, is in my
opinion pre-eminent.'[28]

The lute first appears in Europe during the
second half of the thirteenth century, though at
first the evidence is scanty. The *Roman de la
Rose* (*c.*1260) and other French sources of the
thirteenth century use the name *leu.*[29] In the
following century the lute crops up more often.
Machaut, Chaucer, and Boccaccio all mention
it and artists start to illustrate it regularly.[30]
The typical features are the rounded back, short
fretted neck, and bent-back peg box with
lateral pegs. As surviving specimens show,[31]
the earliest lutes were carved out of the solid:
the construction employing a series of separate
ribs was a development of the Renaissance.
There are four strings, attached to a fixed bridge
on the sound-board, and the earliest tuning
employed is thought to have been a series of
fourths, adopted from the *'ūd* and still used by
Arab players today. During the fifteenth

BOTTOM
Modern *tanbura* or long-necked lute, from
Damascus.

century one of the fourths became a third,
giving a tuning of c, f, a, d' to which a top g'
string was added (the pitches were relative
rather than absolute). Details of the plectrum
are forthcoming from many pictorial sources.
The long stem of the quill is shown held
between the third and index finger (as a modern
guitarist holds a flat pick) or between index or
middle finger, or even between the two middle
fingers.[32] The number of frets seems to have
varied considerably: some pictures show as few
as four whilst the design of Henri Arnault,
one-time court physician and astrologer to the
Burgundian court, shows a dozen frets.[33]
However, the typical fifteenth-century lute
had no more than eight frets.

The mandora

Before the appearance of the standard lute,
there is plenty of evidence for the existence of a
smaller, more compact version called the
mandora (from the Greek *pandoura*). Illustrations
of it have been tentatively identified as early as
the ninth and tenth centuries[34] and it is
mentioned in early Provençal poems such as
Flamenca:

L'us mandura e l'autre acorda
Lo sauteri ab manicorda.
(The one [plays] the mandora and the other
tunes the psaltery to the monochord.)[34]

From the twelfth to the fourteenth century,
the instrument is regularly referred to in French
literature as *mandoire* or sometimes *mandola*
and illustrations often reveal the instrument's most
recognizable feature: its sickle-shaped pegbox.
This is not universally shown, however, and
the chief characteristic of the mandora was its
small size: several literary references to the
standard lute show that by contrast it was
regarded as a *big* instrument.[35] The mandora's
initial popularity seems to have been in Spain,
Italy, and Southern France and it gradually
worked its way north in Europe, reaching
England probably at the end of the fourteenth
century.[36] Because of its Greek root *pandoura*,
the mandora has sometimes been confused with
the *tanbura* and thought to have been a type of
long-necked lute. There seems every reason to
believe otherwise, however. Praetorius[37] gives
the tuning g d' g' d'' for the instrument which
may well reflect medieval practice too. Such
tuning in fourths and fifths is likely to have
been used on the rebec with which the mandora
was interchangeable,[38] the two instruments
representing bowed and plucked versions of
the same type.

The long-necked lute

The phrase 'short-necked' has already been used
to describe the standard type of lute and it
serves to distinguish it from the long-necked

lute. This instrument, similar in basic design to the Mesopotamian depictions of the lute from 2000 BC, is illustrated in Europe as early as the ninth century[39] and survives in many parts of eastern Europe and the Middle East today. Instruments such as the Bulgarian *tanbura*, the Turkish *buzuk,* and the Persian *tàr* share a similar appearance and construction: a finger-board two or three times as long as the sound-board, a large number of gut frets, a small oval body and rounded back, and four strings attached to a tailpiece and passing over a movable bridge. The use of a bridge creates as important a distinction from the standard lute as does the long neck. Although such survivals help us to determine what the long-necked lute sounded like, we are not quite sure how widespread its use may have been. The main problem is matching up the instrument with a contemporary name. In Juan de Ruiz's *El Libro de Buen Amor* (*c.*1350) we read:

Ally sale gritando la guitara morisca,
Delas boses aguda e delos puntos arisca.

(There comes out, shouting, the *guitarra morisca* with its sharp sounds and shrill notes.)[40]

This sounds very like the tanbura or buzuk of today: their metal strings do produce a harsh brilliance, quite different from the normal lute, which Ruiz goes on to mention under the name *el corpudo laúd* – the bellied lute. Another Spanish source, the thirteenth-century *Cantigas de Santa María,*[41] includes illustrations of both short- and long-necked types. It seems quite likely that if the Arabic long-necked lute came into Europe through Spain it could have retained in its name some kind of Moorish association, and if this were the case it would help to clear up a number of puzzling references. In 1349 a list of musicians employed by the Duke of Normandy includes players of the *guiterre latine* and the *guiterre moreche;* Machaut twice uses the word *moreche* coupled with lute; and as early as *c.*1300 Johannes de Grocheo mentions a *quitarra sarracenica.*[42] Unfortunately we cannot be sure that any of these names refers to the long-necked lute, though Curt Sachs and other scholars have thought it quite likely.[43] It is possible, however, that the names refer to an instrument of the mandora type (see Lawrence Wright's theory,[49] mentioned below). Ideally one would like to find a name which avoids using the words 'guitar' or 'lute' since the instrument has its own distinctive features belonging to neither type. After the fourteenth century it seems to have dropped out of use in Europe. Tinctoris (*c.*1487) dismisses it (using the name *tanbura*) as a 'miserable and puny instrument which the Turks with their even more miserable and puny ingenuity have evolved from the lyra'.[44] He does, however,

Angel playing a gittern, from the fourteenth-century Ormesby Psalter. (Bodleian Library, Oxford)

The Warwick Castle Gittern (1300–30), showing original back and neck. (British Museum; reproduced by permission of the Trustees)

mention that the *tanbura* has three strings tuned to an 'octave, fifth, and fourth'.[44]

The gittern

Although it has a number of distinctive features of its own, the gittern may loosely be regarded as the medieval ancestor of the guitar. Unlike any of the instruments so far described in this section, it displays the flat back and waisted shape of its descendant. The movable bridge and tailpiece shown on many gitterns distinguish it from the later guitar and link it with the medieval fiddle. Gittern and fiddle are often depicted together and they may to some extent be regarded as parallel developments of the same basic instrumental type: one with a plucking technique, the other with a bowing technique. The fact that frets are sometimes lacking on the gittern confirms this.[45]

A variety of names were used for the gittern; in French *kitaire, ghisterne, quinterne,* as well as *guiterne;*[46] in English *geterne, gyttern,* or even *gythorn.*[47] Although the gittern is mentioned from the early thirteenth century, its heyday seems to have been the fourteenth century. During this period it is depicted in quite a number of carvings and manuscripts and referred to by poets such as Langland, Chaucer, and Lydgate.[45] The gittern sometimes provides accompaniment to the voice, *eg* Absalon in Chaucer's *Miller's Tale:*

He singeth in his vois gentil and smal, . . .
Ful wel acordaunt to his giterninge.[48]

We are particularly fortunate that an actual gittern has survived from the Middle Ages. It dates from about 1300–30 and is now in the British Museum. Although it was unfortunately converted into a violin during the sixteenth century, the body and neck of the original remain. We find the curious neck extension (shown on a few English gitterns) which provides a thumbhole for the left hand. There are four strings, though examples with three or five are also illustrated. During the fifteenth century the gittern seems to have been gradually eclipsed in popularity by the lute. Without wishing to confuse the reader unnecessarily, it has to be pointed out that with certain fretted instuments there is a problem of matching up names and illustrations. According to a theory recently advanced by Lawrence Wright,[49] the instrument so far described as a 'gittern' should properly be classed as a type of citole (or cittern ancestor) whilst the *name* 'gittern' should be reserved for what we now call a mandora, as in *guiterre latine, quitarra sarracenica,* etc., mentioned above.

The citole

With the citole we continue with less well charted territory. The main problem is still matching up the name with instrument illustrations and detailed information is sparse. Literary references begin in the early thirteenth century:

Et quant je fui sus levez
Si commenz a citoler.
(and when I have got up I begin to play the citole.)[50]

There are several suggestions that the citole was a delicate, even decorous instrument: it was apparently most suitable for young ladies to play, and in *Les Échecs amoureux* (*c.*1370) its tone is described as sweet:

Et citoles meismement
Qui sonnoient molt doucement
(citoles also, which played very sweetly.)[50]

The generally accepted view is that the citole was the ancestor of the Renaissance cittern,[51] resting on the assumption that the word *cetera* or *cetra,* mentioned from the twelfth century onwards, refers to the same instrument as the citole. The first clear description we have comes from Tinctoris in his *De Inventione et Usu Musicae* (*c.*1487). He uses the word *cetula.* 'Yet

another derivative of the lyra is the instrume[nt] called *cetula* by the Italians, who invented it. It has four brass or steel strings usually tune[d a] tone, a fourth and back again a tone, and it i[s] played with a quill. Since the cetula is flat, it [is] fitted with certain wooden elevations on the [neck, arranged proportionately, and known [as] frets. The strings are pressed against these by[...]

Citole; sculpture by Benedetto Antelami (late 12th century–early 13th century). (The Baptis[tery, Parma)

to make a higher or lower note.'[52]
instrument which Tinctoris describes is
...tionably the ancestor of the renaissance
..., with fixed frets, a flat back, and a
...ant tuning for its four metal strings,
...the fourth course tuned higher than
...d. This idiosyncratic feature of the
...ance cittern was more widely applied
...the Middle Ages. The earliest account
...tuning of any stringed instrument, that
...me of Moravia (c. 1250), described three
...tunings, one of which is re-entrant.[53]
...lar practice survives in the Near East
...the melody is played on the two outer
...only leaving the middle strings for

...toris also makes the important point
...e cetula was an Italian invention. The
...cetera, cetra, etc. are Italian modifications
...Greek kithara and this ties in rather nicely
...e earliest cittern-like instrument so far
...ied from the visual arts: a sculpture from
...r 1180 in the Baptistery, Parma.[54] Other
...entations over the next three centuries,
...howing the cittern in the hands of angels,[55]
...strate many of the cittern's characteristics
...ing the 'wings' at the base of the neck
...d from the ancient kithara of classical
...Illustrations of the fifteenth century show
...widely spaced frets which suggest that
...tting was diatonic, not chromatic as on
...fretted instruments.[56] It is also clear that
...liest 'citterns' were carved out of the
...ke the gittern and early lute types.
...ing together all the evidence gives us a
...convincing picture of what the earliest
...s were like. But whether citole specifically
...this type of instrument we cannot be
...tely sure.

bowed instruments

...rigin and development of bowing forms
...the most intriguing chapters in the
...y of musical instruments. Before the
...th century there is no trace of bowing in
...rn Europe; yet a mere hundred years
...owing techniques are amazingly
...pread. Considering that the bow itself
...e generic type which had given rise to
...rp, lyre, and lute in Ancient times, it may
...urprising that it took so long before
...e thought of using the bow as a means of
...ng the strings. But once tried, the idea
...t on like wildfire and revolutionized the
...g and playing of stringed instruments.
...t it was just a question of the application
...bow to existing instruments: the lyre,
...e, and other plucked types. The evolution
...types specifically designed to be bowed

Two traditional fiddle types: a three-string *lira*
from Turkey and a two-string *rabāb* from
Morocco. (Author's collection)

was a much more gradual process, and during
the twelfth and thirteenth centuries there was a
proliferation of shapes and sizes. In *The Origins
of Bowing*[57] Werner Bachmann illustrates no
less than twelve quite distinct shapes of early
fiddle types, and his exhaustive survey makes
clear the problem of systematic classification.
To start with there seems to have been no
correlation between different names and
different types of construction: *rubebe, rebec,
giga, lira, fidula,* and *viella* were all applied fairly
indiscriminately by medieval writers to the
various types of bowed instrument. Any
modern attempt at classification involves using
names such as 'fiddle' and 'rebec' more precisely
than they were used in the Middle Ages. Thanks
to the researches of Werner Bachmann and
Mary Remnant, however, a vast amount of
information about early bowed instruments is
now available and readers requiring a more
thorough survey than the scope of this book
permits are advised to consult their authoritative
writings on the subject.[58] Bachmann includes
some fascinating details of medieval
techniques of construction.

The use of the bow developed initially
outside Europe, probably in Central Asia during
the ninth century, and spread first through the
empires of Islam and Byzantium. The earliest
bows may actually have been a development of
the plectrum. Many European illustrations
show long rod-like plectra which could easily

be used as friction sticks by scraping instead of
plucking the strings. During the transitional
period the same plectrum was probably used to
produce different sounds on the same instrument
by ringing the changes on striking, plucking,
and bowing techniques. From that stage it was
an easy step to equipping the 'bow' with
horsehair or some other suitable material in
order to make the string resonate more
effectively.

Behind the early experiments with bowing
there seems to have been an underlying desire
to find a stringed instrument which could
match the human voice. According to the
Baghdad scholar Al Farabi, who lived in the
tenth century, 'The instruments which most
closely approach the human voice are the *rabāb*
and the wind instruments.'[59] The bow gave
stringed instruments a new sustaining power:
unlike the lute or psaltery, bowed instruments
could play a continuous melodic line, vying
with the voice in flexibility of tone and phrasing.
Nevertheless, in the ancient civilizations of
Asia, the status of the new bowed instruments
seems to have been fairly low: they were
regarded as belonging to the common people
rather than the court. Al Farabi tells us that
'Owing to its construction the sound of the
rabāb is not as strong as that of certain other
instruments. From this point of view, the *rabāb*
is also inferior to most others.'[60]

Inferior or not, by the eleventh century the

bow had reached Europe through Byzantium
and Arab Spain. It is Spain which provides us
with the earliest evidence of bowing in Europe,
including the early eleventh-century miniature
in a Catalan Bible showing a large three-stringed
instrument supported on the knee and played
with a bow shaped like the letter P.[61]

Rebec and fiddle

From the profusion of European fiddle types in
the late Middle Ages, there emerged two distinct
forms: the slender pear-shaped type which
became generally known as the rebec and the
waisted figure-of-eight shape which was most
commonly called the fiddle: *fidula* or *viola* in
Latin, *fythèle* or *vielle* in French. The use of the
last name has led to great confusion – partly
because the word *vielle* was later exclusively
used for hurdy-gurdy and partly because it is so
readily mistranslated as *viol*. As a result, several
quite eminent histories of music still perpetuate
the idea that the viol was a *medieval* instrument,
whereas in fact it was a development of the
fifteenth century.

Even when the rebec and fiddle had achieved
their separate identities, there was still a wide
divergence of types. Details of general
appearance, bows, pegs, peg boxes, sound-holes,
stringing, and playing position varied
considerably. Nor did the question of nomenclature become any less vexed. As late as 1530
John Palsgrave's *Lesclarcissement de la Langue
Francoyse* provides translations as follows:

Croude an instrument	*robecq*
Croudar	*ieuevrde [joueur de]rebecq*
Fyddell	*rebeq*
Fydlar or crouder	*rebecquet*
Rebecke an instrument of musyke	*rebec*
I fyddell	*Ie ieoue du rebecq*
Can you fydell and playe upon a tabouret to?	*Scauez vous iouer du rebecq et sus le tabouryn, aussi[?]*[62]

As Mary Remnant says, this brings confusion
to the point of ridicule. The name rebec and its
continental equivalents (French, *rebebe,* later
rebec; Italian, *ribeca;* Spanish, *rabel*) derived
from the Arab *rabāb*. The body with its rounded
back was carved out of the solid and had a flat
soundboard added. Whilst the number of
strings varied from one to five, Jerome of
Moravia tells us that the thirteenth-century
rubeba had two strings tuned in fifths[63] and
Virdung (1511) prescribes three strings tuned in
fifths, which seems to have been typical in the
later period. In 1528 Agricola depicts a whole
family of three-stringed rebecs which he calls
kleine Geigen ohne Bünde (little fiddles without
frets).[64]

During the Renaissance there were certainly
rebecs of different sizes: the smallest were

Treble rebec, adapted from a folk instrument.

Medieval fiddle. Reconstruction by Robert Hadaway.

sometimes distinguished by names such as *ribecchino* or *rubechette* and there is also a reference to *grosse Rebebn*.[64] The large bass instrument (and probably the tenor also) would have been played gamba-wise, held between the knees. There is evidence that rebecs of various pitches and sizes existed in earlier times too.[65]

During the Middle Ages, however, the most typical rebec was a fairly small instrument of soprano pitch like its plucked relative the mandora. It is shown being played resting on the shoulder, across the chest, or resting on the armpit. Lateral drone strings (*ie* strings to the side of the fingerboard which are not stopped by the fingers) are sometimes found, though they occur much more commonly on the fiddle.[66] Fretted rebecs are shown in a number of illustrations including the *Cantigas de Santa María*,[67] and the presence of frets emphasizes the instrument's close relationship with the mandora. Folk music survivals and modern reconstructions suggest that the rebec had a thin, nasal tone which can be very penetrating particularly when played in a resonant acoustic.

It seems to have been especially associated with song and dance: in *The Miller's Tale* Chaucer describes how Absalon played on his rebec, singing a descant the while:

In twenty manere koude he trippe and daunce
After the scole of Oxenforde tho,
And with his legges casten to and fro,
And pleyen songes on a smal rubible;
Therto he song som tyme a loud quynyble.[68]

In spite of its prevalently secular associations Tinctoris selects the rebec, along with the fiddle, as his two 'chosen' instruments. He describes them as 'those that induce piety and stir my heart most ardently to the contemplation of heavenly joys. For these reasons I would rather reserve them solely for sacred music and the secret consolations of the soul than have them sometimes used for profane occasions and public festivities.'[69] Nevertheless it was the royal households who gave rebec players employment, not the Church, and it was as an instrument for dancing that the small rebec survived as the *kit* or *pochette* into the eighteenth century.

In European court society of the Middle Ages the most important bowed instrument was unquestionably the fiddle. 'Further, among all the stringed instruments I have seen, the *viella* deserves to take precedence' writes Johannes de Grocheo, and he also tells us that a good fiddler should be able to 'play anything' since the fiddle 'combines in itself the attributes of all other instruments, and distinguishes most sensitively between all forms of music'.[70] For the privileged classes playing the fiddle was something to be practised not for its usefulness but for its own sake. Whole orchestras of fiddles were maintained at the court of Alfonso 'El Sabio'; fiddlers accompanied their lords on journeys, playing on horseback as they rode; they were also part of the Queen's retinue. In the medieval German epic of Tristan, the Knight spends his days out hunting with the king whilst in the evening he entertains him with songs, accompanying himself on harp and fiddle.[71] Fiddlers were in demand for banquets, weddings, receptions, and celebrations of all kinds. The famous medieval May Song, *Kalenda Maya*, started life as an *estampida* in the

repertoire of two jongleurs who played it their fiddles.[72] The essence of their art was improvisation. In a German account of the *Parsifal* story we read: 'Then Sir Gawain a if there were no good fiddle players prese There were indeed many worthy fellows their artistry was so great that they were n constrained to play old dances.'[73] In other words, they made up new ones.

Until the end of the Middle Ages the fid was, like the rebec, carved out of one piec wood with the sound-board added. The b was flat, or nearly so, and the neck was ver distinct from the body. The playing positi varied, being held on the shoulder, across t body or, in the case of large instruments, between the knees. The existence of this 'gamba' type, most commonly illustrated the twelfth and thirteenth centuries, has le some authorities to designate it a separate t of fiddle with the name 'medieval viol'. In of the already existing confusion this is per best avoided. Although the number of stri was variable, as far as tuning is concerned have some specific information from Jeror

a, a Dominican monk who lived in
250. According to his *Tractatus de*
the three standard tunings for the fiddle

tunings given by Jerome of Moravia
after Bachmann).

tunings offered the fiddler some
he could choose the appropriate one
ng to the compass and tessitura of the
had to play. The idea of doubling the
ng, though it may seem rather odd to us,
doubt a very practical one. The top
were at the highest tension and therefore
e most liable to break. If one of them
during a performance at least the
g gave the player a 'spare' so that he
arry on. Gut strings were clearly thought
gile in the Middle Ages and players
ly slackened them off when not in use.[75]
owest string was often a lateral drone
although it was not stopped by
ers, it could be plucked with the left
t any rate when the fiddle was played
tally, violin fashion. A common method
ing was to take in several or all the
at once, and the flat bridges shown on a
r of fiddles and rebecs show that
ents were designed for the purpose. A
with open fifths and octaves would
fit this style best.

or two final points may be made about
ddle and rebec. The standard arrange-
f bridge and tailpiece was not ubiquitous.
nstruments employed a kind of com-
ridge and tailpiece, thus effectively
ing the sounding length of the string in
to the body.[76] Whilst the ordinary
r or ménéstrel was content with a
unadorned instrument, there are
ts of fabulous instruments marvellously
r bedizened with jewels to bear witness
owner's wealth.[77] The bow or
tyk' varied enormously and performers
ly made use of several: a short bow
quick strokes of dance music, a longer
a sustained part in a chanson.[78]
the 'gamba' position involved under-
owing, for the 'violin' position of
g an overhand grip was adopted. In
l medieval bows seem to have been
sed of rather fewer strands of horse hair
odern ones.[79]

Some uncertainty remains over fingering
technique. Did players change position or not?
According to Jerome of Moravia the answer is
no. After describing the notes attainable in the
first position on the *rubeba* he wrote 'et non plus
rubeba potest ascendere' and proceeded to
indicate the same for the *viella*.[80] Alternative
tunings certainly facilitated staying in the first
position. However, the higher frets shown on
some fretted rebecs and fiddles could scarcely
be reached without some change of position[80]
so it seems possible that players may have used a
second or even third position on occasions.

The bowed lyre
Bowing techniques were also applied to the
European form of the lyre. Out of the delightful
selection of names given to it during the Middle
Ages – *cruit*, *crot*, *rota*, *rotta*, *chrotta*, *hruozza*,
crwth, *croud*, *crowd*, *crouthe*, and *chorus* – modern
scholars have not quite yet agreed on what to
call this instrument. Bachmann (following
Sachs) opts for 'bowed lyre'. Remnant (following Galpin) prefers 'crowd'. The name which
has remained longest in use, however, is the
Welsh 'crwth', used to describe the folk
instrument which survived in Wales until quite
recent times.

Like the lyre already illustrated (page 23) its
bowed successor was made out of one piece,
the resonator and pillars of the yoke being
hollowed out and the sound board added.
Instead of knobbed pegs turned by hand, as on

Courtly fiddle and flute players. Fourteenth-
century German manuscript. (University Library,
Heidelberg)

the rebec and fiddle, the crwth regularly
adhered to the old lyre tradition of plain pegs
which required a tuning key. Some illustrations
show the musician in the act of tuning, whilst
others show the key attached to the yoke by a
thread and dangling down the side of the
instrument.[81] To start with players seem to have

managed without a central fingerboard in which
case the strings had to be stopped either with
gentle pressure from the inside of the finger, or
else by using the fingernails rather in the
manner of hurdy gurdy tangents.[82] Both
techniques involve a *sideways* movement of the
fingers pulling the string towards the yoke,

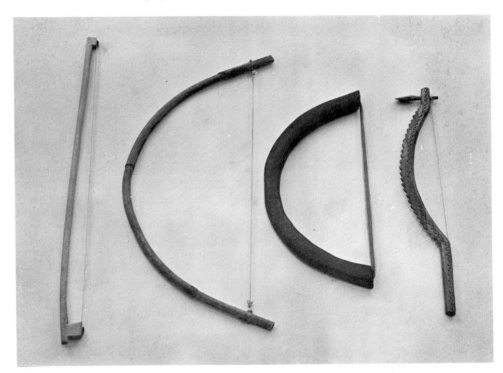

Traditional bows from (*l* to *r*) Turkey, Tunisia,
Morocco, and Yugoslavia, which preserve some
of the variety of medieval types. (Author's
collection)

Arming of a Knight. Fourteenth-century miniature,
showing lute and fiddle. Notice the very large
bow. Although the subject of the miniature is
the Trojan war, the artist depicted the sort of
scene he knew. During the Middle Ages
musicians travelled in their master's retinue and
accompanied them on long journeys and military
campaigns. (Bibliothèque Nationale, Paris)

rather than *back* towards an imaginary sound-board. To any classically trained string player it sounds horribly inconvenient but similar techniques are still used today on a multitude of bowed instruments without a proper finger-board such as the Indian *sarangi*, the Arab *rabāb*, and the Yugoslav *gusle*.

A fascinating example of the bowed lyre without fingerboard which just survived into the twentieth century is provided by the *tallharpa* of Swedish Esthonia, whose traditional techniques were chronicled by Otto Andersson.[83] His photographs of veteran players show the instrument almost lying flat across the knees, the bow gripped underhand with the first finger resting on the wood. Andersson says of one player: 'He stopped the strings with his nails or the hardened back of his fingers, which touched the strings obliquely from below, and he did not seem to find this backhanded method of playing in the least awkward . . . The way in which the strings were stopped gave the tone a peculiar quality; it had a soft and gentle effect, somewhat recalling the violin *con sordino*.'[84] Like the typical medieval bowed lyres of the eleventh and twelfth centuries the tallharpa had only three or four strings, of which the lowest con-sisted of unstopped drone strings. All the strings

Early bowed lyre, depicted in a mid-eleventh-century book of tropes from St Martial, Limoges. (Bibliothèque Nationale, Paris)

were sounded at once, a characteristic of bowed lyre technique which is made essential by the instrument's shape: the bow has to remain parallel to the body and cannot be angled as on the rebec or fiddle. Confirmation of the technique comes from the flat bridges shown in medieval illustrations and found on existing examples of both tallharpa and crwth.

The Welsh crwth provides the most developed example of the bowed lyre. It has six strings, a central fingerboard running between the sides of the yoke and its most idiosyncratic feature is the way the bridge also acts as a sound post. Whilst the shorter foot rests on the soundboard the larger one passes through a sound hole and rests on the back of the instrument. A bowed lyre shown on the seal of Roger Wade the Crowder dating from not later than 1316 shows a similar appearance with the later Welsh crwth and may possess this feature too.[85] Although this particular example has only four strings, there is evidence from the twelfth century onwards of five- and six-stringed instruments: some examples with more than ten strings have been noted.[86] Although we have no direct evidence for medieval tunings, the following Welsh tunings quoted in the eighteenth century seem quite plausible: g, g', c'', c', d', d'', and a, a', e', e'', b', b''.[87]

The tromba marina

Perhaps the most curious application of bowing techniques was to the monochord. The instrument which resulted – the *tromba marina* (French *trompette marine*; German *Trumscheit*) – was certainly curious and some readers might be inclined to agree with Virdung (1511) who said it was a useless instrument or with Glareanus (1547) who said it made him laugh. A French sculpture of the twelfth century gives us our first glimpse of the tromba marina:[88] the three-sided body is about four feet long and tapers towards the pegbox. There is a single string but at this stage no sign of a bow, suggesting that the instrument was still plucked. By the fifteenth century it had acquired two strings of unequal length and is regularly depicted in action, usually in the hands of angels. A variety of oblique playing positions are shown, varying from resting the larger end of the instrument on the ground to pointing it up in the air. The bowing action however is consistent: the tromba marina plays only natural harmonics and whilst the left hand (usually with the thumb) touches the strings very lightly at nodes near to the head, the right hand draws the bow across the strings *above* it, near the nut.

Like the monochord, the tromba marina was full of theoretical possibilities and it certainly fascinated the Swiss monk Henricus Glareanus.

Reconstruction of a large bowed lyre of the crwth type by Christopher Wright. The tuning screws on the tail-piece are a modern addition, to facilitate fine tuning.

In his compendious musical treatise the *Dodecachordon* (1547)[89] he devoted a substantial amount of space to the instrument. He tells us how he borrowed a tromba marina and started to experiment in earnest: 'I attacked the problem by myself' he says. The practical details which he includes are most useful and a selection is given here:

'Players go about through the streets with the instrument's point fixed at the breast . . . The instrument produces a more nearly agreeable tone at a distance than it does close at hand . . . They have created the rattling sound by means of a certain curved bridge, whose one wider and thicker foot supports the string at the triangular

base, and whose other shortened foot, to w[hich] they have affixed a solid substance made of[ ] ebony or another hard and shining materia[l] causes this vibrating sound. I had to laugh a[t] this device of men.'[90]

The use of this special type of bridge, balanced on one foot leaving the other free[ ] enough to rattle, became the unique featur[e of] the tromba marina, though we are not sur[e] what stage it was introduced. Various mate[rials] were used to 'doctor' the vibrating bridge[:] Glareanus even mentions driving in a very[ ] nail which must have produced a devastati[ng] effect. A variety of unsatisfactory explanat[ions] have been given about the origin of the instrument's various names.[91] The association with the trumpet is obvious enough through the use of natural harmonics, but the reason for the qualification 'marine' is obscure. Some authorities have derived the word from Mary (*ie* Marian) and one German name for the instrument is *Marientrompete*. In spite of sometimes being called *nun's fiddle* (German *Nonnengeige*) there seems to be no foundation for the theory that the tromba marina was used as a kind of trumpet substitute in convents. Glareanus used the name *tympani schiza*, his Latinization of *Trumscheit*.

In spite of a certain inherent absurdity the tromba marina continued to flourish during the baroque period and even acquired a specific repertory of music.[92] Later instruments (like the gigantic specimen in the Victoria and Albert Museum) were made larger in order to facilitate the playing of the upper harmonics, where the finger positions became very close together. On the small medieval tromba marina it seems unlikely that the player ascended much beyond the eighth or ninth harmonic, and the instrument's use must have been limited to simple fanfares or drones. The unequal string lengths imply a tuning in fourths or fifths.

The existence of a wide variety of percussion instruments in the Middle Ages is well documented in both literary and iconographical sources. Folk music has preserved one or two types more or less intact, such as the French *tambourin* and the Spanish castanets, whilst the musical traditions of the East provide us with examples of small cymbals and tambourines with heavy brass jingles. For the rest there is enough evidence of practical details for convincing reconstructions to be made.[1] What is totally lacking is precise information from the Middle Ages or early Renaissance about how percussion instruments were used. They must have been regularly employed for dance music but what other sorts of music did they take part in? In spite of the numerous angels shown holding cymbals, triangles, and tambourines, the regular use of such instruments in church music seems unlikely. When they were used, what sort of techniques were employed? And what sort of rhythms did the drummers use? Did they stick to a basic beat or indulge in wild improvisations like Middle-Eastern players today? This is the most uncharted area of early music performance practice and our answers must consist in the main of inspired – or, as the case may be, uninspired – guesswork.

As Jeremy Montagu has pointed out[2] there are one or two basic guidelines. Pictures provide valuable information about the way sticks and instruments were held: the playing position for cymbals and tambourines, for instance, was quite different from that used by orchestral players today and so the playing styles must have been different too. Jeremy Montagu makes the following important point: 'Before AD 1500, all drum names in European languages had a *ram*- or *tab*- root; only during the sixteenth century did the *trom*- and *drum*- words come into use. So much of our drum terminology is onomatopoeic that I believe that the name of the instrument is also and that strokes such as flams, drags, and rolls should not be used in music earlier than the first half of the sixteenth century, but that plain strokes only should be used.'[3]

As with all aspects of early music performance we should never underestimate the skill of medieval and renaissance players, within the limits of their own styles and techniques. Many literary references make one long to know just what medieval percussionists could do given the right opportunity. The French poem *Les Écheçs amoureux* (*c*.1370) describes music for a dance at which the instruments were chosen 'Pour le grant noise qu'ils faisoient'. They include:

Trompez, tabours, tymprez, naquairez, Cymballes, (dont il n'es mes quaires)[4] (trumpets, tabors, timbrels, nakers, cymbals such as you never heard.)

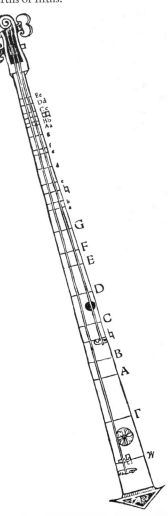

tromba marina based on instruments
ted by Van Eyck and others.
struction by Christopher Wright.

RIGHT
Calibrated tromba marina, from Glareanus' *Dodecachordon* (1547).

In the account of medieval percussion instruments which follows, due acknowledgement must be made to the research and writings of James Blades in this field and for a more detailed analysis readers are referred to the relevant chapters of his fascinating book *Percussion Instruments and Their History*.[5] For the sake of convenience all the percussion instruments will be dealt with here, even though two of them – kettledrums and side drum – properly belong to the Renaissance. Most of the instrumental types described are of very ancient origin indeed, drums, rattles, and scrapers being the commonest instruments of primitive man.

The drum types

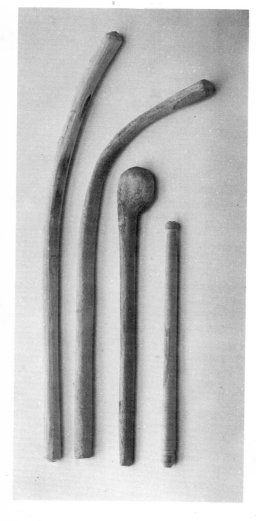

Many different types of animal seem to have provided drum heads in the Middle Ages and Renaissance including pigs, goats, and even wolves, though sheep or calf skin was the most common choice. The usual method of fixing the skin to the shell was by ropes attached directly to the skin. This presupposes fairly thick skins at a fairly low tension, otherwise the skins would tend to tear easily when struck. Some pictures show heads nailed directly to the shell, others permanently laced on, either method leaving the instrument rather susceptible to weather changes (drum heads become flabby when damp), but the use of ropes or cords which could be slackened or tightened up afforded some control of tension. The method of rope tensioning which has proved most successful is that still used on certain military drums today: the two drum heads are roped together zig-zag fashion and leather buffs or 'tug ears' are used to narrow the V-formation and tighten the heads. The edge of the drum head was probably often strengthened by being sewn on to a rope ring, but the wooden hoops used in the construction of military drums today were a development of the sixteenth century. Snares, however (usually one or two strands of gut), are regularly illustrated from medieval times onwards on many shapes and sizes of drum including the nakers. Drum sticks reveal a great profusion of shapes both in pictures and in surviving folk-music practice.

Nakers and tabor

Along with the shawm and the trumpet, the nakers shared the honours in a typical Saracen military band during the time of the Crusades. Europe inherited not only this ancient instrument but the name – *naqqāra* in Arabic – which emerged variously as *nacaires* (French) and *naccheroni* (Italian) as well as the English *nakers*. Marco Polo describes how in 1266 King Kaidu and the great Khan waited for a battle to begin

with the sound of *nacars*[6] and Joinville writing in 1309 about the crusade of Louis IX mentions the terrifying effects of the Saracen *nacaires*.[7] Besides retaining their military association nakers were used for a wider variety of European music including processions and dance music. Players occupied an important place in the royal household from the time of Edward I onwards.[8] Edward III's musicians included four nakerers as well as three taborers[8] and Froissart distinguishes between the two types of instrument when he described the king's victorious entry into Calais in 1347 as 'a foisson de trompettes, de tabours, de nacaires et de buccines'.[9]

The technique of the nakerer involved a pair

of sticks and certainly differed from that of the taborer who was basically a one-stick man, whether or not he doubled on a pipe as well. The drums themselves consisted of two spherical bowls of about eight inches in diameter. The favourite material was copper although pottery and wood were also used. Many illustrations show the nakers slung round the waist by a strap or belt: sometimes one drum is slightly larger than the other but more often they are the same size. Modern reconstructions suggest that nakers could not be tuned to specific notes and their function must have been rhythmic rather than harmonic. Rope tensioning does make possible a contrast of timbre which is effective, but many medieval nakers must have been permanently laced up like the instruments found in North Africa and India today.

Whilst the nakers may well have afforded opportunities for virtuoso display, the tabor employed a simpler single-stick technique. It was the most popular drum of the Middle Ages and the many variants of its name all stem from the same root: *taberett* and *tabor* in English, *taboret* and *tambour* in French, and so on. Confusion arises over the use of the French *tambour* for tambourine, string-drum, and tabor and the Italian *tamburino* and German *Tamburin* for both tambourine and tabor. There was no standard shape or size for the tabor as the reader can see for himself if he compares the illustrations from Mersenne's *Harmonie Universelle* with those of the pipes and tabor in chapter 1 (pp 13 and 14). The essential features of the tabor are its cylindrical shape and two drum heads with a snare on the top one, *ie* the one which is beaten. Since only the right hand was used for playing, a small drum could be held by the left hand, though larger sizes were more conveniently slung from the waist. The tabor usually employed the method of tensioning already mentioned. As with the

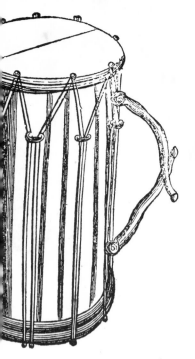

from Mersenne's *Harmonie Universelle*

rs, taborers found regular employment in
vice of the nobility as well as that of the
: Galpin gives as examples 'the Tabrer of
Audham' and 'Guillot the Tabrer of the
Warwick'.[9]

drums and side drum

eginning of the sixteenth century saw
tant new developments in the art of
ning. The medieval nakers gave way to
endour of the larger kettledrums, and the
whilst it continued to flourish as a
strument, was rivalled by the side
with its two-stick technique. Not all
dvances in martial music pleased every-
his *Musica getutscht* (1511) Sebastian
ng has this to say about the big army
drums of copper, called *tympana*: 'These
are to the taste of those who cause much
et to pious old people, to the sickly and
eakly, the devout in their cloisters and
who have to read, study, and pray. I
believe that the devil must have had the
ng and making of them, for there is no
re nor anything good about them.'[10]
aristocracy, however, took great
re in these new delights, which came to
e once again from the Arab world. In
King Ladislaus of Hungary sent envoys to
Charles of France accompanied by
drums on horseback, and according to one
Benôit, drums of such size had never
een before.[11] From eastern Europe the
drums are included in the famous *Triumph*
ed for the Holy Roman Emperor
milian I and in 1542 Henry VIII 'sent to
a for kettledrums that could be played on
back and for men who could play them
ly'.[12]

The shell of renaissance kettledrums was
usually made of copper or brass with a diameter
of anything between two-and-a-half feet
(Arbeau) and seventeen-and-a-half inches
(Praetorius). The depth was quite shallow and
could be as little as twelve inches. In order to
facilitate accurate tuning German makers
introduced tensioning screws to replace the old
system of rope tensioning. Two hoops are
usually employed, one made of wood, the other
metal. To the first, called the 'flesh hoop', the
drum head is attached by lapping the edges of
the drumskin over the hoop. In the second,
called the 'counter hoop', which fits above it,
the lugs for the screws are fixed. Tuning was
crucial to the kettledrum because its role was
harmonic as well as rhythmic: to supply a tonic
and dominant 'bass' part to the ceremonial
fanfares of the trumpet band.

The side drum appeared at the beginning of
the sixteenth century and employed the same
kind of hoop construction for the drum heads
whilst retaining the old rope-tensioning. Unlike
the modern orchestral instrument, the
renaissance side drum inherited the flexibility of
shape and size of its ancestor the tabor. In
his *Orchésographie* of 1588,[13] Arbeau illustrates a
large side drum about two-and-a-half feet in

TOP
Side drum and pair of kettledrums from
Virdung's *Musica getutscht* (1511). All the drum
heads are fitted with hoops and the kettledrums
are equipped with tensioning screws.
BOTTOM
Mounted kettledrums and trumpets from
The Triumph of Maximilian I (1526). Again the
tensioning screws can be seen.
ABOVE RIGHT
Side drum and player from Arbeau's
Orchésographie (1588).

depth and diameter. And for the first time we
get some precise examples of what percussionists actually played. Besides giving us a mine of
information about dancing and dance steps,
Arbeau prescribes the basic drum rhythms
of the dances:

♩ ♩♪ ♩ ♫   for the pavan,

♩ ♩♫♫   for the basse danse,

and so on. These straightforward 'basic
beats' seem more suited to the single-stick
technique of the old tabor and they probably
represent the sort of thing which taborers had
played for centuries. Arbeau also discusses the

military uses of the side drum and describes
how the player can maintain a clear rhythm for
soldiers on the march. He also says: 'In addition
to the marches, saltarations, and war dances
noted above, the drummer employs a succession
of lighter and quicker strokes composed of
quavers, combining them with loud blows of
the sticks, which resemble the discharge of
many arquebuses, and this is done when the
soldiers approach near to the enemy.'[14]

The specialized techniques of the side drum,
such as the roll, flam, drag, and paradiddle
developed in the first instance to fulfil a
practical object: to encourage friend and
frighten the foe. To this end side drums often
accompanied the shrill sound of flutes and fifes,
a similar partnership to that of the old pipe and
tabor.

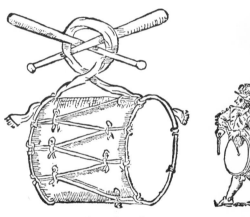

Tambourin and tambourine

As mentioned in chapter 1, the three-holed pipe
was sometimes coupled with other percussion
instruments besides the tabor. A combination
which remained popular in France long after the
Middle Ages and Renaissance was the pipe and
string drum. Various names have been used for
the string drum including *Scheitholt* and *tambourin*
(literally small *tambour*) which also describes the
long cylindrical tabor still used in Provence to
accompany the pipe. In the fourteenth century
it was apparently known as the *chorus* (another
confusing name) and had two strings; in the
fifteenth century it had three.[15] The nature of
the instrument is simple enough and is related to
the folk zither. The thick gut strings are
stretched over an oblong sound box and tuned
to the key-note and fifth of the pipe so as to
provide a drone accompaniment. All the strings
are struck at the same time with a small stick
held in the right hand and the instrument can be
suspended from the right forearm. The
tambourin was not inseparable from the pipe,
however, and during the Middle Ages it no
doubt accompanied a variety of instruments.

As already mentioned *tambourin* is also used
for the tambourine (Italian *tamburino*, Spanish
panderete, German *Tamburin* and *Schellen-*

33

Béarnais string drum, beater, and three-holed pipe. (Pitt Rivers Museum, Oxford)

ABOVE
Modern Egyptian tambourine. Notice the pairs of heavy jingles and the playing position. (Author's collection)

BELOW
Two Boys and a Girl making Music by Jan Molenaer (1609/10?–68). An apparently impromptu ensemble of a violin, rommelpot made from a jug, and an improvised drum consisting of a helmet played with spoons. This was the sort of company the violin kept in its early days: notice the playing position, on the shoulder rather than under the chin. (National Gallery, London)

trommel) which we in England called by the less confusing name of *timbrel*. The familiar single-headed frame drum fitted with jingles was introduced into Europe during the Crusades. In the Near East it was often played by women and although European artists often depicted the timbrel in the hands of angels its associations were frankly secular. The playing positions illustrated often correspond with those used in the Middle East today. One hand holds the instrument with the fingers in contact with the skin head whilst the other hand strikes it delicately with the fingers or palm, never the clenched fist. A variety of subtle rhythms are obtained by using the fingers of both hands and the technique is similar to that used on the *darabuka* or hand drum. The Middle-Eastern tambourine has changed little in eight hundred years: the jingles are thicker and heavier than on a modern orchestral instrument and their shape is smoothly concave rather than domed. Praetorius and others before him show us that small pellet bells were sometimes attached as well as jingles. Pellet bells were often attached to accoutrements and clothing in the Middle Ages – saddles, fiddle bows, jesters' caps – and to this day they are worn by Morris dancers, so that their bright sound can make an independent rhythmic contribution to the dance.

The rommelpot

Here we move into the realm of popular music-making: it is doubtful whether the rommelpot (the Dutch name means 'rumble-pot') was ever regarded as a serious instrument. On the contrary it was obviously great fun, judging by the cheerful expressions on the faces of players depicted by such artists as Frans Hals ('The Man with the Rommelpot'[16]) and Jan Molenaer. The instrument is a type of friction drum. A membrane, such as a pig's bladder, is attached to a suitable receptacle such as an earthenware pot or jug and a stick is inserted through the middle. The action required is not scraping the stick to and fro but rubbing it gently with moistened fingers. The resulting noise has given rise to many of the onomatopoeic names for the rommelpot: *puttiputti* (Italian), *zambomba* (Spanish), and *Brummtopf* (German). In Flanders rommelpots were associated with seasonal rites, especially Christmas celebrations.[17]

Melodic instruments

The Middle Ages and Renaissance offered much less variety of tuned percussion than that found in the symphony orchestra today. There were three principal types of percussion instrument capable of playing a melody: the xylophone, the dulcimer (already dealt with in the previous chapter), and the chime bells or *cymbala*.

Chime bells

Bells traditionally occupy an important place in worship and religious ritual of all kinds and there were (apart from the small pellet bells previously mentioned) two main types in use in the Middle Ages. Those with metal tongues or clappers which were used to ring out a merry peal or to summon the congregation to service like the church bells of today lie outside the scope of this book. The other type consisted of a series of accurately tuned cup-bells, usually without tongues, which were regularly illustrated throughout the Middle Ages. They were struck with a pair of small beaters or hammers and were used for musical theory and instruction as well as participating in Church music.

Apart from chime-bells and *clokarde*, a word which came into use about 1400 meaning a set of chime-bells, most medieval names for the instrument are derived from the Latin *cym*[...] Hence, *cymbal* (English), *cymbale* (French), *Zimbel* (German), and so on. As often happ[...] the name tells you the origin of the instru[...] chime-bells are related not so much to the [...] of church bell just mentioned but to what [...] call cymbals today. Medieval cymbals (see [...] below) had a high central dome similar in [...] shape to the cup-bells, and both instrumen[...] developed from the hollow discs of wood [...] metal which were struck together in pre-Christian times. In the case of the cup-bell[...] playing action changed from striking one [...] against the other to striking a whole series [...] bells with hammers.

Most illustrations show the bells suspen[...] on a simple wooden frame. The number i[...] set varied from three to as many as fifteen, [...] though the usual compass would seem to [...] been a diatonic octave $c'' - c'''$, often with [...] addition of a flattened as well as a sharpene[...] leading note, b''. For once we have fairly [...] detailed information about compass and c[...] struction because bells were a favourite su[...] for writers and theorists: even the closely-[...] secrets of bell metal were regularly reveale[...] roughly 80 per cent copper to 20 per cent t[...] The scientific aspects of bell making with [...] calculations, proportions, and ratios captiv[...] the medieval mind just as the bright sound [...] bells with its clear harmonic make-up capt[...]

Like the monochord, bells were used ⟨tea⟩ching the scale and its intervals, notably ⟨in c⟩hoir schools. And it was a natural ⟨extensi⟩on of this practice that they should ⟨accom⟩pany plainsong during the service too. ⟨They ar⟩e sometimes depicted hanging by the ⟨side of⟩ the organ, the only other instrument ⟨with an⟩ undisputed part in church music. There ⟨is defin⟩ite evidence for the use of bells in certain ⟨liturgic⟩al dramas[19] and in England they are ⟨linked⟩ with the performance of the Te Deum.[20] ⟨But t⟩he largest sets of bells would have ⟨exceed⟩ed the requisite compass for many chants, ⟨and it is⟩ quite likely that the player simply ⟨change⟩d the octave when the part went outside ⟨ran⟩ge.[21] When bells are accompanying ⟨voices,⟩ doubling the voices one or two ⟨octaves⟩ higher, such a change easily goes ⟨unnoti⟩ced.

the fact that by the sixteenth century the xylophone was well established. Agricola (1528) shows an instrument with twenty-five bars and Mersenne (1635), though his instruments are more restricted in range, thought that the xylophone was a useful instrument for acoustical experiment. 'Further one can determine what the pitch is of all sorts of bodies by means of these xylophones . . . so as to conclude some new things of their manifest or occult qualities.'[23]

Other types of instruments

Cymbals and triangle
The origin of both cymbals and triangle lies in the East. Together with the bass drum they

Detail from *Christ in Glory* (c.1430) by Fra Angelico. Angels are playing trumpets, pipe and tabor, cymbals, tambourine, and shawms. (National Gallery, London)

⟨...⟩ eleven tuned cup bells (diatonic range ⟨...⟩ with f♯″ and b♭″). Reconstruction by ⟨W⟩hitechapel Bell Foundry.

Woodcut from *Theorica Musica* by Franchino Gaffurio, Milan (1492). Acoustical experiments using bells (with clappers) and tuned glasses of water.

Woodcut from the *Dance of Death* series (1523–5) by Hans Holbein. This is the earliest known illustration of the xylophone.

⟨X⟩ylophone
⟨The fi⟩rst mention of the xylophone comes in ⟨Arnolt⟩ Schlick's treatise on organ building ⟨publish⟩ed in 1511,[22] and the first illustration of ⟨the on⟩es in Holbein's *Totentanz* (c.1525), pin⟨point⟩ing an association with the macabre which ⟨the xy⟩lophone has never entirely shaken off. ⟨But i⟩t is of such ancient origin and widely ⟨know⟩n in primitive societies, some simple ⟨ancest⟩or of the xylophone was very likely in ⟨ancient⟩ medieval Europe, albeit undocumented. ⟨The G⟩erman name *Stroh-fiedel* (straw fiddle) ⟨strong⟩ly suggests that this was the case, as does

made up in the eighteenth century what was known as 'Turkish Music' – the typical percussion instruments of a Turkish military band – and composers used all three together for special effects (for example Mozart in his opera *Il Seraglio*). Before 1600 neither cymbals nor triangle seem to have had such restricted associations. Their illustrated use ranges from wild Bacchanalian orgies to delicate church music accompaniment in the hands of angels. Whilst the former seems likely enough (we know that the triangle, like the tabor, was used with the three-holed pipe) the latter remains

obscure. It is difficult to imagine the contribution which cymbals or triangles could make to the performance of early church music, whether plainsong or polyphony. It was probably their biblical associations which led artists to depict the instruments so often, though the accuracy and consistency of certain details make it clear that these cymbals and triangles were real-life instruments and not vague derivations from classical times. Evidently, as Curt Sachs says of the cymbals, 'though they were never regular implements of European art music, neither were they entirely absent'.[24]

Cymbals are generally shown as being six to ten inches in diameter with a higher central dome than modern orchestral instruments.[25] They were thicker too and the typical playing position was that of ancient cymbals: held horizontally not vertically. The distinctive feature of the triangle (though by no means universal[26]) was a series of rings hanging on the lower bar, linking it with the ancient *sistrum*. Whether such triangles were sometimes shaken like rattles, or whether the rings simply jangled in response to the vibrations created when the instrument was struck with a beater,

Triangle and beater, from Mersenne's *Harmonie Universelle* (1636). The instrument is in a typical closed equilateral form. Without an opening at one corner the resonance is effectively damped, making the jingling rings the main feature of the sound. When there is an opening at one corner, however, it is all too easy in performance for the jingles to fall off.

Castanets, from Mersenne's *Harmonie Universelle* (1636).

Nineteenth-century English policeman's rattle and children's Easter rattle from Czechoslovakia. (Author's collection)

Jew's harp player from *The Triumph of Maximilian I* (1526).

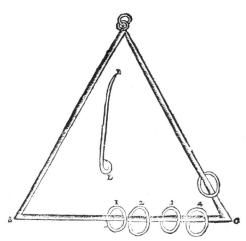

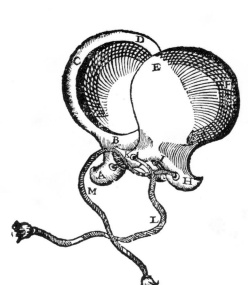

we do not know. But the rings certainly continued to be employed right down to the nineteenth century. Not all medieval triangles were triangular in shape: some were trapezoidal or stirrup-shaped. Mersenne (1635) employs the delightfully confusing name *cymbale* and states that the triangle was used by beggars to accompany the hurdy-gurdy.[27]

Clappers, castanets, and rattles

'All the knuckle bones and the small sticks of wood or other material that one holds between the fingers or in other fashion, and which are handled so dexterously and quickly and with such regulated cadences that it is impossible to explain them, can be related to the castanets and the xylophones.'[28] So writes Mersenne approvingly of a whole range of simple percussion instruments, some of which, like the marrow bones and the cleavers, could be adapted from domestic materials or utensils. Hence Bottom in *A Midsummer Night's Dream*: 'Let us have the tongs and bones.'[29]

The most sophisticated of these wooden clappers were the castanets which probably originated in Spain. In the *Cantigas de Santa María* of Alfonso 'El Sabio' (1232–84) there is a reference to the use of castanets not only in songs but also in Church music.[30] Mersenne says that castanets are 'very much used in Spain where the sarabandes are danced to the sound of the instruments'[31] and like the sarabande castanets spread to other parts of Europe too.

Many of these simpler percussion instruments had a practical non-musical function. Wooden clappers and rattles were used to scare away birds and to provide alarm signals: the old

policeman's rattle belongs to this tradition. Rattles were associated with various religious customs too and they acted as bell substitutes during Holy week 'when the bells are gone to Rome to be blessed by the Pope'.[32] This particular tradition has survived up to the present century in countries such as Belgium and Czechoslovakia.

The jew's harp

No apology is made for following the precedent set by both Praetorius and Mersenne and including the jew's harp amongst the percussion instruments. The classification of this instrument remains elusive, since the action involves a plucking or strumming motion with the hand whilst the variations in tone are produced by altering the position of the tongue and shape of the mouth cavity, which acts as a resonator. The truth is that nobody quite understands how the jew's harp works, let alone how it should be classified, and at least one attempt has been made to classify it as an aerophone or wind-vibrator rather than an autophonic instrument or self-vibrator.[33] Praetorius, rather neatly, classifies it as a 'mixed' instrument.[34]

Equal disagreement reigns over the origin of the name. One explanation is that the jew's harp was a despised instrument and took its name from a despised people ('this instrument serves the lackeys and people of low position', says Mersenne).[35] Another is that *jew's* harp is a corruption of *jaw's* harp, and although this is to some extent borne out by the existence of the German name *Maultrommel* (literally mouth-drum) it does seem strange that the name does

not occur until the sixteenth century, a period when the Jews suffered a great persecution in Europe, whereas the instrument itself is as old as the hills. A third and rather ingenious explanation is that jew's harp is a corruption of the French *jeu d'harpe*.[36] A slightly earlier version of the name is *jew's trump* (first recorded in 1545).[37] The French called the instrument *rebube* and later *guimbarde*, whilst Virdung (1511)

uses the name the *Trumpel*. The names with 'trump' root are perhaps something to do with the instrument's trumpet-like use of overtones or harmonics. Although a jew's harp can produce only one basic note, determined by length and thickness of the tongue, a skilful player can vary the harmonic structure of the note so as to give a convincing impression of different notes.[38]

Modern jew's harp.

ian with his musicians, woodcut by Hans
air from Der Weisskunig (1505–16). The
d side of the woodcut shows an organist
a small positive organ (marked with the
nitials) with an assistant working the
behind them are four singers and a
layer. In the centre there is a harpist and
ght an oblong keyboard instrument
ls or clavichord?). On the table there is a
gamba (?), flute, recorders, cornett, and
rn, and piled up on the floor a kettledrum,
pair of drumsticks, sackbut, lute case, and
marina. (Oesterreichische National–
ek (MS. coll. no. 3032), Vienna)

6 Woodwind

During the Renaissance the development of woodwind instruments was prolific. No other family produced quite as many new varieties nor did other types of instrument proliferate in such a multitude of individual treble-to-bass sizes. One can only marvel at the ceaseless inventiveness and skill of renaissance craftsmen, particularly in Germany, where woodwind instruments were exceedingly popular. The German root of many of the new names – *Krummhorn, Rauschpfeife, Kortholt, Rackett* – suggests a German origin for several of them and the city of Nuremberg in particular was an important centre for the production of woodwind as well as brass instruments. Recorders, crumhorns, and rauschpfeifen as well as trumpets and sackbuts were supplied from Nuremberg to many courts and cities throughout Europe, including the court of the Holy Roman Emperor Maximilian I at Innsbruck.[1] The principal centre for design, however, seems to have been Venice and many of the surviving woodwind instruments of the sixteenth century are of Italian origin.[2] German courts certainly imported from Venice and it is quite likely that the magnificent royal collection built up during Henry VIII's reign[3] contained instruments of Italian origin. A number of Italian musicians turn up in the records of the King's Music[4] for the first half of the sixteenth

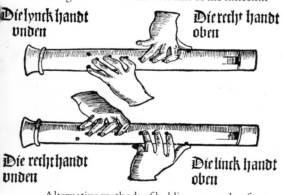

Die lynck handt vnden   Die recht handt oben

Die recht handt vnden   Die linck handt oben

Alternative methods of holding a recorder, from Virdung's *Musica getutscht* (1511). Notice the alternative finger-holes provided for right-hand and left-hand little fingers.

century, including Peter de Casanova, Zorzi de Cremona, Vizenzo de Venetia, Ambrose de Myllan, and five members of the Bassani family who remained in the royal service for several generations and have been credited by some writers with the invention of the bassanello, *c.*1600.[5] Makers normally supplied woodwind instruments in complete consorts: the Brussels Museum of Musical Instruments possesses a set of six crumhorns from the second half of the sixteenth century said to have been made for Duke Alfonso II of Este (reigned 1559–97), still nestling in their original custom-

made case (see p 49). Because of the lack of standard pitch, buying a ready-made consort was the only way of ensuring that the instruments would play in tune together. Not only that, but the instruments would be voiced in the same way too: many of the problems of balance and intonation in early music ensembles today are caused by the lack of properly 'matched' instruments. Renaissance makers differed considerably in their approach to certain details of construction and both tone and volume must have varied as a result. Although there was a great deal more standardization than there had been during the Middle Ages, it is an over-simplification to talk about 'the' renaissance recorder or 'the' renaissance crumhorn.

As far as materials were concerned, boxwood was the favourite for the smaller instruments and maple for the larger ones. Makers continued to employ a basic one-piece construction: even the largest recorders and shawms were made in this way. The Renaissance witnessed tremendous improvements in the art of wood-turning: most woodwind instruments had to be turned and bored on a lathe, and surviving instruments reveal a high standard of workmanship, with a smooth finish to the bores and very precisely drilled finger-holes. Whereas all woodwind players today hold their instruments with the left hand above the right, during the Renaissance a 'correct' position had not been established, and it was also common to play with the right hand uppermost. On instruments with seven finger-holes, alternative holes were provided for the little finger, offset to the left and right of the other finger-holes. Whichever hole was not required was stopped up with wax. Improvements in metal-work were important too, for the protective bands of metal which reinforced reed-caps and key-covers, and for the development of crooks and keywork. Long S-shaped crooks were essential on the largest shawms, dulcians, and recorders in order to bring the reed or mouthpiece within reach of the player's mouth. Keys, usually of the open-standing type, were added sparingly and again are generally found only on the larger instruments. It was the development of the alto shawm which first made a little-finger-key necessary in order to cover the lowest hole, which was otherwise out of reach of the player's hand. The swallow-tail shape was designed to be operated by either left or right-hand little finger; when pressed down, it closed a metal flap with a sewn-on leather pad. The key was kept in the open position by a brass leaf-spring and the whole mechanism was protected by a perforated key-cover. On shawms and recorders this was a barrel-shaped wooden device known as the *fontanelle*: it simply rested in position and could be slid

upwards when required. On crumhorns, curtals, and other instruments whose shape or cross-section made the fontanelle impractical, the key-covers were in the form of a metal box, which could also be easily removed in order to inspect the key mechanism.

Besides the introduction of keywork, the principal innovations of renaissance makers lay in the development of the reed-cap of the crumhorn and its relatives and the use of 'double' or parallel bores connected by a U-bend, as on the various precursors of the bassoon. Perhaps the most striking feature of the renaissance woodwind is their prevailing deepness of pitch. Apart from the soprano shawm, with its brilliant upper register, the chief glory of the reed instruments lay at the bass end of the various families, which often descended to sepulchral regions well below the bass stave. The largest sizes of shawm, curtal, sordun, or rackett added a wonderfully rich sonority to their respective consorts and must have provided a useful means of doubling bass lines an octave lower, a practice recommended by Praetorius.[6]

Very little music was written specifically for woodwind instruments during the Renaissance, although some rare examples will be mentioned during the course of the chapter. Nevertheless, players had a considerable repertory to draw on

Little-finger key with fontanelle removed, from a modern soprano shawm by Gunter Körber.

Two types of renaissance key-cover. Top: little-finger key with wooden fontanelle from a modern soprano shawm by Gunter Körber. Bottom: thumb key with metal box-cover from a modern alto curtal by Moeck.

since most instrumental part-music, esp the dance music, was suitable for a wide of instrumentation. The *Danserye* of Tie Susato, published in 1551,[7] is described title page as 'zeer lustich ende bequaem spelen op alle musicale Instrumenten' (p and appropriate to be played on instrum all kinds). Anthony Holborne's *Pavans, Galliards, Almans and other short aeirs* (15 contains the more specific suggestion 'fo Violins, or other Musicall winde Instrum Amongst other purely instrumental form woodwind instruments are also suitable canzonas and some of the simpler types o fantasy. Especially on the continent, woo instruments also regularly doubled or re voices in music of all kinds: *chansons, fro madrigals*, and certain types of Church m

Interesting evidence concerning the professional use of woodwind instrumen provided by a number of sixteenth-centu inventories.[9] Henry VIII's Inventory[10] re an overwhelming majority of woodwind compared to any other type of instrumen more than seventy flutes, more than seve recorders, twenty-five crumhorns, twent shawms, thirteen *dulceuses* (a problem: se page 42) as well as bagpipes and a tabor p Other inventories also include a high prop of woodwind: that of the Accademia

promising member of a large renaissance family provided the prototype for re-modelling: tenor flute, alto recorder, soprano shawm, and bass curtal. Even the bass rackett re-emerged briefly in a new baroque form. But the limitations of the wind-cap instruments precluded further development. With their unchanging tone, fixed dynamics, and inability to overblow, the crumhorn, cornamuse, kortholt, and the rest must have been nearly obsolete by the time Praetorius' *Syntagma Musicum* appeared. With the revival of interest in renaissance music today, however, these instruments are enjoying a new lease of life and are well on the way to becoming more popular and widespread than they ever were during the Renaissance.

Reed instruments without reed-cap

Little precise information is available about reeds and reed-making during the Renaissance. One of the most useful sources is James Talbot's manuscript,[14] compiled at the end of the seventeenth century, which includes reed measurements not only for the new oboe and bassoon, but for the old shawm as well. Since reeds are so vulnerable to loss or accident it is not surprising that hardly any have been preserved intact from the Renaissance, although the collection of the Kunsthistorisches Museum, Vienna, includes one or two rare examples.[15]

All the reed instruments, with or without reed cap or pirouette, seem to have employed a similar style of reed. The raw material was the *arundo donax* which grows in the marshes of Spain and Provence and which has been used by reed makers from the time of the earliest reed instruments right up to the present day. The method of manufacture was similar to that used later for bassoon reed-making,[16] though the reeds were shaved much flatter without the central spine typical of the German style of bassoon reed today. Even the smaller sizes of instrument required relatively broad, thick reeds; there was nothing approaching the delicacy of a modern oboe reed with its long narrow blades gouged to twenty-two thousandths of an inch or less.

The shawm

Since a confusing variety of names was applied to the shawm during the Renaissance it may be helpful to summarize them as follows:

1. From the Latin *calamus* meaning reed. English *shawm* or *shalm*, French *chalemie* and *chalemele*, Spanish *chirimia*, German *Schalmei* or *Schalmey*. The French word *chalumeau* has been applied to the shawm as well as a detached double-reed bagpipe chanter (Mersenne uses it in this sense) and the single-reed precursor of

Shawms from Praetorius' *Syntagma Musicum*. Left to right: *kleindiscant,* soprano with detail of reed and pirouette, alto, tenor with crook and pirouette, and bass.

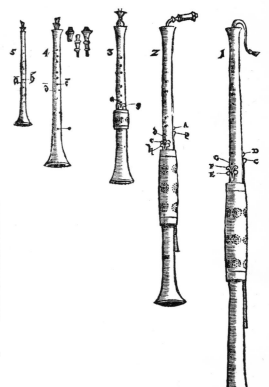

king music with shepherds: ivory carving by [o]f Angermair, from the coin cabinet of [or]th of Lorraine (made 1618–24). The mixed [ab]le consists of (clockwise from top left) [...], rackett, sackbut, small recorder, [...]es (allegorical rather than real), and large

recorder with unusually decorated cap. In the background are a crumhorn, shawm, and flute. A hunting horn and bagpipes can be seen slung from the waist of two of the players. (Bayerisches Nationalmuseum, Munich)

[...]onica, Verona, 1569,[11] lists several sets of [a]nd recorders including a complete chest [...]nty-two recorders, two tabor-pipes, five [...]orns, and a curtal. At the Berlin Hofkapelle [...]2[12] there were fifteen recorders, nine [...]three shawms, seven *Schreipfeifen*, [...]crumhorns, and a *Dulzan* (curtal). [...]ial evidence and surviving accounts of [...]mances[13] confirm a wide and varied use [...]odwind instruments during the [...]ssance: sadly, many of the most delightful [...]mental inventions of the sixteenth century [...]ed an active life of less than a hundred

years and were swept away by the manifold changes of composition, musical style, and instrumental practice which occurred during the early baroque period. The new dominance of the violin family demanded a range and flexibility which no renaissance woodwind instrument could offer. A glorious period of activity was followed by a decline in woodwind playing until the emergence of the new baroque designs of flute, recorder, oboe, and bassoon from the French workshops of the Hotteterres and others during the later seventeenth century. In each case the most

Set of modern rackett reeds mounted on their staples (as supplied by Moeck). Left to right: great bass, quart bass, bass, and tenor.

Modern soprano shawm in C by Moeck, based on an instrument in the Brussels Museum of Musical Instruments. Notice the long bell section.

lip-fatigue and offered some protection to the reed. The player placed the reed on the staple so as to suit his embouchure, leaving just the right amount of reed projecting above the rim of the pirouette. The design of the pirouette was an aid to controlled playing, rather than a handicap as is sometimes stated. It is unfortunate that many of the modern reproductions of soprano shawms are made without a pirouette and supplied with oboe reeds. Their emasculated

Detail of soprano shawm reed and pirouette

of four hundred years ago. Northern Spain also the home of another interesting shawm survival: the *dulzaina,* found all over the northern part of the country, is a small key shawm, played without a pirouette. Typo-logically it is derived from the bagpipe cha like the Breton bombarde, and must have b relatively rare during the Renaissance, altho Mersenne illustrates an instrument of this k Despite the absence of a pirouette, the dulz still produces a very penetrating sound.

A feature of all shawms is a number of ve holes, variously placed between the little-fi hole (or key) and the end of the bell. This se of the bore is often quite extensive, occupyi more than half the overall length on some instruments, and it makes an important contribution to the tone and carrying powe It may also have prompted the addition of t extra keys on the larger shawms to extend t range downwards by three diatonic notes. O the bass shawm pitched in F, for example, t little finger operates two keys instead of one

Modern Spanish shawm survivals. Left: keye *tiple* from Barcelona. Right: *dulzaina* from Madrid. (Author's collection)

the clarinet. The most common meaning of *chalumeau,* however, is a simple rustic reed-pipe (the word is still used in Switzerland in this way[17]).

2. From the Latin *bombus* meaning drone or buzz.
English *bombard, bumbard,* French *bombarde,* German *Pumhart,* and various other corruptions. Agricola (1511) uses *Bombhardt* and Praetorius (1619) uses *Pommer* which became the standard German version of the name. Although *bombard* originally referred to the larger types of shawm (see chapter 1, page 9) the distinction was not always maintained. Praetorius says that shawms are designated by the term *bombarde* or *Pommer* irrespective of their size[18] and the Breton *bombarde* of today is a small folk shawm only a foot long.

3. From the French *hautbois.*
During the late fifteenth century this new name occurs in France. Marcuse[19] interprets it literally as 'high wood' and states that it referred to the higher-pitched shawms. It seems equally likely that the name derived from the shawm's status as one of the *haut* (as opposed to *bas*) instruments and that *hautbois* really meant *loud* wood. In England various anglicized versions of the name occur during the sixteenth century: *hautboys* are regularly called for in the stage directions of plays by Shakespeare and his contemporaries.[20] Most European languages adopted the name for the shawm's descendant, the oboe.

4. From the English *wait,* a watchman.
A common English name for the shawm was the *wait* or *wayte-pipe,* occurring as early as the fifteenth century. During the Renaissance the name *wait* came to mean town bandsman and by extension the instrument which the waits most commonly played: the shawm.[21] In 1530 Palsgrave defines wayte as 'an instrument, hauboys' and as late as *c.*1700 James Talbot describes both treble and tenor waits.[22]

5. Another confusing name may be mentioned here – the Italian *piffaro,* etymologically related to the German *Pfeife* and the English *fife.*[23] In the sixteenth century it was used as a general term for any kind of pipe: specific meanings included *flute* as well as shawm and there has been regular confusion with *piva* (bagpipe).

Unlike its oriental parent, the European shawm of the late Middle Ages and Renaissance employed a broad cane reed which was controlled by the player's lips. On the largest sizes of instrument (from the bass downwards) the reed was placed on the end of a crook, as on the modern bassoon. On the smaller sizes (from the tenor upwards) the reed was placed on a staple, inside a pirouette. Praetorius actually shows the tenor shawm with a short crook *and* a pirouette at the end of it. The pirouette (also used on the renaissance rackett) was a funnel-shaped reed-shield against which the player could press his lips whilst taking the projecting part of the reed into the mouth. The pirouette, made in a variety of shapes, helped to avoid

sound is a far cry from the piercing brilliance of the renaissance shawm, the ubiquitous outdoor instrument of its age. 'At great feasts . . . they are to play upon shagbut, cornetts, shawms and other such instruments going with wind' wrote Richard Brathwaite in 1621;[24] the shawms' contribution must have been the most distinctive and by far the most penetrating of the three instruments he mentions. As Anthony Baines says: 'Of all musical sounds that from day to day smote the ears of a sixteenth-century town resident, the deafening skirl of the shawm band in palace courtyard or market square must have been the most familiar.'[25]

Such sounds are still to be heard from the Catalonian *coblas* of north-eastern Spain which play for the *sardana,* the 'national' dance of the region.[26] In bands such as the famous *coblas* of Barcelona which play in the square outside the Cathedral on Sundays, two sizes of renaissance shawm survive, the *tiple* (treble) and *tenora* (tenor). Although they are now fitted out with quite elaborate keywork, added during the last century, the basic design and sound have not changed since the sixteenth century. The *tiple* and *tenora* display the pirouette, the widely conical bore, and terminal bell of the renaissance shawm. Even the reed possesses the flared shape illustrated by Mersenne and others. The effect of a dozen or so *tiples* and *tenoras* playing together is thrilling and even though their repertoire of nineteenth-century marches is so different from that of the renaissance bands they provide a direct link with the playing traditions

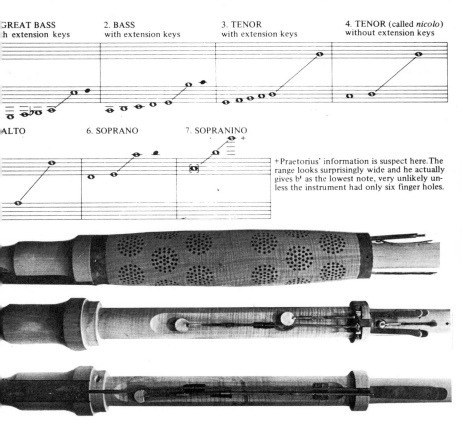

GREAT BASS
h extension keys

2. BASS
with extension keys

3. TENOR
with extension keys

4. TENOR (called *nicolo*)
without extension keys

ALTO

6. SOPRANO

7. SOPRANINO

+Praetorius' information is suspect here. The range looks surprisingly wide and he actually gives b' as the lowest note, very unlikely unless the instrument had only six finger holes.

Modern bass shawm by Moeck. Notice the large fontanelle.

n ranges from Praetorius' *Syntagma Musicum*.
M

rn bass shawm: detail of keywork. Top:
ew showing fontanelle in position; the
inger keys are above, the thumb keys
. Middle: front view with fontanelle

removed showing little-finger keys. The small additional key for the third finger between the swallow tails is not original. Bottom: back view with fontanelle removed showing thumb keys. The bottom end of the lowest key is under the metal box cover.

g F and E respectively when closed. D and
obtained by closing two thumb-keys at
ck of the instrument. The key mechanism
four holes is protected by a very large
nelle. With the crenellated metal band
nonly found round the bell, the shawm
together a fairly tough instrument
le of standing up to the exigencies of
or life. On occasions the wear and tear
have been considerable. Anthony Baines[27]
ions a dispute amongst the town bandsmen
gsburg which reached its climax when
f them aimed a blow at the bandmaster's
head with a bass shawm.
etorius describes the full range of
ssance shawms in his *Syntagma Musicum*
akes clear certain peculiarities of the
y. From the bass upwards (*see figure*)
ms were built in sizes a fifth apart: tenor
alto in G, soprano in D, and a *Kleindiscant*
No doubt, the fact that the smaller shawms
pitched in sharp keys was useful when
played with cornetts as was the regular
ice in the town or royal bands. But when a
e band of shawms played together there
problem, as Praetorius observes: 'it

becomes difficult to match them all together in intonation; for the outermost instruments of the set are then separated by five fifths, a relationship very difficult to deal with'.[28] In other words, whatever key the piece was in, it would necessarily be uncomfortably far from the basic scale of one or two members of the family.
In practice shawm bands (or the more common 'mixed' band of soprano shawm, cornett, two alto shawms, tenor sackbut, and bass shawm[29]) normally played their music a tone higher than written. This transposition was mainly to accommodate the soprano shawm which at the bottom of its range lacked the c' found in most soprano parts and on which f' was an unsteady note of poor quality. Praetorius sensibly suggests[30] that makers should produce two much-needed sizes of shawm, a tone lower than the standard models – *ie* an alto in F and a soprano in C. Whilst his advice does not seem to have been heeded at the time, modern makers have followed it to such an extent that today instruments built in the original key are very hard to come by. It should be noted that, in England and France at least, the nomenclature of the two original shawm sizes was rather at

Set of German shawms, sixteenth–seventeenth century: (*l* to *r*) soprano, alto, alto with extension keys, tenor, great bass, bass, tenor, alto. (Staatliches Institut für Musikforschung, Berlin)

Itinerant Musicians Brawling (detail), copy of a painting by Georges de la Tour (1593–1652). The pirouette and reed of the shawm are clearly shown. (Musée de Chambéry)

variance with that of other instruments. The *treble* shawm meant the soprano in D – not the alto as we should expect – whilst the *tenor* shawm referred to the alto in G. Together with the bass, they seem to have been the sizes most regularly used.[31]
During the later seventeenth century a narrow-bore type of shawm was developed in Germany and the Low Countries known as the *Deutsche Schalmei* or *Schalmey*. It represented an attempt at compromise between the old shawm and the newly developed oboe. But no compromise was really possible since the oboe represented an entirely new line of development

from the shawm and fulfilled a quite different purpose. It is worth noting that, versatile as the oboe is, it has never been much use as a band instrument in the open air, where the shawm's vastly superior carrying power is desirable.

The bassanello

Nearly a century before the appearance of the baroque oboe there seems to have been some attempt to tame the extrovert brilliance of the shawm. In 1577 in an inventory made of the estate of the Archduke Karl of Austria there occurs the first mention of the *bassanello*.[32] Praetorius tells us that this was a soft version of the shawm, invented by and named after the Italian composer Giovanni Bassano.[33] A number of scholars find Praetorius' attribution suspect: Curt Sachs[34] thinks it unlikely for chronological reasons (the first known date in Bassano's life is 1585) and points out that it was not until the nineteenth century that the practice of naming instruments after their inventors became established. Other writers,[35] however, have credited the members of the Bassano family resident in England with the invention. If this were the case, however, it does seem strange that the instrument is only mentioned in German sources. Unfortunately there are no surviving examples and for our most detailed information we must rely on Praetorius, who gives the following sizes:

Bassanello ranges from Praetorius' *Syntagma Musicum*.

All the bassanelli have the reed set on a crook and seven finger-holes (with a little-finger-key for the lowest) but no thumb-hole. The overblown range was evidently quite useful: Praetorius says that 'with good reeds, bassanelli can be brought quite high'.[36] He particularly recommends the sound and pure intonation of the smallest bassanello and says it is very suitable for tenor parts in mixed ensembles. Praetorius' illustrations show instruments with a delicately expanding conical bore and an amount of bulbous turned decoration which is surprising for the period. Altogether the bassanello is a rather intriguing instrument and well worth some attempt at reconstruction today.

There may possibly have been some kind of 'soft' shawm in existence in England at the beginning of the sixteenth century. In the Lord Chamberlain's Records for 1509 there is a

reference to liveries for nine players of 'The styll shalmes'.[37] This was before the arrival of the Bassano family, however, and there is no reason to suppose that still shawms, whatever they may have been, were identical with bassanelli.

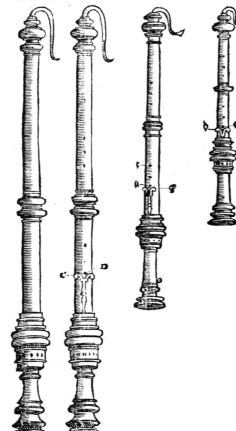

Bassanelli from Praetorius' *Syntagma Musicum*. Left to right: great bass (two views), bass, tenor.

The curtal or dulcian

Although it is such a splendid instrument to look at, and is certainly ideal for playing the bottom part in a renaissance wind band, the bass shawm suffers from several serious disadvantages. It is heavy to hold, cumbersome to carry about, and although the fundamental range up to f is full and secure the overblown register is disappointingly weak and wheezy, fading out altogether above the note C'. Dissatisfaction with the bass shawm led to its gradual replacement by the bass curtal, a much more handy and versatile instrument. Of all the sixteenth-century woodwind innovations, the development of the double-bore principle (two parallel tubes drilled in the same block of wood and connected by a U-bend at the bottom) has proved of the most lasting value. It is all the more frustrating that we know so little about where the earliest developments took place, and

we cannot even be sure that the curtal was the first double-bore instrument to be produced. Anthony Baines[38] points out that the embryo of the bassoon can be seen in certain early types of bagpipe on which some kind of doubling back of the tube is quite common. On surviving examples from Bohemia and elsewhere there is a thick section of the long drone pipe which contains three parallel drillings joined alternately top and bottom to produce a flattened S shape.

This saves a foot or more in the overall length of the drone and may, as Anthony Baines suggests, have provided the impetus for the double-bore experiments of the sixteenth century. Since the bagpipe drone is cylindrical, however, it is possible that the earliest double-bore instruments may have been cylindrical

Modern bass curtal by Moeck. The split key for the little finger is a modern addition, giving low F/F♯.

also. It is much easier to drill a pair of cylindr[ical] bores than to ream out a pair of conical ones it is tempting to wonder whether the *dulceus* described in Henry VIII's Inventory[39] as *shor[t]* instruments may have been some kind of *cylindrical* double-bore prototype. This is pu[re] conjecture, however. The first real evidence for the conical-bored curtal from about 1540 onwards. An early mention comes in 1546 when the Verona Academy bought a *fagotto* and a *dolzana* from a soldier:[40] although the meaning of these names is ambiguous at this stage, one of them must have meant a curtal. In 1562 the Verona Academy lists a *Fagoto* w[ith] its reeds and by 1585 there were *fagotti*. Amo[ng] the Flemish Band of Marie, widowed Quee[n of] Hungary, two *fagotes* are listed in 1559. The earliest English reference comes in 1574 in th[e] Household Accounts of Sir Thomas Kytson [of] Hengrave Hall, Suffolk: '1574 Dec. For an instrument called a curtall XXXs'.[42] The following year a double curtal was in the possession of the Exeter Waits. By the last quarter of the century the curtal had establis[hed]

ar place for itself in the town bands. The
ration of the City of London bought one
and several continental bands are pictured
e bass curtal playing alongside cornetts,
s, and sackbuts. In about 1582 Stephen
n wrote: 'The common bleting musicke
rone, hobuis and curtoll' (ie bagpipe,
, and curtal).[43] But unlike the shawm the
rtal was not solely restricted to being a
strument. It was useful for doubling the
e in church music – hence the name
–Fagott – and it had a role to play in court
oo. In 1589, at the wedding of Duke
nd of Medici to Christine of Lorraine
took place in Florence, one of the
des was accompanied by 'Tromboni,
i, dolzaini et fagotti'.[44]
h of the early evidence for the curtal's
ce comes from Italy, as do a number of
iest surviving instruments, and it is
hat the initial development took place in
t any rate, Italy was the home of a
experiment which contributed one of
tal's family names – fagotto – and may

have contributed to the development of the
double-bore principle in general. Before the
year 1521 a certain Canon Afranio of Ferrara
(c.1489–c.1565) was already experimenting with
an instrument which he called a Phagotum,
employing a pair of U-tubes. At a banquet in
Mantua in 1532 the Canon played a solo on 'il
suo fagoto' and an illustrated description of the
phagotum was published in 1539.[45] Together
with a sheet of playing instructions dated 1565
this provides comprehensive information[46]
about one of the most extraordinary musical
inventions of the sixteenth century, sufficient
for a convincing modern reconstruction to be
made.[47] Because of the amount of information
available, the phagotum has been regularly
mentioned in reference books, but because of its
name it has often been misunderstood as a kind
of bassoon prototype. The phagotum was, in
fact, a kind of bagpipe and the only feature it
shared with the curtal was the use of parallel
bores. Following Lyndesay Langwill,[48] we may
contrast the features of the two instruments
as follows:

Phagotum	Curtal
Bellows-blown	Mouth-blown
Single reeds	Double reeds
made of metal	made of cane
Twin U-tubes,	Single U-tube,
c.22 inches high	c.4 feet high
Cylindrical bore	Conical bore

On the instruction sheet of 1565 the word
fagoto is used to describe each of the larger
pillars of the phagotum with their parallel
bores and by this date the word was already
being used for the curtal.

From what has already been said, the reader
will have observed that not only is the evolution
of the curtal a rather obscure subject but that it
is further confused by the variety of names
which are applied to the instrument. As with
the shawm a summary may be found helpful.

1. From Canon Afranio's phagotum.
Italian fagotto, German Fagott, Spanish fagote.
The name phagotum represents a Latinization of
the Italian fagotto (a bundle of sticks) and was
presumably applied to Afranio's instrument by

way of a nickname. The one-piece curtal could
in no way be said to resemble a faggot or bundle
of sticks, and must presumably have derived the
name fagotto from the phagotum.

2. From the Latin curtus (= short).
English curtal, sometimes spelt curtoll, curtail,
and other variants.
This was the main English name for the
instrument, and like bombard it was borrowed
from artillery: curtal had previously denoted a
type of short-barrelled cannon. The continental
equivalents, however, courtaut (French) and
Kortholt (German), referred to cylindrical types
of double-bore instrument, not the curtal.

3. From the Latin dulcis (= sweet).
German Dulzian, English dolcian, Italian
dolzone, and other variants such as dolzan,
dulcan, dolcan, etc. This name, particularly
common in Germany, is confusing because of
its similarity to the mysterious medieval douçaine
and the equally mysterious dulceuses of Henry
VIII's Inventory. To make matters worse the
dulzaina, which is mentioned several times

ian bagpipe with doubled-back section of
pipe. (Pitt Rivers Museum, Oxford)

The phagotum: the original drawings of 1539,
showing back and front views.

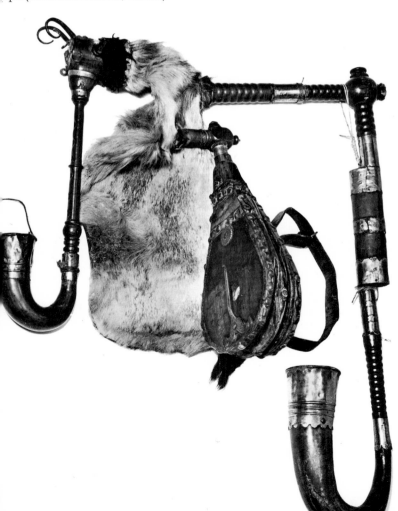

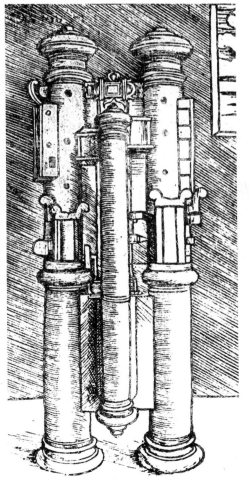

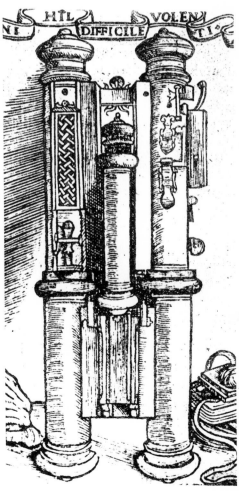

Detail of alto and tenor curtals with perforated
bell-caps.

Smaller sizes of curtal by Moeck showing the
thumb-holes. Left to right: soprano (with a
modern style of keywork), alto, and tenor (with
original type of keywork and metal box-cover).
(Author's collection)

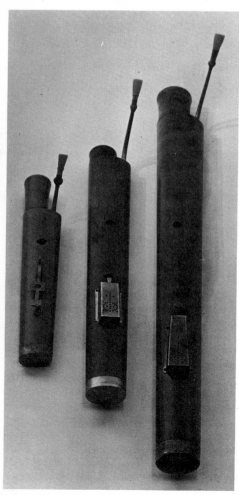

during the Renaissance, was evidently a
cylindrical instrument with a single bore, like
the cornamuse, despite its use today for the
small keyless shawn of Northern Spain.

4. From the Latin *bassus* (= bass).
French *basson,* Spanish *bajon,* Italian *bassone,*
English *bassoon.*
This name has been in use since the early
seventeenth century, though it did not come
into regular use in England until the following
century.

It is worth noting that up to the mid-seventeenth
century, all these names referred to the curtal.
After the emergence of the bassoon proper they
were indiscriminately applied to the new
instrument as well as the old: by the eighteenth
century so great was the confusion that the word
Fagott was even used for the old bass shawm.[49]
In churches and town bands the curtal continued
to be used throughout the baroque period: the
Denner workshop in Nuremberg produced
some very fine curtals[50] as well as examples of
the new baroque woodwind.

A variety of names were used to distinguish
the different sizes of curtal. As already
mentioned the most common size was the bass,
known in England as a *double* curtal and abroad
as a *Chorist-Fagott* or *fagotto chorista.* The prefix
double on the continent, however – as in
Doppelfagott or *fagotto doppio* – referred to an
instrument pitched a fourth or fifth lower than
the bass curtal. Diminutions such as *fagottino* or
bajoncillo signified smaller sizes, like the English
single curtal.

Despite the plethora of new names, the curtal
still retained much of the shawm's basic design,
re-formed into a U-tube. The bore followed
the widely expanding conical bore of the
shawm and the tone was still rather bottom-
heavy: to lighten the quality of the lower notes
some curtals were made with a perforated
bell-cap, looking rather like a pepper-pot, which
acted as a mute. Such instruments were known
as *gedäckt* (covered) and Praetorius says that the
tone is 'much less strong and considerably softer
and lovelier'.[51] Some of the overblown notes in
the second octave (g upwards on the bass) are
rather unsteady and uneven in tone, but can be
'humoured' by using special fingerings
involving the thumb-holes, and the bass curtal
can ascend as high as g', giving it a useful range
of two-and-a-half octaves. The tone has a
'dolce' quality compared to the shawm as the
name *dulcian* suggests. There are two keys, the
standard one for the little finger and a thumb-
key (for low E on the bass). The lowest three
notes, governed by the thumbs only, are much
more manageable than on the shawm with its
clumsy extension keys. The two bores, reamed
out in opposite directions, are connected at the
bottom by a small passage cut between them

and sealed at the base with a wooden (later cork)
plug. Some of the larger curtals were made in
two halves like the cornett so that the bore could
be very carefully finished off: the twin channels
are gouged out, the two sections glued together
and finally bound round with leather.
Praetorius gives the following sizes of curtals:

Curtal ranges from Praetorius' *Syntagma
Musicum.*

Praetorius makes enthusiastic mention
even larger curtal – a great bass, lying an
below the ordinary bass and descending t
which he says is still under construction b
Hans Schreiber, one of the Electoral cham
musicians at Berlin. 'If he should succeed
this,' writes Praetorius,[52] 'he will indeed h
produced a unique and remarkable instrum
for even on the organ it is often difficult to
construct the two lowest notes of the larg
trombone stops – the 16 foot C and D – so
sound quite pure. But time will tell.' Whe
Hans Schreiber ever completed his great-
dulcian is unknown: but such an instrume
has been produced today by Rainer Webe
Bayerbach and it fully lives up to Praetori
expectations.

It has been stated that the smaller curtal
especially the soprano and alto, are weak a
deficient in tone. Whilst it is certain that t
smaller sizes were much less common than
bass, and surviving specimens are compara
rare,[53] practical experiment reveals that th
midget curtals (as Anthony Baines affectio
calls them) have a resonant reedy sound w
character all their own, and their size lend
itself to dexterous fingerwork. The idea o

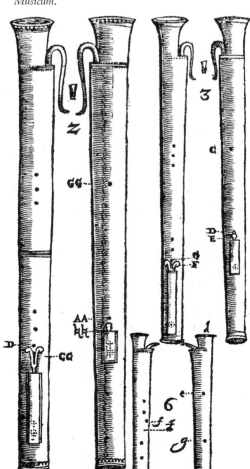

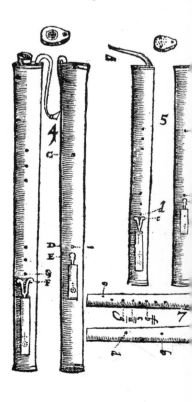

Five sizes of curtal from Praetorius' *Syntagm
Musicum:* each instrument is shown twice, b
and front. Left to right: *Doppel-Fagott* or qu
bass, *Chorist-Fagott* or bass, *gedäckt Chorist-F
or covered bass, and covered tenor. The alto
soprano are shown beneath the others.

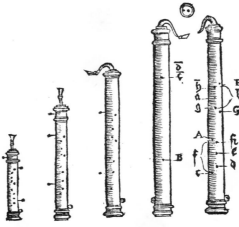

Consort of sorduns from Praetorius' *Syntagma Musicum*.
FAR RIGHT
Courtaut from Mersenne's *Harmonie Universelle*.

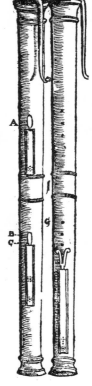

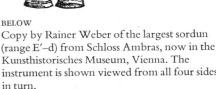

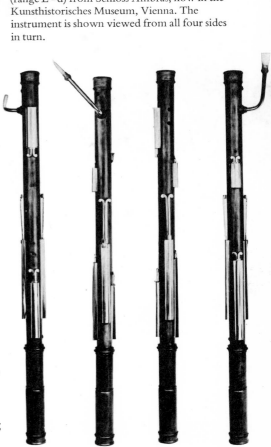

BELOW
ass curtal. Exact copy by Rainer Weber
rly 16th-century instrument in the
lian Museum, Augsburg.

BELOW
Curtal with extended bell from Mersenne's
Harmonie Universelle. The position of the thumb
keys on the reverse side is shown beneath: the
upper one governs low B♭.

BELOW
Copy by Rainer Weber of the largest sordun
(range E′–d) from Schloss Ambras, now in the
Kunsthistorisches Museum, Vienna. The
instrument is shown viewed from all four sides
in turn.

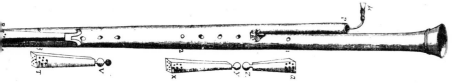

of curtals playing *en famille* cannot have
nknown in the Renaissance: indeed, some
tradition seems to have been carried on
roque and classical times. A surprising
r of tenoroons and octave bassoons were
uring the eighteenth century and at least
ce of ensemble music survives for them.[54]
s, alas, no such specific repertoire from
naissance, although during the first half
eventeenth century a number of
sers included the bass curtal in
sitions for both church and chamber,[55]
st them Michael Praetorius, Giovanni
li, and Heinrich Schütz. The earliest solo
s the *Fantasia Basso solo* (bass curtal plus
uo) by Fray Bartolomé de Selma y
rde, published in Venice in 1638.
omé – a Spanish curtal-playing monk –
the service of the Archduke Leopold of
a, and if this composition is anything to go
must have been a virtuoso player, with a

brilliant finger technique and mastery of the
complete compass of the instrument. The
fantasia descends several times to low B♮ and by
this date a bell extension and third key had been
introduced in France. Mersenne (1635) describes
the *basson* as having *three* keys and illustrates an
instrument with extended bell. Anthony Baines
has suggested that this extension came about in
order to accommodate the cellos in Louis XIII's
court band, which were tuned a tone lower
than normal.[56]

The sordun and courtaut
As has already been mentioned, it is easier to
drill cylindrical bores than conical ones, and so
it is not surprising that renaissance makers
experimented with narrow *cylindrical* double
bores. A cylindrical bore has an additional
advantage, in that it permits the instrument to
be made still shorter; when sounded with a reed
it has the acoustical properties of a stopped pipe

and produces a scale an octave *lower* than on the
equivalent length of expanding conical bore.
So whilst a bass curtal is roughly half the length
of a bass shawm, a bass sordun or courtaut is half
as short again. The tone is much softer and more
muffled, however, and very similar to that of a
rackett: hence the other name given to the
instrument, *sordone* (Italian), *Sordun* (German),
sourdine (French), all derived from the Italian
sordo, mute. The sordun has no bell; the sound
simply emerges from a rather insignificant
lateral hole at the top end of the instrument
near the crook.

The sordone is first mentioned by Zacconi in
1592[57] and an inventory made in 1596 at Schloss
Ambras near Innsbruck enumerates two basses,
three tenors, two descants, and one 'smaller'
descant.[58] Four of these have survived and are
now housed in the Kunsthistorisches Museum,
Vienna; the larger sizes reveal a system of
keywork uniquely elaborate for the period.
The sordun described by Praetorius is much
simpler: the instruments he illustrates are
keyless, though he says: 'Sorduns have twelve
visible holes – and some have two keys as well.
Besides these there is a hole below for moisture
and one on top from which the sound issues.'[59]
Of the twelve finger-holes, eight employ the
standard woodwind fingerings using the thumb,
six fingers, and little finger whilst others (for
the lowest four notes) use the remaining thumb
and little finger as well as the middle joints of
each index finger. Praetorius gives the following
sizes of sorduns (*overleaf*):

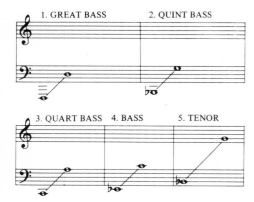

1. GREAT BASS   2. QUINT BASS

3. QUART BASS 4. BASS   5. TENOR

Sordun ranges from Praetorius' *Syntagma Musicum.*

Mersenne[60] shows yet another design of sordun – under the name *courtaut* – equipped with six short projecting tubes which he calls *tetines*. These are to help the player locate some of the remoter holes, a particularly tricky business with the holes governed by the middle joints. Mersenne's courtaut was designed for left- or right-handed players and the unwanted *tetines* had to be stopped up with wax. Because of its cylindrical bore the sordun should theoretically be able to overblow at the twelfth (as the clarinet does). The bore is too narrow for any overblown range to be at all successful, however, and in practice the instrument is restricted to the fundamental notes.

The rackett

The ingenuity of renaissance makers was not content with a mere pair of parallel tubes and in the rackett produced the *ne plus ultra* of multiple-bore construction. Once again the ingenious inventor remains unknown though the instrument is likely to be of German origin. The first reference to it (as *Raggett*) occurs in Württemberg inventories of 1576 followed by a Graz inventory of 1590 which includes *Rogetten*.[61] The well-known painting of the Munich court band in the time of Orlando di Lasso[62] (1532–94) shows a rackett player amongst a delightful mixed consort which also features flute, recorder, cornetts, sackbut, lute, viols, *viole da braccio,* and harpsichord. Another depiction is to be found in the outstandingly beautiful ivory cabinet by Christof Angermair (*c.* 1600–32), carver at the Munich court (see p 39). A number of racketts survive in museums at Vienna, Munich, Leipzig, and elsewhere.[63]

The rackett's narrow cylindrical bore consists of no less than nine parallel channels drilled in a wooden or ivory cylinder and connected alternately top and bottom. The wide reed is inserted into a pirouette similar to that of the shawm and the outlet of the bore is a small lateral hole at the base of the instrument. Because of the internal convolutions, the size of

Bass courtaut by David Owen, reconstructed according to the details given by Mersenne.

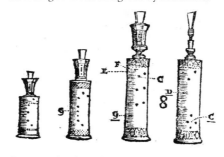

Consort of racketts from Praetorius' *Syntagma Musicum.* Left to right: tenor, bass, quint bass (two views).

the rackett is amazingly tiny compared to its pitch. The smallest size, the tenor (with a bore of only 6 or 7 millimetres), is a mere four-and-a-half inches in height: yet its lowest note is the G on the bottom of the bass stave. The great-bass rackett descends as low as the double-bassoon in spite of being only just over a foot high. It is surprising how full and reedy a consort of racketts can sound, despite the constrictions of the narrow bore and multiple U-bends. Praetorius was rather disparaging about the effect of a complete *stimmwerk :* 'In sound racketts are quite soft, almost as if one were blowing through a comb. They have no particular grace when a whole set of them is used together ; but

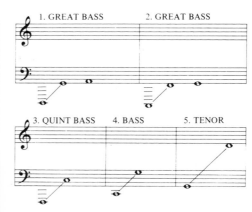

1. GREAT BASS   2. GREAT BASS

3. QUINT BASS 4. BASS   5. TENOR

Rackett ranges from Praetorius' *Syntagma Musicum.*

when viols da gamba are used with them, or when a single rackett is used together with other wind or stringed instruments and a harpsichord or the like, and is played by a good musician, it is indeed a lovely instrument. It is particularly pleasing and fine to hear on bass parts.'[64]

The painting and sculpture already mentioned confirm the German practice of using a single rackett in a mixed ensemble and the larger racketts are very effective when doubling the bass line an octave lower. Praetorius seems to have had a particular interest in woodwind instruments which operated at 16-foot pitch. He says: 'I myself designed and recently had constructed a rackett which can be brought down to the 16 foot C, and which in its lower register is similar to the largest diapason stops of the organ.' Of course, when playing in consort the whole rackett family operate at 16-foot pitch, an octave *lower* than standard instruments, just as the smaller sizes of recorder operate at 4-foot pitch, an octave *higher* than normal.[65] Praetorius states that racketts, like sorduns, are not readily overblown, although a good player can obtain one or two 'falsetto' notes on a good instrument.

The various names for the rackett derive from its squat appearance and convoluted bore. The German *Rankett* and other variants already mentioned are usually derived from the old German word *rank* meaning crooked. Anthony Baines[66] has suggested that since the rackett does resemble a small firework, the derivation may be from *Raquete* (a rocket). Later German names were *Wurstfagott* (sausage-bassoon) and *Faustfagott* (fist-bassoon). The Italian *cortali* denoted racketts and the Italian *cervellato* (sausage) provided the most common French name *cervelat,* sometimes spelt *cervelas.*

Since a number of modern writers[67] describe the renaissance rackett but illustrate its baroque descendant the later history of the instrument may be briefly mentioned here. During the later seventeenth century the bass rackett in F was entirely redesigned. It was given a wider

expanding conical bore instead of a cylindrical one, a coiled crook inserted at the side of the instrument instead of a pirouette, and a centrally placed bulbous bell to enhance the tonal projection. The disposition of finger-holes, wayward on renaissance racketts, was entirely rationalized and a number of *tetines* (presumably derived from the sordun) were added to facilitate the fingering. The result was in effect a compact narrow-bore bassoon, light in tone and enchanting in appearance. The development of the baroque rackett (effective range B♭' or g') has been attributed to the Nuremberg maker J. C. Denner (1655–1707) and an instrument from his workshop (dated 1709) survives in Vienna.[68] According to Sir John Hawkins at least one rackett was produced in early eighteenth-century London, though this may have been an attempted reconstruction of the renaissance type. The maker was Thomas Stanesby, famous for his recorders, flutes, oboes and bassoons. Hawkins's account is so amusing as to warrant quoting in full.

'Stanesby who was a diligent peruser both of Mersennus and Kircher, and in the making of instruments adhered as closely to the directions of the former as possible, constructed a short bassoon or Cervelat . . . for the late earl of Abercorn, then Lord Paisley, and a disciple

Two bass racketts by Moeck, showing comparative sizes. Left: renaissance bass, with cylindrical bore. Right: baroque bass, with expanding conical bore. (Author's collection)

usch, but it did not answer expectation: on of its closeness the interior parts d and retained the moisture of the breath, rts dilated, and broke. In short the whole p.'[69]

ether in its cylindrical or conical version, kett is quite a tricky instrument to make.

ern consort of racketts by Moeck. gh the basic design remains the same, the g system has been rationalized and four dded, as on the baroque rackett. Left to great bass, quart bass, bass, tenor.

artölde from Schloss Ambras. historisches Museum, Vienna)

ger-holes have to be drilled often quite at a variety of different angles in order up with the appropriate section of the Because of the depth of some of the holes fine tuning is more difficult than on woodwind instruments and great care e taken to seal all the U-joints. It would uch easier if the instrument was made a section of cylindrical *metal* tube which

could be bent into any shape you fancy. Such an idea must have crossed the mind of the maker of the *Tartölde* listed in the 1596 inventory of the music room of the Archduke Ferdinand at Schloss Ambras and now in the Kunsthistorisches Museum, Vienna.[70] These unique instruments are basically racketts (not shawms as sometimes stated) made out of coiled brass tubing concealed inside a painted brass dragon. The looped brass crook is designed for a reed without pirouette, and unlike most racketts, the internal structure has escaped the ravages of time so that the *Tartölde* are still in playing condition.

The reed-cap instruments

All the instruments so far mentioned in this chapter demand a similar expertise in playing to that of the modern oboe or bassoon. The player must develop the correct embouchure for his instrument and learn how to control the reed so as not only to make some gradation of tone and dynamics but to be able to adjust his intonation to the ensemble in which he finds himself and assist the weak or out-of-tune notes on his instrument. The basic scale of any renaissance reed instrument should be in tune with itself, but the chromatic notes can only be obtained by cross-fingering which tends to weaken the tone and often produces one or two unsteady notes requiring 'humouring' on the player's part. On instruments pitched in C, for example, the fingerings for A♭, F♯, and E♭ in the basic scale can be rather unsatisfactory, though the professional players of the Renaissance certainly overcame any such shortcomings as a matter of course. However,

in the days when musicians were expected to double on a variety of instruments (and in the courtly entertainments already mentioned quite a bit of doubling must have gone on) it was useful to have instruments which did not require the mastery of a special embouchure. From the late fifteenth century onwards there developed a new genre of woodwind instrument in which the reed was kept out of contact with the lips by means of a reed-cap. The player simply blows through a slot in the top of the cap, using a fairly strong breath pressure in order to activate the reed which is mounted on a staple and vibrates independently as on the bagpipe. The reed-cap, which survives today on the bagpipe practice chanter, represents an extension of the principle of the older hornpipe and bladder-pipe, though all the renaissance reed-cap instruments employed double, not single, reeds. It must not be imagined that once the reed is hidden away inside a reed-cap all the player's troubles are over. Cane reeds fluctuate wildly with changes in temperature or humidity and require careful maintenance on reed-cap instruments just as they do on bagpipes. Even when equipped with plastic reeds, as on most modern reproductions, reed-cap instruments are by no means easy to play in tune. But with a well made and well regulated reed, the problems are a lot easier than on the shawm or curtal. Most reed-cap instruments cannot overblow at all and have a very restricted compass. This usually means that with only one octave to cope with the finger-holes can be placed so as to assist the chromatic notes: on the cylindrical-bore reed-cap instruments such as the crumhorn, cross-fingerings work extremely well. Since their pitch is governed entirely by breath pressure, reed-cap instruments play at a fixed dynamic level: any fluctuation in pressure produces an equivalent change in pitch. Tonguing through a reed-cap produces a characteristic sharp attack which is very effective in an ensemble. A consort of crumhorns, *cornamusen*, or *rauschpfeifen* produces a fresh, invigorating sound quite unlike any other. The nearest sound is, of course, that of the renaissance organ, so many of whose stops were modelled on the sounds of contemporary woodwind instruments. But when each line in a consort is played by a different instrument, there is a much greater separation than on the organ, and the human breath imparts a living quality which the organ's bellows cannot quite match.

The crumhorn
The earliest and by far the most common of the reed-cap instruments was the crumhorn. The name first occurs in 1489 as an organ stop in Dresden,[71] suggesting that the instrument had already been in use for some time. The name

means literally 'curved horn' and is associated with the old English *crump* and the German *krumm* meaning crooked. Hence *Krumbhorn*, *Krummhorn* (German), and the French *cromorne* (not met with till the seventeenth century).[72] Other names used for the instrument also refer to its shape: *tournebout* (French), *corno torto* or

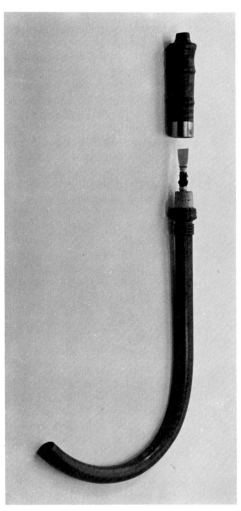

Alto crumhorn in G by Moeck (with cap removed to show reed), based on one of the sets of crumhorns in the Museum of Musical Instruments, Brussels, shown on page 49.

simply *storto* (Italian), and *orlo* (Spanish). In Italian usage *piva* and *cornamusa* both referred to the crumhorn as well as the bagpipe.[73] The crumhorn is made by turning and boring a length of boxwood and then steaming round the lower end to produce the characteristic fishhook shape. The curve has no effect on the sound whatsoever and is purely decorative: presumably it was inherited (like the suffix *horn*) from a medieval crumhorn/bladder-pipe prototype, which had a curved horn-bell like the hornpipe. It is easy to see how the crumhorn

developed from the bladder pipe: the rather
vulnerable bladder could easily become damaged
and players simply learnt to do without. Apart
from the bladder itself the two instruments seem
to have been very similar by Virdung's time
(1511) with a cylindrical bore, six finger-holes,
and a slightly funnelled-out bell. Although they
are not shown, there must have been one or
two vent holes in each bell section, otherwise
the instruments would have produced a very
peculiar scale. Virdung shows four sizes, as does
Agricola (1538), and Praetorius gives the
following:

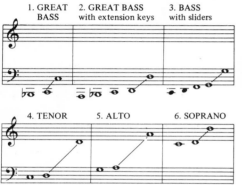

Crumhorn ranges from Praetorius' *Syntagma
Musicum*.

Modern alto crumhorn in F by Moeck, with two
extra keys for high a′ and b♭′. (Author's
collection)

In spite of the fact that Praetorius states that
crumhorns had *six* finger-holes plus thumb-hole,
his own illustrations reveal seven finger-holes.
In his usual practical way, Praetorius was
conscious of the restriction imposed by the
crumhorn's basic octave-and-a-note compass
and in Volume III of his *Syntagma Musicum*
describes how crumhorn players should
transpose music to use their resources to the
best advantage.[74] Since bass parts tend to have
the widest range, the largest crumhorns were
often equipped to cope with additional low
notes. One method was to fit two keys for the
little finger instead of one: the vent-holes were
provided with brass sliders to pre-set the pitch
of the extra (lowest) note when both keys were
closed. Praetorius' *Bass Chorist* is of this type.
Alternatively, as with Praetorius' great bass in
C, crumhorns were fitted with three extension
keys like those of the larger shawms. However,
there are no surviving examples or illustrations
with extension keys for the *upper* end of the
register such as are fitted by most modern
crumhorn makers.

The standard four-part consort of crumhorns
was not soprano, alto, tenor, and bass as we
might expect but alto, two tenors, and bass;
furthermore the alto was pitched in G, as
Praetorius shows, a tone higher than most altos
made today. It is a pity that in the modern
revival of early instruments an unwritten law

seems to have grown up stating that everything
that blows shall be in either C or F; there really
is a need for G and D instruments too, alto
recorders and crumhorns in G being particularly
useful. As far as crumhorns are concerned, the
soprano in C seems to have been a comparative
rarity: few such instruments have survived,
neither Virdung nor Agricola mentions a smaller
size than the alto in their texts[75] and Praetorius
gives his alto the name *cantus*. By virtue of its
narrow bore the soprano crumhorn does tend
to be a rather weak instrument, deficient in
tone: the alto makes a much better 'lead'
instrument for a consort. A surprising amount
of music fits the a.t.t.b. consort as it stands,[76]
including the pavan marked specifically for 4
crumhorns from Johann Schein's *Banchetto
Musicale* of 1626 and the majority of Susato's
Danserye of 1551. Although Susato does not
suggest using crumhorns in his edition, the fact
that he opened up his music shop and printing
business at the sign of 'In de Kromhoorn'
suggests that he had a particular affection for the
instrument. Other works associated with
crumhorns include:
1. The six-part madrigal *Guardan almo pastore*[77]
by Francesco Corteccia, from the Medici
wedding celebration of 1539, which was first
played by cornett, soprano crumhorn (*stortina*),
and four other crumhorns (*storte*), and then sung
by six shepherds, doubled by the same instru-

Pavan for four crumhorns, from Schein's
Banchetto Musicale (1617). Modern edition by
Dieter Krickeberg (Bärenreiter, BA 4499).

A similar combination was used in
cia's music to the Florentine *intermedii*
; the third *intermedio* features a *cornetto*
d five *storti* accompanying voices.[78] On
casion the composer seems to have had a
lar dramatic effect in mind, since the
represented Frauds and Deceptions.
ere in the intermedii the nasal buzz of
orns seem to have been employed as a
effect; three crumhorns helped to cele-
e Age of Bronze in 1548[79] and one
panied Calumny, Ignorance, and Fear
.[80]

six-part psalm setting *Erzürne dich nicht*[81]
by Thomas Stolzer. In a letter he
mends that it be played on *Khrumphörner*
suits them throughout, which is not the
th every composition, especially those in
parts'.[82]

five-part *Pazzamezze* and *Gaillarde*
CLXXXIII and CCLXXXIV) from Praetorius'
chore (1612)[83] These two dances by
=Francisco Caroubel) are mentioned by
rius in his introduction[84] as being suitable
umbhörner or other instruments. Curiously
h they not only require drastic downward
osition but some adjustment of the inner
well since all three exceed the 9-note
Professional woodwind players in those
ust have been fairly adept at 'editing'
arts as they went along in order to suit
mpass of their instruments.

umber of anonymous works in a set of
ooks now in the Royal Danish library in
hagen which seem to have been compiled
-sixteenth century for the wind band of
Albrecht of Prussia.[85] The outstanding
a splendid five-part setting, basse-danse
of the popular Flemish tune *Tandernaken*,
for a.t.t.b.b.[86] Some of the other pieces
e the downward transposition mentioned
etorius before crumhorns can be used.
ransposition facilitates the performance
ide variety of dances and chansons not
cally intended for crumhorns.

Bernard Thomas has pointed out,[87] the
er of different types of music represented
above list is impressive, ranging from
to an Italian madrigal and Church music.

Consort of crumhorns (two sopranos, two altos,
two tenors, bass); German, sixteenth or early
seventeenth century. (Staatliches Institut für
Musikforschung, Berlin)
Consort of crumhorns (soprano to great bass)
from Praetorius' *Syntagma Musicum*.

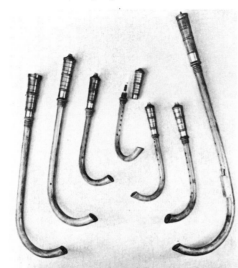

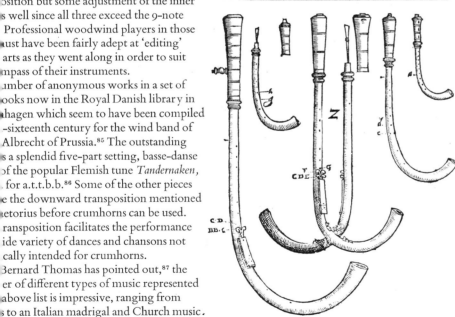

Set of six crumhorns still in their original case.
Italian, second half of the sixteenth century.
(Museum of Musical Instruments, Brussels)

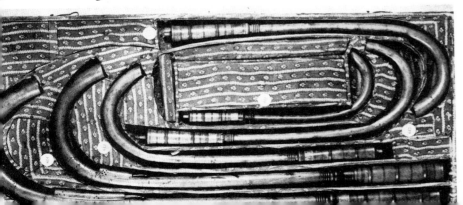

Despite public reaction today to the crumhorn's
appearance or to its sound when badly played,
the crumhorn was far from being a joke. Its role
in musical life was a limited but serious one, and
a consort of crumhorns, like their keyboard

Three crumhorn players; engraving by Heinrich
Aldegrever, 1551. (Graphische Sammlung
Albertina, Vienna)

equivalent the regal, was ideally suited to
solemn slow-moving music such as Schein's
pavan.

It was in Germany, Italy, and the Low
Countries that the crumhorn and its reed-capped
relatives seem to have been most popular. In
spite of Henry VIII's collection of twenty-five
crumhorns[88] there is no occasion when they are
known to have been used, nor a single piece of
English music which is associated with reed-cap
instruments. A rare literary reference occurs in
Sir William Leighton's *Teares or Lamentations
of a Sorrowful Soule* (London 1613): 'With
Crouncormes musicke laud the King of Kings
with one accord.'[89] Curiously enough it was in
France that crumhorns lingered on the longest.
In 1650 'les cromornes et les trompettes marines'
appear amongst the instruments of the *Grande
Écurie du Roy*: several members of the Philidor
family doubled on crumhorn and tromba
marina (an unlikely combination if ever there
was one) as well as oboe and fife and there is a
surviving suite *pour les cromornes* by Degrignis
(1660).[90] It is thought that the crumhorns of the
Grande Écurie may have differed considerably
from the renaissance type. Mersenne (1635)

illustrated a thick sausage-like crumhorn with
the finger-holes at the side and a curiously
insecure looking reed-cap. A number of
museums possess crude leather-covered
instruments of this kind.[91]

Tournebout from Mersenne's
Harmonie Universelle.

Quartet of angelic crumhorn players. Detail from
a painting by an unknown Czech artist (1520).
(National Gallery, Prague)

The cornamuse

'Corna Muse are straight like bassanelli. They
are covered below, and around the bell have
several little holes, from which the sound issues.
In sound they are quite similar to crumhorns,
but quieter, lovelier, and very soft. Thus they
might justly be named still, soft crumhorns,
much as *cornetti muti* could be called soft
cornetts.'[92]

So writes Praetorius, giving us the clearest
description that we have of this instrument.
No cornamuse has survived, nor does Praetorius
illustrate it, so we cannot be sure of its outward
appearance. He states that the cornamuse had no
keys[93] and his family sizes reveal in each case the
limited range of a ninth, characteristic of
reed-cap instruments.

The name *cornamuse* (derived from the
medieval Latin *cornamusa*) is a confusing one
since it most commonly means bagpipe, as in
the French *cornemuse* today. When we find the
name included amongst the instrumental
ensembles heard at courtly entertainments it
must be the reed-cap instrument rather than the
bagpipe which is meant. The music at the
banquet held in Munich to celebrate the
marriage of Albert V of Bavaria to Renée of
Lorraine in 1568 included a mixed consort of
harpsichord, trombone, recorder, lute,
cornamusa, mute cornett, viol, and *piffero*.[94]
Anthony Baines[95] believes that in Italian usage

cornamusa actually meant crumhorn and not the softer, straight instrument described by Praetorius. Another ambiguous name crops up in the Munich account of 1568: there was a heterogeneous ensemble consisting of *dolzaina, cornamuse,* shawm, and mute cornett.[96] *Dolzaina* (from the Latin *dulcis,* sweet) takes us back to the confusion of douçaine/dulceuse/dulcian (see page 43).[97] No *dolzaina* has survived, nor is it ever depicted, nor unfortunately does Praetorius mention it. However, Zacconi (1592)[98] tells us that it had a compass of a ninth and with the addition of two keys could ascend by two further notes (these keys must have been very similar to the 'extra' keys fitted by most crumhorn makers today). To all intents and purposes the dolzaina must have been very similar to the cornamuse: a straight cylindrical-bore reed-cap instrument. Whatever the distinction between the two may have been we shall probably never know.

The kortholt
The reed-cap principle was applied to the cylindrical double-bore instruments too. The kortholt (literally *kurz Holz,* short wood) is basically a courtaut or sordun provided with a reed-cap. Praetorius[99] admits to being rather short on information about it and he was puzzled by the disparity in pitch between the kortholt that he had seen and the equivalent size of sordun. He does not give a complete table of ranges but he does illustrate the instrument, calling it *Kortholt oder Kurzpfeiff.* The illustration shows a bass size of kortholt: for the top two notes keys are provided, no doubt similar to those on the dolzaina mentioned by Zacconi. Modern makers have assumed that a complete *stimmwerk* must have existed and added three other sizes to produce a complete 4-part consort.

The doppione[100]
The double-bore reed-cap instruments certainly occupy one of the most murky corners of renaissance instrument history. Even the indefatigable Praetorius confesses of the *doppione* that 'In spite of my efforts I have not been able to examine such an instrument'[101] and concludes vaguely that it must be like the kortholt, sordun, or cornamuse. However, he gives the following

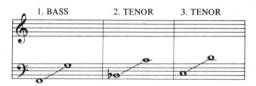
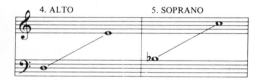

Cornamuse ranges from Praetorius' *Syntagma Musicum.*

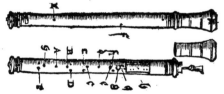

Kortholt from Praetorius' *Syntagma Musicum.*

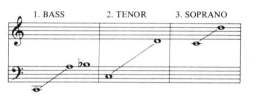

Doppione ranges from Praetorius' *Syntagma Musicum.*

ranges, which correspond with those giv[en by] Zacconi (1592), who Praetorius tells us is [the] source of information. Cerone (1613) cop[ies] Zacconi also, but uses the name *doblados.*[10...]

In one respect we are more fortunate th[an] Praetorius, since two doppioni have surv[ived] albeit in rather worm-eaten condition, fo[r] examination. They are now in the collect[ion of] the Teatro Filarmonico of Verona, which [also] includes recorders, flutes, crumhorns, and cornetts. From a recent exhaustive survey [a] number of rather curious facts have emerg[ed]
1. On both doppioni there was originally [a] reed-cap although this is now missing.
2. There is provision for *two* crooks or sta[ples at] the top of each instrument, and consequen[tly] there must have been *two* reeds for each instrument.
3. The doppioni have parallel *conical* bores.
4. Both bores expand towards the bottom [end] of the instrument: in other words instead [of a] continuously expanding bore (as on the cu[rtal]) there are two expanding bores which mee[t at] a common U-joint.
5. Each bore has the basic set of seven woo[den] finger-holes but one set is placed much lo[wer] down the instrument than the other.

The authors of the survey mentioned ab[ove] (Rainer Weber and J. H. van der Meer) co[nclude] that the two bores of the doppioni were *alternatives,* designed to be played separate[ly.] Only one reed at a time was employed, of course, the player selecting the appropriate [one] for the bore which he was to use. Thus the doppione was a two-in-one instrument rat[her] as, on a grander scale, the early two-manu[al] harpsichord was, with its lower keyboard [tuned] a fourth below the upper one. Each doppi[one] offered a pair of consort sizes: (1) soprano/a[lto,] (2) alto/tenor, (3) tenor/bass, (4) bass/great[bass.]

The Verona instruments correspond to 2 [and] 3, whilst the instruments mentioned by Za[cconi,] Cerone, and Praetorius correspond to 1, 3, [and 4.] The ranges given by these writers can be se[en] to be only partially correct: for the two sm[aller] doppioni only half the instrument was take[n] into account, giving the characteristically limited range of a ninth; for the largest the combined range of both bores is given. Rai[ner] Weber and J. H. van der Meer also conclu[de] that the Verona doppioni started life as ree[d-cap] instruments, but were later blown directly [in] the manner of a sordun or courtaut.

Rauschpfeife and schreierpfeife
All the reed-cap instruments dealt with so f[ar] belong to the 'bas' or soft class; even the crumhorn, more strongly voiced than the [rest,] lacks the carrying power necessary for out[-] doors. *Rauschpfeifen* and *schreierpfeifen,* how[ever] are reed-cap shawms and their place is wit[h the] 'haut' instruments of the outdoor band.

FAR LEFT
Alto and soprano cornamuse: reconstructions by Moeck. Notice the vent holes round the covered bell. The instruments are provided with two extra keys to extend the range upwards. (Author's collection)
MIDDLE
Four modern sizes of kortholt by Moeck.
l to *r*: bass (front view), tenor (back view), alto (front view), soprano (back view). (Author's collection)
LEFT
The Verona *doppioni* as restored by Rainer Weber, with new caps.
BELOW
Detail of upper end of the *doppione,* with reeds and crooks for direct blowing.

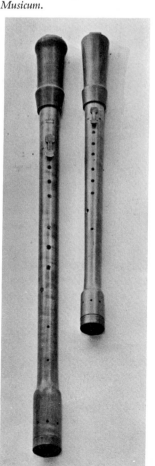

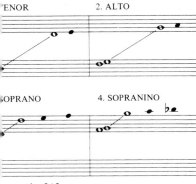

rauschpfeife ranges.

...ing to Marcuse[104] the name *Rauschpfeife*
...ed from the old German *Rusch* (=rush)
...ans simply *reed-pipe*. Confusingly both
...g and Agricola use the name *Russpfeife*
...ribe a short wide-bore recorder with four
...oles (see below, pp 57–8). The origin
...ame *Schreierpfeife* (Italian *schryari*) is
...: perhaps it had something to do with
...rument's 'screaming' tone quality
...=to cry). Of the two, rauschpfeifen
...have been more common: there is a
...voodcut showing five of them being
...on horseback in the *Triumph of*
...*ilian I* and 5- and 6-part consorts of
...pfeifen survive in collections in Berlin
...gue respectively.[105] Together these
...ents cover the soprano to bass registers:
...llest instrument (in Berlin) is a little over
...ong and is equivalent to the *kleindiscant*
..., the largest (in Prague) is over four feet
...d is suitable for bass parts. The omission
...chpfeifen from the *Syntagma Musicum* is
...curious, although Praetorius does
...te a type of reed-cap shawm which he
...*Bassett Nicolo*. This is an alto instrument in
...with extension keys and, apart from the
...p, is identical in design to the other large
...s shown by Praetorius. He gives the
...ss as a basic 9-note range from f–g′ plus
...xtension keys going down to c.
...r as rauschpfeifen are concerned, the
...nporary nomenclature for the various
...not clear: modern makers produce the
...own above.
...ause the rauschpfeife has an expanding
...l bore like the shawm, it overblows at the
...and unlike other reed-cap instruments
...two useful extra notes are obtainable
...second octave. The larger sizes have a
...inger-key and fontanelle for the lowest
...A late French type of reed-cap
...h is described by Mersenne[106] under
...ne *hautbois de Poitou*: he gives three
...oprano, alto, and bass. The soprano is
...lent to the *chalumeau*, the chanter of the
...use (French bagpipe), and the same
...ment could either be played separately
...reed-cap or as an integral part of the

ABOVE
Woodcut from *The Triumph of Maximilian I*
showing five shawms (left) and five rauschpfeifen
(right). The difference between the pirouette of
the former and the reed-cap of the latter is quite
clear.
LEFT
A modern consort of rauschpfeifen. Left to right:
sopranino and two sopranos by Gunter Körber,
alto in G by Rainer Weber. (Author's collection)

bagpipe. Mersenne shows the bass *hautbois de
Poitou* with a doubled-back bore, like the
curtal, though this type of instrument is not
heard of elsewhere. In France an ensemble of
hautbois et musettes de Poitou was still included in
the royal band in the time of Lully, who used
them to introduce the finale of his music to
Le Bourgeois Gentilhomme.[107] Their folk
descendants are still to be heard in Brittany
today: the *bombarde* (small shawm) always plays

in combination with the *biniou* (bagpipe).

The *Schreierpfeife* or *Schryari* is rather more
of a mystery since no specimens are extant. In
1541 the Nuremberg trumpet maker Georg
Neuschel offered Duke Albrecht of Prussia some
Schreyende pfeiffen he had received from Lyons
and Venice which he said were far louder than
shawms.[108] Several German inventories include
a consort of *Schreierpfeifen* and Praetorius gives
the following sizes:

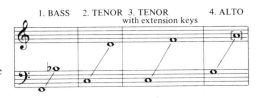

Schryari ranges from Praetorius' *Syntagma
Musicum*. He omits to indicate the upper limit
of the alto schryari.

He tells us that the instrument is non-over-blowing with a 'strong and fresh' tone[109] and his illustrations reveal several interesting

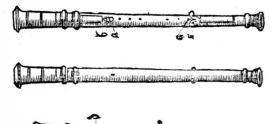

Schryari from Praetorius' *Syntagma Musicum*. Top to bottom: bass (two views), tenor, and alto with covered bell (two views).

features. The larger sizes have *upward* extension keys operated by the index finger, like those shown on the kortholt: in his table Praetorius gives the range of two types of tenor schryari, one with the extra keys and one without. The smallest size is an alto on which the bottom end of the instrument is covered, but provided, Praetorius tells us,[110] with numerous vent holes. The tenor and bass are open-ended with a small flared bell. The most surprising feature however is that the exterior of the schryari is conical, but tapering *away* from the reed cap. Whether this indicates that the bore is contracting instead of expanding it is impossible to say, but if the schryari did have a contracting bore it would have been an extremely unusual instrument. Curt Sachs has suggested that it may have been of oriental provenance.[111]

In conclusion it may be helpful to summarize the different categories of renaissance reed instruments by means of a table. The phagotum and *Tartöld* have not been included since they may be regarded as 'sports' rather than established instrumental types.

CONICAL BORE		CYLINDRICAL BORE
shawm		crumhorn
curtal		cornamuse
bassanello		dolzaina
rauschpfeife		sordun
schreierpfeife		kortholt
doppione		rackett

SINGLE BORE	DOUBLE BORE	MULTIPLE BORE
shawm	curtal	rackett
bassanello	doppione	
rauschpfeife	sordun	
schreierpfeife	kortholt	
crumhorn		
cornamuse		
dolzaina		

WITH PIROUETTE	WITH WIND CAP	WITHOUT WIND CAP OR PIROUETTE
shawm (*except for bass sizes downwards*)	crumhorn	bassanello
	cornamuse	curtal
rackett	kortholt	sordun
	dolzaina	doppione(?)
	rauschpfeife	
	schreierpfeife	
	doppione(?)	

The bagpipe

A word may be added at this point about the renaissance development of the bagpipe. Although not a reed-cap instrument in the sense described above, it does involve a similar separation of the reed from the mouth, and to an extent all reed-cap instruments can be regarded as derivatives of the bagpipe. Whilst the crumhorn, rauschpfeife, and their relatives are essentially ensemble instruments, the bagpipe remained an ideal solo instrument. Although two or three rustic pipers probably improvised simple part-music as they still do in Southern Italy or Spain today, and regiments of military pipers played in thrilling unison, the bagpipe's limitations[112] clearly prevented it from any involvement in the mainstream of renaissance music. There was still some association with the court: Henry VIII's Inventory[113] includes five bagpipes 'with pipes of Ivorie' and as late as Elizabeth I's reign a solitary bagpiper, Richard Woodwarde, is listed amongst the King's Music.[114] But during the Renaissance the emphasis gradually shifted from court to country, as the Elizabethan actor Robert Armin makes clear in *A Nest of Ninnies*. 'At Christmas time, when great logs furnish the hall fire . . . and indeed all revelling is regarded . . . amongst all the pleasures provided, a noise of minstrels and a Lincolnshire bagpipe was prepared; the minstrels for the great chamber, the bagpipe for the hall; the minstrels to serve up the knight's meat and the bagpipe for the common dancing.'[115] As an instrument of rustic and popular merrymaking the bagpipe has been immortalized in the paintings of Pieter Breughel and his contemporaries.

During the sixteenth century the bagpipe started to form its special ties with Scotland and Ireland. Most Scottish towns employed a town piper and drummer to perform much the same function as the English 'waits'. Yet it appears that in the Scotland of those days the music of the pipes was not to everyone's taste, for in 1630 the town of Aberdeen decided to dispense with the services of its bagpiper. 'The Magistrates discharge the common piper of all going through the town at nycht, or in the morning, in tyme coming, with his pype – it being an incivill forme to be usit within sic a famous burghe, and being often found fault with, als weill by sundrie nichtbouris of the toune as by strangers.'[116]

Meanwhile the Irish had developed the great war-pipe or *píob mhór*. In his *Dialogo della musica antica e della moderna* (1581) Vincenzo Galilei says of the Irish and their *píob mhór*: 'To its sound, this unconquered, fierce and warlike people march their armies and encourage one another to feats of valour. With it also, they accompany their dead to the grave, making such mournful sounds as almost to

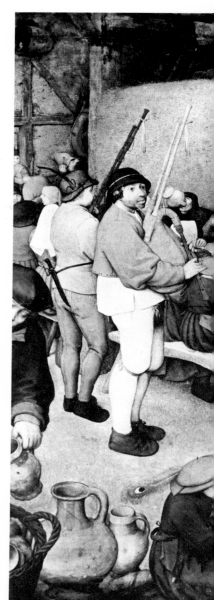

Two bagpipers, from *The Peasant Wedding* Pieter Breughel the Elder. (Kunsthistorische Museum, Vienna)

force the bystander to weep.'[117] Small sets 'indoor' bagpipes were popular during the Renaissance too, especially in France. Praetorius[118] describes a small French instr which was bellows-blown: this was the an of the eighteenth-century *musette* and the Northumbrian small-pipes and Uillean pip of today. The size, construction, and tuning renaissance bagpipes varied so enormously no detailed analysis will be attempted here readers are once more referred to the book Anthony Baines and Francis Collinson.[119]

...utes

...the Renaissance the word 'flute' con-
...o be used as a generic term denoting
...corder and transverse flute and when it
...on its own without some kind of
...ation we cannot always be quite sure
...instrument is meant. On the continent
...as sometimes used specifically for the
...r: there is no ambiguity about the
...Praetorius (1619) and the *flauto* of
...(1535). On other occasions there *is* a
...a of identification: although both
...ius[120] and Philibert Jambe de Fer[121] tell
...talians called the recorder 'flauto', this
...eem to be an over-simplification. The
...do for three flutes from Peri's *Euridice,*
...Sinfonia con un Triflauto') could be
...or transverse flutes or recorders.[122] The
...was that the continental languages lacked
...valent to the convenient English word
...er'. In England a regular distinction
...the two instruments does seem to have
...ade during the sixteenth century and
...and 'recorders' are often mentioned side
...According to the chronicler Holinshed,
...in 1510, King Henry VIII was

...ising himself dailie in shooting, singing,
...s, wrestling, casting of the barre,
...g at the recorders, flute, virginals . . .'[123]

Henry VIII's Inventory[124] includes over
seventy 'flutes' and over seventy 'recorders' and
the Lord Chamberlain's records of the *King's
Musick* list seven recorder players and seven
flute players for the funeral of Queen Elizabeth
in 1603.[125] Yet by the time of the Restoration
the transverse flute had dropped out of use
altogether in England and Purcell and his
contemporaries invariably referred to the treble
recorder in F as a 'flute'. When did this change
in nomenclature begin? It would be fascinating
to know, if only to establish which instrument
should be used in Thomas Morley's *First Book
of Consort Lessons* (1599)[126] and other consort
music[127] scored for the typically English
'broken consort'[128] of treble viol or violin,
'flute', bass viol, lute, cittern, and bandora. The
celebrated picture of Sir Henry Unton's
wedding shows a broken consort with a
transverse flute, yet in the set of manuscript
part-books containing a number of Morley's
pieces (now in the Cambridge University
Library) the flute part-book is labelled 'the
recorder part'.[129] Furthermore Praetorius, who
writes with admiration in his *Syntagma
Musicum,* Volume III, about the novel and
extraordinary effect of the English broken
consort, twice mentions the use of 'eine
Querflöit oder Blockflöit' (transverse flute *or*
recorder).[130] Perhaps as Sydney Beck has con-
cluded[131] the flute and recorder were to some

extent alternatives in the broken consort, just
as the treble viol and violin were. But as far as
English nomenclature is concerned, although
'flute' *generally* referred to the transverse
instrument during the sixteenth century it
cannot be established that it *always* did so.

On the continent a variety of names
developed in order to distinguish clearly between
flute and recorder. Back in medieval times the
different playing positions of the two instruments had provided a means of distinction
(*flaustes traversaines* and *flaustes dont droit joues
quand tu flaustes*[132]): hence the use of *traverso* or
traversa (Italian) and *Zwerchpfeife, Querflöte,* or
Querpfeife (German, cross flute) for the transverse flute and *flauto dritto* (Italian, straight flute)
for the recorder. Another distinction was
offered by the supposed country of origin. As
mentioned in chapter 1, the transverse flute
was especially cultivated in Germany in
medieval times and became known as the *flûte
d'Allemaigne*[133] during the Renaissance. Later
the recorder became known as the *flûte
d'Angleterre* because of its popularity in this
country. Another distinguishing feature was
the number of finger-holes. The transverse
flute was occasionally known as the *flûte à six
trous* whilst the recorder was regularly called
flûte à neuf trous: if the arithmetic sounds suspect
it is because of the alternative holes provided for
the little finger (ie 1 thumb-hole+7 finger-holes
+1 alternative little-finger-hole=9). The
transverse flute was also sometimes called
fiffaro or *fifre,* though the fife or *fistula militaris*
was in fact a separate instrument (see below).
The recorder was also called *Blockflöte or
Plockflöte* after its 'block' or fipple and *flûte
douce* because of its 'dolce' tone quality. Finally,
mention should be made of the German name
Schwegel, shinbone: it most commonly meant
the three-holed tabor pipe, but unfortunately it
was also used for the transverse flute and in the
Austrian Alps for the recorder as well.[134]

It is hardly surprising to find some confusion
between the recorder and flute at this stage in
history, since the two instruments possessed a
similar sound, technique, and function and their
careers overlapped in many ways. The most
important similarity is the way in which flutes
and recorders normally operate at four-foot
pitch, an octave higher than normal. The 'bass'
flute or 'bass' recorder for example is in reality
an alto instrument although it supplies the bass

to the rest of the consort. Flutes and recorders
maintained their four-foot role when playing
in a mixed ensemble, often playing their parts
an octave higher than written. Praetorius
comments on this practice and on the fact that
it is difficult to tell at what pitch a recorder or
flute is playing, since they tend to sound an
octave *lower* than is actually the case. Speaking
of the tenor instrument (lowest note c' or d')
he says: 'This recorder, and the cross flute in
this register as well, may not only be used as a
descant instrument . . . but also as a tenor, an
octave lower. Various musicians believe that
this type of recorder and cross flute actually is a
true tenor instrument in sound and that its
lowest tones – the C or D in the tenor register
– produce a low pitch in the organ-maker's
measure [Praetorius means c or d]. I too, was
actually of the opinion for a time, for with the
ear it is quite difficult to perceive the true
pitch.'[135]

Although Praetorius does not mention the
Morley *Consort Lessons* in this connection, it
seems likely that the 'flute' part should sound
an octave higher than written, whichever
instrument plays it. As it stands the part lies
uncomfortably low for either bass flute or
recorder and in practice often just gets lost.
The use of a tenor flute or recorder not only
solves the balance problem but offers a much
greater range of expression and dynamics as
well. Altogether the Morley *Consort Lessons*
and the other surviving broken consort music
provide the recorder/flute player with a considerable challenge to his technique and
musicianship. No other renaissance woodwind
instrument can lay claim to a regular partnership with the most aristocratic and refined
instruments of the day or a part share in some
of the most exquisite chamber music of the time.

Besides the *Consort Lessons,* flutes and
recorders were associated in a number of other
sixteenth-century publications. In a songbook
published by Arnt von Aich in about 1518
the title-page offers alternative methods of
instrumental performance: '. . . lustick zu
syngen. Auch etlich zu fleiten, schweglen, und
anderen Musicalisch Instrumenten artlichen zu
gebrauchen.'[136] (joyful for singing; some are
also suitable for recorders, flutes, and similar
musical instruments).[137]

Unfortunately Arnt von Aich does not tell
us *which* pieces are most suitable. The Parisian
publisher Pierre Attaingnant, however, who
ran one of the most successful publishing
businesses of the time, was more specific. In
two chanson collections published in 1533[138]
and evidently aimed at capitalizing on some
kind of vogue for consorts of flutes and
recorders, Attaingnant carefully marked up all
the pieces which are most suitable for either
instrument. On the title page he explains that

Masque music for a wedding feast – detail from a
mural painted *c.*1596 (artist unknown), showing
various scenes from the life of Sir Henry Unton,
Queen Elizabeth's ambassador to France. The
ensemble is that prescribed by Thomas Morley's
Consort Lessons of 1599. (National Portrait
Gallery, London)

¶ Dingt et sept chansons musicales a qua-
tre parties desquelles les plus couenables a la fleuste dal-
lemant sont signees en la table cy dessoubz escripte par a.
et a la fleuste a neuf trous par b. et pour les deux par a b.
Imprimees a Paris en la rue de la harpe deuant le bout
de la rue des Mathurins prez leglise sainct Cosme par
Pierre Attaingnant. Pense April. m. D. xxxiii.

Amour me poingt	a b	v	Je ne puis pas	a b	vi	Bien de bon cueur	a	viii
Amours amour	a	iiii	Iectez moy sur lherb.	a	ix	Pour qy boc ne frig.	a	xiii
Allos vng peu pl° avat	a b	v	Iamais vng cueur	a b	x	Si bon amour	a	xvi
Amour me voyant	a b	ix	Ie ne diray mot		xiiii	Tous amoureux	a b	vii
Alles soulspirs	b	xi	Ie nauoye point	a	xv	Troys ieunes bourg.	b	x
Be vous seruir	a b	i	Les yeulx bedes	a b	iiii	Qa mirelidrogue		iii
Elle veult dō:	a	xi	Mirelaridon		i	Voyant souffrir	a b	xii
Gentil mareschal		iii	On dit quamour	a b	xii	Vng petit coup		xv
Bellas amour	a b	viii	Parle qui veu't	a	xi			
Dayne et amour	a	xiii	Par vng matin	a b	vii			

Superius.
Cum priuilegio ad sexenniu

Title page of the second of Attaingnant's two
chanson collections of 1533.

Flute and recorder with their ranges, from
van Eyck's *Der Fluyten Lust-hof,* 1646.

the chansons which are 'les plus convenables a
la fleuste d'allemant' (transverse flute) are
marked with the letter *a*, those suitable for 'la
fleuste a neuf trous' with the letter *b* and
those suitable for both with *ab*. Although the
reasons for Attaingnant's choice are not always
clear, his selection of chansons provides some
fascinating hints about the relative qualities
of recorders and flutes.[139] In particular the
flutes seem to be able to cope with a wider
range than the recorders. Both instruments
make a tantalizingly brief appearance in the
score of Monteverdi's Vespers of 1610.[140] In the
Quia respexit section of the *Magnificat* there are
obbligati lasting only a few bars first for two
fifari and then two *flauti*.[141] As late as 1646 both

flute and recorder crop up together in the pre-
paratory instructions of *Der Fluyten Lust-hof*[142]
by Jacob van Eyck. Whilst the *Dwars-fluit*
(transverse flute) is credited with a two-and-a-
half-octave range, the *Hand-fluit* (recorder) has
a compass of two octaves and one note. This
disparity in range is confirmed by other writers
including Agricola (1528 and 1545) and
Philibert Jambe de Fer (1556): the latter
emphasizes the gentleness of breath pressure
required for the recorder.[143] In other ways the
technique of flutes and recorders seems to have
been generally similar. Different types of
tonguing were called for, double-tonguing
being needed for very fast divisions; Agricola
even mentions a kind of flutter-tonguing.[144] He

also makes it clear that even in the fastest
passage every note should be tongued. The
existence of brilliant divisions such as those of
van Eyck, together with the examples given in
various instruction books, suggest that
sixteenth-century flute and recorder players
possessed a very accomplished technique indeed.
However when recorders or flutes played
together in consort there were evidently tuning
problems then as now. Round about 1530 a
new metaphor was adopted into the French
language: *accordez vos flûtes* meaning 'agree
amongst yourselves'.[145]

Altogether more information is forthcoming
about the flute and recorder than about the
majority of renaissance woodwind instruments.
For a thorough summary of the evidence about
the renaissance flute, the reader should consult
the article on the subject by Joscelyn Godwin[146]
together with that by Bernard Thomas[147]
investigating the practical application of the
evidence. It is to be hoped that their work encourages a greater understanding and appreciation of the renaissance flute, sadly neglected
today in comparison to the renaissance
recorder. During the sixteenth century flutes
were tremendously popular: they were widely
illustrated and often form the largest item in
inventories, as in that of the Stuttgart
Hofkapelle in 1589 where there was a staggering
total of 220 flutes compared to 113 cornetts, 48
recorders, and 39 viols.[148]

The transverse flute
The renaissance flute has a cylindrical bore with
six finger-holes and a very small round mouth-
hole which demands a rather different
embouchure from the baroque or modern flute.
According to Mersenne 'it is a great deal more
difficult to make this flute speak than the
others which are blown at the end [*ie* recorders]
since everyone can use the latter but few know
how to sound the former because of the difficulty
found in placing the lips as required on the
first hole'.[149] Besides the basic sound production,
the renaissance flute is a tricky instrument to
handle in other respects: a number of notes are
naturally out of tune and need 'helping' by
turning the instrument in order to alter the
angle of embouchure. Curiously enough this
essential aspect of technique does not appear to
be mentioned by any renaissance writer.[150]

According to most of the sources, flutes were
made in three principal sizes separated by a
fifth: alto in A, tenor in D, and bass in G. The
smaller sizes were made in one piece, and the
bass was sometimes jointed, as shown by
Praetorius. A study of surviving instruments,[151]
however, suggests that many were in fact
pitched a tone lower than this, *ie* alto in G,
tenor in C, and bass in F. If this were the case a
great deal more ensemble music would suit a

consort of flutes than is the case with the
A-D-G tuning. Bass parts do tend to go
to F, and the nature of renaissance music
makes B♭ and E♭ fairly common notes (
uncomfortable on flutes pitched in 'sharp
This hypothesis receives some support fr
Volume III of the *Syntagma Musicum,* whe
suggestions which Praetorius makes abou
music which is suitable for flutes rather c
dict his illustrations of flutes in Volume II
their A-D-G tuning.[152]

In spite of being known as a *German*
ment, the idea of a flute consort caught o
France before it did in Germany. Writin
the *fleuste d'Allemand* in his memoirs, the
la Vieilleville says: '. . . les François s'en a
mieulx et plus musicalement que toute au
nation, et jamais en Allemaigne n'en fut j
quatre parties, comme il se fait ordinaire
en France.'[153] (The French make better an
more musical use of it than any other nati
and in Germany it is never played in four
as is the custom in France.)

The earliest account of the compass of
flute comes in the first edition of Agricola
Musica instrumentalis deudtsch, published i
1528, where each flute is given an astonish
three-octave range. In later editions Agric
somewhat modified his ideas, perhaps, as
Joscelyn Godwin suggests, as a result of ha
experienced the highest notes as described
Philibert Jambe de Fer '. . . ilz sont fort cr
rudes, pour la vehemence du vent qui y es
necessaire, et pour ceste cause sont peu usi
l'experience vous en rendra plus certain.'
(Because of the force of breath pressure re
quired, they are very crude and harsh and

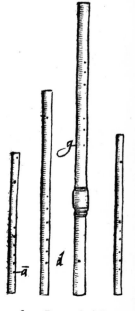

Consort of flutes, from Praetorius' *Syntagm*
Musicum: alto, tenor, and bass together wit
Schweizerpfeiff, a military fife.

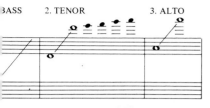

BASS   2. TENOR   3. ALTO

...nges from Praetorius' *Syntagma*
... He omits to indicate the upper limit
...ass flute.

...n consort of renaissance flutes (bass, tenor,
...o) by John Cousen after various originals.
... the very small mouth-hole, even on the

...son are little used . . . actually hearing
...vould make you positive of this.)
...t theorists agree on a comfortable two-
...compass for the flute: the range given
...etorius may be taken as standard for the
... Clearly the tenor flute with the possi-
...of extra 'falsetto' notes was the most useful

...he three sizes, the bass is the hardest to
...because of its length. However lightly
...it becomes tiring to hold and most basses
...e a very wide stretch of the fingers, far
...r than on the equivalent size of recorder
...the holes can be bored at more of an
...and so brought within easier reach of
...and. A number of pictures show a
...nal position which is certainly more com-
...le than trying to hold the bass flute
...ntally. This involves a rather different
...f embouchure too: blowing partly
...he instrument instead of *across* it, and in
...aité des Instruments de Musique* (*c.*1640)
...Trichet appears to mean something of
...id when he says that the bass flute is
...'par derrière'.[155]

...art from what has already been mentioned,
...s little definite information about the use
...es in sixteenth-century music. In the
...y *intermedii* there seems to have been a
...olic association with seascapes.[156] In the
...i wedding celebrations of 1539, Francesco
...ccia's music for the second intermedio
...ed three sea monsters playing flutes
...were disguised as a fish's backbone, a
...il, and a sea marsh cane.[157] In Count

Bardi's *intermedii* to *L'Amico Fido* of 1585 there
were flutes in the sea scene, although the gods
descended to the sound of flutes as well.[158]

Some mention should be made of the
military branch of the flute family, which goes
back to medieval times. During the Renaissance
the fife was variously known as *fistula militaris*,
Schweizerpfeife (Swiss pipe), or *Feldpfeife* (field
pipe). The latter names came from the
instrument's use in the Swiss infantry fife-and-
drum corps.[159] The main difference between
flute and fife lay in the length and bore. As
Arbeau succinctly puts it in his *Orchésographie*
(1588): 'What we call the fife is a little transverse flute with six holes, which the Germans
and the Swiss use, and as its bore is very narrow,
only the width of a pistol bullet, it gives a shrill
sound.'[160]

Praetorius gives two sizes (*see overleaf*).

Fifes occupy an important place in the
Triumph of Maximilian I (1512). Three fifers are
shown on horseback with their fife cases at their
sides. They are led by one Anthony 'the fifer'
who carries the following verse inscription:

I, Anthony of Dornstätt, have played my fife
For Maximilian, great in strife,
In many lands and on countless journeys,
In battles fierce and knightly tourneys.[161]

RIGHT
Fifes played on horseback, from *The Triumph of
Maximilian I* (1526). In front of them is Anthony
the fifer, bearing a standard; his fifes are in the
case at his side.

Fife ranges from Praetorius' *Syntagma Musicum*.

The recorder

'Govern these ventages with your fingers and thumb, give it breath with your mouth, and it will discourse most eloquent music. Look you, these are the stops.'[162]

Hamlet's remarks to Rosencrantz and Guildenstern read like an extract from some contemporary manual of recorder instruction. And uniquely among wind instruments, the recorder did have its own published tutor during the Renaissance: the *Opera Intitulata Fontegara*[163] by Sylvestro Ganassi, issued in Venice in 1535. It is appropriate that the city of Venice, which produced so many fine recorders, should also have produced the first recorder tutor. Ganassi (born in 1492) was a court musician to the Doge of Venice and an instrumentalist at the basilica of St Mark's. He played the viol as well as the recorder and produced a book of instruction for the former instrument too: the *Regola Rubertina* (1542/3). Judging by the *Fontegara*, recorder playing had achieved a high degree of technical accomplishment by Ganassi's time. The care taken to explain different methods of articulation, alternative fingerings, and the complex art of improvised ornamentation is impressive. Even more so is the extent of Ganassi's fingering chart which gives the recorder a compass of two octaves and a sixth: a fifth higher than the standard range of the baroque recorder, *after* Hotteterre's improvements. Players (or instruments) capable of such a wide range must have been the exception rather than the rule during the sixteenth century.

Most of the renaissance writers on instruments give us valuable information about the recorder: for a full survey the reader should consult Edgar Hunt's *The Recorder and its Music*.[164] Virdung devotes the last eighteen pages of his *Musica getutscht* to the instrument. He describes three sizes: bass in F, tenor in C, and alto in G and illustrates a typical four-part recorder consort with two tenors. Virdung calls his alto *discant*, showing that this was the standard top-line instrument of the consort, not the soprano which we call *descant* today. He gives each instrument a range of just under two octaves and shows how to arrange suitable music for the consort. The piece he selects is a hymn: *O Haylige, onbeflecte, zart*.

During the century after Virdung's publication the recorder family expanded. Praetorius illustrates no less than eight sizes, from the tiny *exilent* in G (what we would today call a

ABOVE
Title-page of Ganassi's *Fontegara* (1535).

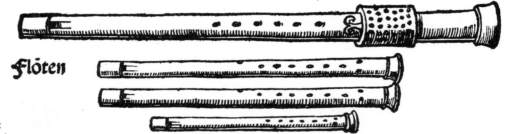

BELOW
Recorders from Virdung's *Musica getutscht*: bass, two tenors, alto.

sopranino) down to the great bass in F.

'A complete set such as this can be procured in Venice for about eighty thaler' Praetorius tells us.[165] If only that were still the case! These days the largest sizes are very expensive to make and comparatively few modern reproductions have been produced. The great bass must always have been an awkward instrument to manage: even though the finger-holes are brought as close to the reach of each hand possible (by boring the outer holes of each group of three at an angle) the stretch req is considerable. With a large windway wh responds to gentle breath pressure, separa from the player's mouth by a long crook, great bass also demands a rather special ty articulation.

Praetorius explains that the wide range recorder sizes offered a number of separate consorts within the family, which were m up, like Virdung's consort, of three adjace instruments.[166] You could have an ensembl soprano, alto, and tenor, for example, pla their music an octave higher than written, 4-foot pitch, or the deliciously mellow combination of bass, quart-bass, and great which operated at 'normal' 8-foot pitch. T latter is what Mersenne called the *grand jeu* phrase borrowed from organ terminology he describes the effect of the full consort: these flutes form the small group, while th which will follow after form the large gro but they can all be tuned [*ie* played] toget as are the large and small stops of the orga

Praetorius preferred the deeper soundin instruments. In Volume III of his *Syntagma Musicum* he says: 'When a canzona, motet *concert per choros* is to be played on recorde alone, without other instruments, it is ver good and fitting to use the whole range of recorders, especially the five largest kinds, the small ones are much too loud and pier This gives a very soft, sweet, and pleasant harmony, especially in rooms and chambe He goes on to say that in a church the larg recorders cannot be heard very well and recommends using a curtal as the bass whe combining recorders with voices.[169]

1. GREAT BASS   2. QUINT BASS

3. BASS   4. TENOR   5. ALTO
8va

8va 6. SOPRANO   7. SOPRANO   8. SOPRANINO

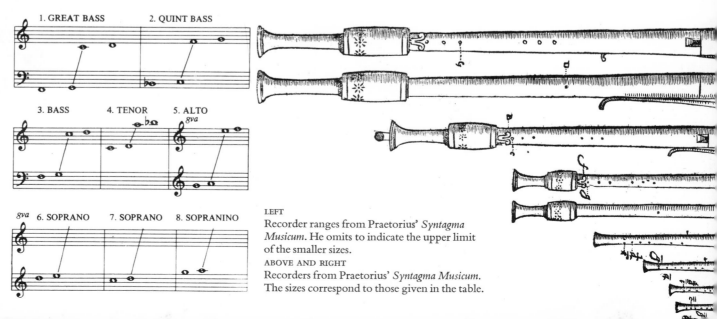

LEFT
Recorder ranges from Praetorius' *Syntagma Musicum*. He omits to indicate the upper limit of the smaller sizes.
ABOVE AND RIGHT
Recorders from Praetorius' *Syntagma Musicum*. The sizes correspond to those given in the table.

rising as it may seem, even larger sizes
...der were built than Praetorius' great
... Having reached the limit of what was
...ble with the placing of finger-holes,
...resorted to extension keys after the
...pattern. Mersenne illustrates such an
...ent and the collection of the Vleeshuis
...p,[170] preserves a great bass with three
...n keys descending to low C.[171]
...es the joint flute/recorder repertoire,
...e a number of interesting sixteenth-
...references to the use of the recorder
...Guillaume Vorsterman's *Livre Plaisant*
...ile, published in Antwerp in 1529,

...rn 'great consort' of recorders – tenor,
...rt-bass, great bass – by John Cousen,
...various originals. Notice how the bass is
...hrough a slot in the back of the cap:
...were reserved for larger sizes.

includes the well-known chanson by Jacobus
Barbireau (d. 1491) *Een Vrolic Wesen* in what is
almost certainly an arrangement for recorder
and lute.[172] A copy of a song book published
by Georg Forster in 1539 has been preserved
with certain pieces marked up by hand for the
flöt.[173] Recorders were regularly used in church,
not only in Germany but in Spain too. The
accounts of Seville Cathedral record several
purchases of recorders and the instruments were
employed to give musical variety to the
services. In a directive of 11 July 1586: 'At
greater feasts there shall always be a verse
played on recorders. At Salves, one of the three

verses that are played shall be on shawms, one
on cornetts and the other on recorders; because
always hearing the same instrument annoys the
listener.'[174] In 1549 a *caxa de flautas grandes* was
bought for Guatemala Cathedral[175] – surely
as Lawrence Wright suggests[176] the earliest
known evidence of recorder playing in the
New World.

As far as the other whistle instruments of the
Renaissance are concerned, the most important
was the tabor pipe which regularly crops up in
the inventories. Like the bagpipe it retained its
medieval function as a solo instrument and
was not used in consort. The tabor pipe has

The extended great-bass recorder in the Museum
of Musical Instruments, Brussels. This is a copy
by Mahillon of the instrument in the Vleeshuis
Museum, Antwerp.

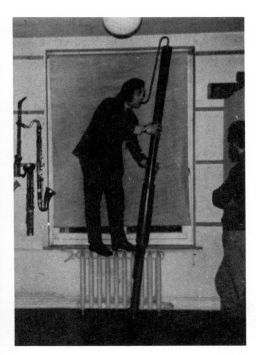

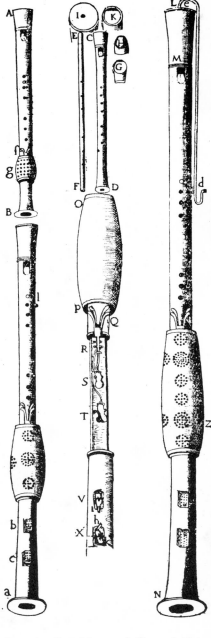

Recorders from Mersenne's *Harmonie Universelle*,
including an extended great-bass. Mersenne
shows the detail of keywork with the fontanelle
removed.

already been dealt with in chapter I together
with the six-holed pipe, gemshorn, and
flageolet. Three other types should be mentioned briefly. Virdung illustrates a four-holed
Russpfeif which looks as if it is made from bone.
Agricola devotes a chapter to a small four-
holed recorder on which one stops the end as
well as the holes and Praetorius illustrates a
similar instrument. Praetorius also illustrates
Dolzflöten: whistle instruments made to look
like transverse flutes, similar to the folk instruments still found in India and Pakistan today.
Antony Baines suggests that they may correspond with the *Zwerchflöten* (as opposed to
Zwerchpfeifen) found in some inventories.[177]

Despite the considerable refinements and
improvements in the construction of woodwind

instruments which took place during the
Renaissance, it is instructive to remember that,
on paper at least, much more novel and far-
reaching developments were proposed. By way
of a postscript to this chapter, the reader is
referred to the many sketches for musical
instruments and musical machines in the
notebooks of Leonardo da Vinci.[178] Eight of the
sketches show the application of a complete
system of keywork to wind instruments.
Although the drawings are in the nature of
preliminary jottings rather than fully worked

7 Keyboard

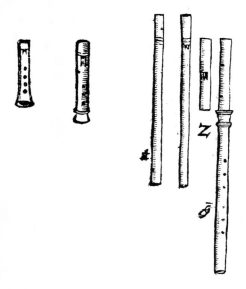

out designs, Leonardo clearly envisaged the possibility of a keyed trumpet and a keyed *zufolo* or pipe: the instruments are equipped with something like a miniature keyboard and mechanical stopping devices. It was not until 1840 with the work of Theobald Boehm that a complete keywork for wind instruments, replacing the principle of finger-stopping, was introduced into instrumental construction. As Emanuel Winternitz has pointed out,[179] the sketches of Leonardo anticipate Boehm's epochal invention by three centuries and a half.

From the tiny amount of solo organ music which has survived from before the fifteenth century we cannot be sure just how extensively the medieval organ may have been used as a solo instrument. But its main functions must have been to give support to the voices in church and to play a part in the concerted vocal and instrumental music of the court. During the Renaissance, however, the art of the keyboard became predominantly a solo art. From the fifteenth century onwards first the organ and subsequently the harpsichord and virginals acquired a vast solo repertory of their own. As with the solo lute repertory, the range of music is enormous. Composers took delight in making keyboard settings of every type of vocal piece: motets, mass movements, chansons, frottole, and madrigals. They seized on the new dance forms of the Renaissance – the pavan, galliard, alman, and coranto – and the new instrumental forms – the canzona, fantasia, and *in nomine*. And they developed new idiomatic keyboard types such as the prelude, the toccata, and the variation. Playing keyboard instruments became popular with amateurs as well as professionals, and amongst the middle classes as well as at court. As Castiglione remarks in his book *Il Cortegiano* (1528): 'all the keyboard instruments are very harmonious because they give the harmonies with great perfection, and many things can be performed on them which fill the spirit with melodious sweetness'.[1]

The number of publications from the second half of the sixteenth century[2] shows that printing keyboard music was good business, though the enthusiast often built up his own manuscript collections of favourite pieces. That of the organist Thomas Mulliner[3] gives us a fascinating cross-section of music from mid-sixteenth-century England, and a number of such collections were made for the harpsichord or virginals, the most famous being *The Fitzwilliam Virginal Book*.[4]

The Renaissance produced a number of outstanding composers whose output was principally or even exclusively of keyboard music and who were themselves famous performers. The German organist Paul Hofhaimer (1459–1537) earned high favour with the Holy Roman Emperor Maximilian I. He frequently accompanied the emperor on his journeys and is depicted playing a positive organ in the *Triumph of Maximilian I*.[5] The Spanish composer Antonio de Cabezón (1510–66) became organist and clavichordist to the Emperor Charles V at the age of eighteen. He continued in the royal service under Philip II, with whom he travelled to Italy, Flanders, and England. The epitaph on Cabezón's tombstone described him as 'the first organist of his time, whose fame fills the world'.[6] Amongst the English virginalists, John Bull (1562–1628)

became celebrated on the continent as a great virtuoso. He toured through France, Germany, and the Netherlands and ended his days as organist at Antwerp Cathedral. Bull became a close friend of Jan Pieterszoon Sweelinck (1562–1621) whose organ recitals at the Oude Kerk in Amsterdam attracted pupils and admirers from all over Europe. He was known as the 'Glory of Amsterdam', and the merchants of the city showed their appreciation by making up a purse for Sweelinck in 1604, and

Paul Hofhaimer playing a positive organ in *The Triumph of Maximilian I*. Behind him is a regal in a case, and what is probably a case for the organ.

subsequently presenting him with a *clavic[in]* and a finely woven cloth to cover it.[7] The organists' jobs which were most highly th[ought] of – and the best paid – during the sixteen[th] century were those of first and second org[anist] at the basilica of St Mark's, Venice. A suc[cession] of distinguished composers occupied the p[ost] including Andrea Gabrieli (1510?–86) and Claudio Merulo (1533–1604). St Mark's w[as the] first church to have two large organs buil[t ...] their existence, together with the basic de[sign]

Maximilian wanted to show how, 'by orde[r of] the Emperor', Hofhaimer had 'artistically increased and enlightened music'.

A prelude by John Bull from the *Fitzwilliam Virginal Book*. (Fitzwilliam Museum, Cambridge)

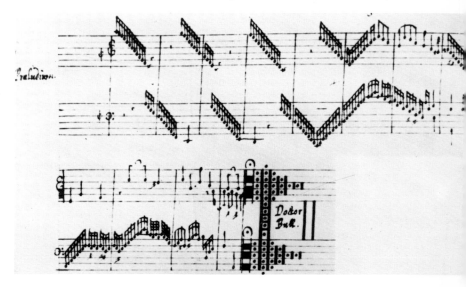

uilding with its various galleries for
ers, helped to develop the antiphonal
cori spezzati for which Venice became
at the end of the sixteenth century.
details as these serve as a reminder of
rent schools of keyboard playing and
ition which developed during the
ance. With them grew up different
of making too, each with their own
tinctive traits. There could scarcely be a
contrast between the English organs of
eenth century, with only one manual,
ls, and a few flute stops, and those of the
erman School with three manuals, a
ard, and a host of colourful mixtures,
nd reeds to choose from. There is an
marked difference between the
forward harpsichords and spinets of the
lian makers and the rather grander
ords and virginals of the Flemish
All in all the amount of information
e about early keyboard music and the
ents, makers, and players is encyclopedic.
the brief survey which follows readers
rred to the works listed in the
es.

general point may be made about the
eyboard instruments in *ensemble* music
the sixteenth century. Artists regularly
hem being played in consort and other
illustrate the sort of company they kept.
of the *intermedii* of 1565 celebrating the
g of Francesco de Medici to Joanna of
, the instrumental music played before
logue at the opening of Heaven was
for: four double harpsichords (*gravicembali*
four viols, two trombones, two tenor
rs, one mute cornett, one transverse flute,
o lutes.[9] At the banquet held in 1568 in
h for the wedding of Albert V of Bavaria
dolce (soft regal) played with six *viole da*
, a cornett, and five trombones, whilst a
hord accompanied singers in one piece
another joined a mixed ensemble of
one, recorder, lute, *cornamusa,* mute
t, viol, and *piffero*.[10] In such ensembles the
the keyboard must have been primarily
al one, and although we have no precise
ation about how players may have
ed' their part, the style may to some
have anticipated the continuo of the
aroque period. With the advent of opera
and the new musical habits of the
eenth century, keyboard instruments,
with the harp, lute, and chitarrone,
e indispensable to music of all kinds
e of the harmonic support which they
provide.

e mention should be made of the system
ng employed on keyboard instruments
the renaissance and early baroque
s. As early as 1511 Arnolt Schlick gives a

clear account of how an organ should be tuned
and anticipates the system of 'mean tone'
temperament.[11] Unlike the systems of equal
temperament in use on keyboard instruments
today, mean-tone tuning involves a kind of
juggling with the relationship between
semitones which favours the most commonly
used keys and intervals at the expense of other
less common ones. Schlick directed that
ascending fifths should be made flat so as to
accommodate the thirds, particularly: F–A,
G–B♮, and C–E. He describes the interval from
G♯ to E♭ as the 'wolf' and recommends the
player to avoid using C♯ or A♭ as keynotes at
all.[12] Mean-tone tuning is an uncompromising
system but when properly understood it can
give a new depth to early keyboard music.
Its fallibilities worried the theorists, however.
In his *Istituzioni armoniche* published in Venice
in 1558, Zarlino illustrates a harpsichord which
solved all the problems by offering nineteen
divisions to the octave. All the 'sharps' are split
– so that there were alternatives for G♯ and
A♭ for example – and extra keys were provided
between E and F and B and C. Impractical as it
sounds, this instrument was actually constructed
and played on by Luzzasco Luzzaschi, organist
to the Duke of Ferrara.[13] It still existed as late as
1770 when Charles Burney came across it in
Florence on his travels. Praetorius describes a
similar instrument which he says might 'justly
be called an Instrumentum Perfectum – if not
perfectissimum'[14] and a number of other
experimental harpsichords were made along the
same lines. But Praetorius makes clear that the
fretted instruments of the day used a system of
tempered tuning different from the keyboard
instruments. 'The harpsichord, symphony, and
the like . . . are rather incomplete and imperfect
in that they do not afford chromatic notes such
as can be produced on lutes and viols da
gamba.'[14] It would be interesting to know if
keyboard players of the sixteenth and
seventeenth centuries adopted a different
system of tuning when they played in an
ensemble. In his *Discourse on Ancient Music and
Good Singing* Count Giovanni de' Bardi
emphasizes that there was a problem: 'And
more than once I have felt like laughing when I
saw musicians struggling to put a lute or viol
into proper tune with a keyboard instrument
. . . In your consort, then, you will as far as
possible avoid combining lutes or viols with
keyboard instruments.'[15]

The renaissance organ

At the end of the Middle Ages the large church
organ was still a fairly unwieldy instrument.
As William Leslie Sumner says in his book *The
Organ*: 'Large instruments built in fine cases
were found in many parts of Europe in the
fifteenth century. They were intractable to play,

Al fresco consort of spinet, lute, recorder, and
bass viol. Anonymous Italian painting, sixteenth
century. (Musée de Bourges)

capable of sustaining only the crudest counter-
point and sometimes only single-line melodies
played with mixtures containing repeated
octaves and fifth sounding ranks . . . When the
tone was mollified by the reverberation of a
vast Gothic cathedral there can be no doubt
that its powerful diapason chorus would have
considerable emotional effect.'[16]

Nevertheless, it was during the later fifteenth
century that several major improvements were
made in organ construction. During this period

Title page of Schlick's *Spiegel der Orgelmacher und
Organisten* (1511), showing a single-manual organ
with pedalboard.

there was an upsurge of interest in organ
playing and composition in Germany, and
amongst a number of collections[17] by far the
largest and most important is the famous
Buxheim Organ Book (*c.*1470).[18] This collection
frequently demands an agile finger technique
and on occasions pedal technique too, pedals
being actually specified in a few pieces and
implied in others.[19] The high standard of organ
playing in Germany at this time is hardly
surprising after the example of Conrad Paumann
(*c.* 1415–73), the blind organist of Nuremberg.
In about 1450 he entered the service of Duke
Albrecht III at Munich and also served his
successor Albrecht IV. Paumann's career was a
thoroughly international one: in 1470 he visited
the courts of Ferrara and Mantua and in the
following year he played the organ at
Regensburg for the Emperor Frederick III. A
contemporary eulogy describes Paumann thus:

Meyster ob allen maystern:
Solt man durch kunst einen meister kron,
er trug wol auf von golt ein kron.
(Master above all masters:
If one crowns a master because of his art,
He would surely wear a crown of gold.)[20]

For the benefit of his pupils, Paumann wrote
a textbook, the *Fundamentum organisandi* (1452),
which is the *locus classicus* of fifteenth-century
organ teaching. From the point of view of
organ *building,* however, the most useful treatise
of this period is the *Spiegel der Orgelmacher und*

Organisten by Arnolt Schlick, published in 1511.[11] This describes in great detail an organ with a compass of three octaves and a third, organized in three sections, each with its own series of separate stops. On the 'positive' there were four registers of flue stops including a mixture and a gemshorn. The 'manual', the main part of the instrument, with eleven registers, was composed of reeds and flue stops, including a *Zink, Regall,* and *Rauspfeiffen,* whilst the pedals' four registers featured a 16-foot flue stop (*Principaln* 16) as well as a *Trommetan oder basaun.* Schlick also gives useful information on how the various registers should be employed.

The changes which had taken place in the construction and design of organs by the beginning of the sixteenth century may be conveniently summarized as follows:
1. The keyboard had been thoroughly 'modernized' to make it as responsive to the touch as that of the smaller sizes of organ.
2. Instead of the permanent 'mixture' sound of the large medieval organ, the registration for each keyboard could be controlled by a series of stops, which worked in a similar way to the old slider mechanism.
3. As well as open and stopped 'flue' pipes operating on the whistle mouthpiece principle there were a variety of 'reed' pipes employing a single vibrating tongue (usually metal) and a resonator, either conical or cylindrical.
4. The different stops were used for contrast and many of them were designed to imitate the sound of contemporary instruments.
5. Couplers were used to join manual to manual or manual to pedals.

During the late Renaissance organ-building flourished as never before. There were improvements, experiments, and refinements, and different schools of makers sprang up all over Europe. By the beginning of the seventeenth century the organ had become, especially in North Germany, Flanders, and Spain, a truly sumptuous instrument with carefully balanced registers and a colourful variety of sound. The tone was always bright and clear, sometimes even harsh. Schlick repeatedly uses the words *scharf schneidend* to characterize the stops he describes.[22] Some stops were positively raucous, such as the *trompeta exterior* or *real* favoured by Spanish makers. The appearance of the renaissance organ was equally sumptuous. The organ cases were often richly decorated with gold, azure, and vermilion; the pipes themselves were often silvered or gilded.[23] One of the most magnificent renaissance organs to have survived more or less intact is that in the royal palace of Frederiksborg in Denmark built in 1612 by Esaias Compenius. All the pipes are made of wood, many of them inlaid with ivory and ebony, and they are encased in a richly ornamented cupboard of oak. The keyboards, including the pedalboard, are faced with ivory and ebony and the stops are of solid silver each in the shape of a human face. The quality of sound still achieves a matching perfection even after three hundred and fifty years. Praetorius mentions Compenius[24] in the large section of his *Syntagma Musicum* devoted to the organ and he includes the specification of the Frederiksborg instrument, commenting on its exclusive use of wooden pipes.[25]

The names of some of the stops illustrate the extent to which organ builders drew on the sounds of contemporary woodwind instruments for inspiration. This was particularly the case in Germany where such a variety of woodwind types flourished during the Renaissance. On the Frederiksborg instrument Compenius included: on the upper manual a 4-foot *Gemshorn* and a 16-foot *Rancket* (= rackett); on the lower manual a 2-foot *Gemshornlein* (= little gemshorn), a 4-foot *Blockpfeiffen* (= 'blockflute' or recorder), an 8-foot *Krumhorn,* and a 4-foot *Regal*; and on the pedals an 8-foot *Gemshorn,* a 4-foot *Querflöten* (= flute), a 16-foot *Sordunen,* an 8-foot *Dolzian,* and a 4-foot *Regal.*[25] That we can still hear these sounds today is thrilling, not only because the organ itself is a masterpiece of organ building but because it provides us with a direct link with the live sounds of the Renaissance. The organ builders could not accurately reproduce the sounds of strings or brass instruments, but with the woodwind they must have been able to copy fairly exactly, even though their method of sound production may have differed from that used on the instrument itself (for example, the use of *single* tongues instead of *double* reeds). The Frederiksborg organ and others of its period provide evidence of the sharply defined attack and uncompromising tone colours which must have been characteristic of renaissance woodwind instruments. The renaissance organ even shared some of their shortcomings: large unstopped flue pipes, like big recorders, tend to be soft and unfocused, whilst the highest notes of the crumhorn stop tend to be rather feeble, just as soprano crumhorns often are.

Whilst it is in the larger instruments that the greatest achievements of the renaissance organ-builders are to be found, the smaller positive and portative types continued to be produced. By its very nature the portative was a very restricted instrument and it gradually dropped out of use during the sixteenth century. But the positive continued to thrive as an invaluable instrument in court, chamber, or church. On the continent it was often equipped with one or two of the new reed stops and after 1600 it became indispensable as a continuo instrument.

The regal

Besides being one of the new reed stops of the renaissance organ the regal had a long career as a separate instrument in its own right. As Praetorius pointed out, the use of the same name is confusing: 'I believe it would be better to name this instrument a regal-works and to call the organ regal stops by the term regal-pipes, in order better to distinguish the one from the other.'[26]

In essence the regal is a small portable reed organ. Praetorius mentions that it could have up to three ranks of reeds (4-foot, 8-foot, and 16-foot) but most regals had just one rank of 8-foot reeds.[27] The instrument has a characteristic incisive attack and penetrating tone: the word 'snarling' has often been applied to it but there is a rich resonance too, especially in the lower register, similar to that produced by a consort of crumhorns. The earliest mention of a reed organ in 1460 when Heinrich Traxdorff of Nuremberg constructed an organ the sound of which resembled that of the shawm. Galpin inferred that the instrument was a regal[28] and his opinion seems to be generally accepted. On the earliest regals the reeds were apparently open but later acquired short resonators of brass or wood.[29] Judging by surviving specimens the regal was more common on the continent than it was in England: this seems likely in view of the English preference for flute stops on the

larger organs. Nevertheless, the Inventor[y?] Henry VIII's instruments[30] reveals an im[portant?] collection of no less than twenty-two reg[als?] including such varieties as 'one faire instr[ument?] being Regalles and Virgynalles', 'a paire [of?] double Regalles with twoo stoppes of pip[es?] couered in purple vellat', and 'v. small si[ngle?] Regalles twoo of them being in Cases of [?] Timbre'.

The descriptions 'single', 'double', and [?] of' were regularly applied to both the reg[als?] to the virginals and the exact meaning of [?] terms remains elusive. Certain of the solu[tions?] which have been offered can be discounte[d.?] A 'double' or 'pair of' certainly did not si[gnify?] a two-manual instrument since no such f[?] regal existed and a two-manual virginal v[as of?] comparative rarity. Nor is it likely that o[ne?] instrument was regularly placed on top o[f?] another in order to make a 'double' or 'pa[ir?] Such a practice was not unknown in the c[ase of?] stringed keyboard instruments: Praetoriu[s?] mentions that the spinet 'is generally plac[ed?] on top of larger keyboard instruments'[31] presumably to provide the player with a [?] contrast of timbre. But in the case of the r[egal?] the existence of the bellows makes the ide[a of?] placing another instrument on top of it [?] impossible. The most likely explanation [of?] 'single' and 'double' is that the words refe[r to?] the instrument's compass.[32] Just as 'single'[?]

Table organ built by the German maker Haase in 1684. There are two ranks of stopped flute pipes (4' and 2') and one regal (8'). (Collection of Noel Mander)

ble' curtal described different sizes of ~~ian~~, so a 'single' virginals or regal would ~~possessed~~ a limited downward compass, ~~st~~ a 'double' would have had the full range. ~~or~~ 'a pair of' this most probably refers to the ~~ion~~ of keyboard between two hands in ~~the~~ same way that we use the expression ~~ir~~ of gloves'. The word 'regal' itself ~~ch~~ *regale*; German *Regal*; Spanish *realejo*) ~~be~~ derived from the Latin *rigabellum* or ~~a~~.[33] Confusingly the name was sometimes ~~to~~ describe a positive organ with a regal ~~as~~ in Henry VIII's Inventory.

~~esides~~ possibly being the birthplace of the ~~Nuremberg~~ is also thought to have ~~uced~~ the compact form of the instrument ~~wn~~ as the Bible or Book regal. This ~~ation~~ is ascribed to the Nuremberg organ ~~er~~ Georg Voll who died in 1565.[34] The ~~ious~~ design allows the keyboard and ~~ators~~ to be packed away inside the 'book', ~~overs~~ of which form the bellows.

Bible regal, in playing position, and encased. (Museum of Musical Instruments, Brussels)

One aspect of the regal mentioned by several authorities is its unstable tuning. Pietro Cerone (1613)[35] says that it is the worst of all instruments in this respect, going out of tune from one hour to the next, and Praetorius (1619) explains at length how the regal is susceptible to changes of temperature:

'I know only too well how much difficulty is caused the organist or director of an ensemble when several regals are to be played together in churches or at court dinners – and especially when in winter a regal must be brought out of the coldness of the church into a warm dining room. It is indeed true that metal pipes are forced down in pitch to such an extent by the cold of winter that they sink by half a semitone, if not more.'[36]

After observing that all organs – and wind instruments in general – fluctuate in a similar way ('and when the stoves are going these instruments become even sharper') Praetorius

concludes stoically: 'Since up to now, no one has been able to establish the true cause for such variation and change, this must be taken for one of the extraordinary works of God.'[37]

In spite of this disadvantage, regals continued to be made throughout the seventeenth and eighteenth centuries (in England a tuner of 'His Majesty's regals' was still receiving a salary as late as 1779[38]). As a stop on the large organ the regal continues in use to the present day, though, as has happened with so many other organ stops, it has lost much of the reedy clangour with which the renaissance makers endowed it. Its highly individual tone colour prompted Monteverdi to use the regal with a consort of trombones in order to create the sinister atmosphere of the Underworld in Act III of his opera *Orfeo* (1607).

The harpsichord
The development of the harpsichord during the fifteenth century introduced a quite new type of stringed keyboard instrument employing a mechanical *plucking* action. The harpsichord is essentially a mechanized psaltery and the same method of sound production is used on the virginals and spinet. Each key on the keyboard operates a mechanical device known as the 'jack', which is equipped with a small plectrum (made of leather or quill) attached to a pivoted tongue. When a player presses down a key on the keyboard the jack rises and the plectrum plucks the string. When the key is released the jack descends and through the ingenious positioning of the spring (usually made of hog's bristle) the tongue pivots back, allowing the plectrum to pass the string silently on its return journey. When the jack returns to its original position a damper (made of felt) silences the vibration of the string. A piece of wood known as the 'jack rail' is fixed over the jacks to prevent them from jumping right out when the keys are pressed down. This action deprives the player of the type of contact with the string offered by the clavichord and means that basically no contrasts of dynamic or tone are possible from a single set of strings. Touch and articulation are still very important, however, and the harpsichord and virginals demand a somewhat different technique from the organ, clavichord, or piano.

The earliest detailed information we have about the construction of a harpsichord comes in a manuscript compiled in the middle of the fifteenth century by Henri Arnault of Zwolle, physician to the Duke of Burgundy;[39] the same manuscript gives details of the *dulce melos* which anticipates the piano's hammer mechanism. A German illustration of this period depicts a *clavicymbalum* with the typical winged outline which the harpsichord adopted from the wing-shaped form of psaltery, but unfortunately

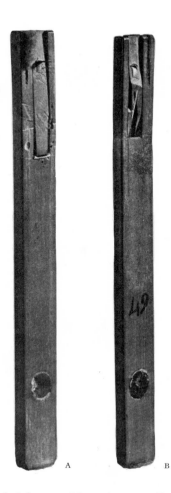

A   B

Jack from an eighteenth-century English spinet shown actual size. The weights are not characteristic in earlier harpsichords. A, front view; B, back view. (Collection of Christopher Hogwood)

the artist omits the action altogether. There are a number of other representations of the harpsichord during the second half of the fifteenth century, including a stone carving in the roof of the nave of Manchester Cathedral (*c*.1465),[40] though the instrument may well have been in existence in some form as early as the beginning of the century. A German poem of 1404, *Der Minne Regeln*, lists *clavicimbalum* as well as *clavichordium* amongst the instruments of courtly love,[41] and this is the earliest recorded use of the name from which the Italian word for harpsichord *clavicembalo* derives. A common corruption is *gravicembalo* and during the baroque period the name was regularly shortened to *cembalo*. Other early names derived from the same root include the German *Klavizimbel* (though in modern German the Italian word is used) and the French *clavecinon* later shortened to *clavecin* (the word was first used by Cotgrave in 1611).[42] Since most early keyboard music left the selection of instrument to the performer it is hardly surprising that names came to be used in a very general as well as a specific way. In the Leckingfield proverbs of Henry VII's time *clavicimbalum* probably means *claviorganum, ie* a combined harpsichord and organ; Virdung (1511) uses the word to describe a rectangular instrument, and Mersenne (1635) uses it for the carillon and keyed xylophone.[43] Praetorius (1619) pinpoints the confusion when he says that in the Netherlands the spinet is called 'Clavicymbels and also Virginals' whilst in England 'all such instruments be they large or small are termed Virginals'.[44] He also tells us that the Germans used the word 'Flügel' to describe the harpsichord because of its winged shape.[45]

The earliest harpsichord surviving today is an instrument by Jerome of Bologna dated 1521, now in the Victoria and Albert Museum.[46] It was in Italy that the first important school of harpsichord making developed and a number of other fine examples are still in existence. Several features of Jerome's instrument are typical. It is built of cypress wood and can be removed from the decorated outer case which is lined with green velvet. There are two sets of jacks and two sets of strings, but their purpose was not to offer contrast of timbre but to give extra brilliance and volume. There is no hand stop to change the registration, and both sets of jacks are permanently 'fixed on'. Although the apparent compass of the keyboard is three octaves and a seventh, the lowest note being E, the actual compass descends to C. This is

achieved by a device known as 'short octave tuning'. The E key was tuned to low C, the F♯ to D, and G♯ to E. This provided an *effective* compass of over four octaves, since the missing chromatic notes – low C♯, D♯, F♯, and G♯ – were in practice not often required. An occasional variant of this system was 'split-key' tuning in which the two lowest accidentals are split into a front and a back section. The back part was tuned to its expected note, the front to the 'extra' low note. Both these devices for extending the compass were applied to other types of keyboard instrument, especially the virginals.

The second great school of harpsichord-making developed in Flanders towards the end of the sixteenth century with Antwerp as its centre, a city where instrument-makers had already flourished for over a hundred years. It was there that Hans Ruckers (*c*.1550–*c*.1620) settled down in 1575 and, after serving his apprenticeship, founded a family business which was to involve his two sons Jan (1578–1643) and Andries (1579–*c*.1645) and produce some of the most splendid keyboard instruments of the age. Ruckers instruments are often referred to during the seventeenth and eighteenth centuries; many of them continued in regular use right up to the end of the eighteenth century, and over a hundred examples of the family's work (harpsichords and virginals) are known today.[47]

The instruments built in the Ruckers workshop between the years 1580 and 1650

conformed to fairly rigid designs, and show a new aim in harpsichord-making: to offer the player some contrast of tone or register. The typical single-manual Ruckers instrument had a short-octave compass of four octaves from C and had two sets of strings, one 8-foot and one 4-foot. Hand stops in the right-hand side of the case brought one or both sets of jacks into contact with the strings as desired. The Ruckers family also produced two-manual harpsichords and they were probably the first makers ever to do so. The idea seems to have originated not as

an attempt to provide more contrast but as a transposing device to help accompanists. The lower manual was pitched a fourth below the upper one,[48] so that a player could easily accommodate, for example, an alto who wanted to sing a song written in soprano pit or a recorder player who wanted to play a treble solo on his descant. It is surprising that such transposing harpsichords are not being revived today when the facility would be as useful as ever. During the baroque period, the transposing keyboard became obsolete and

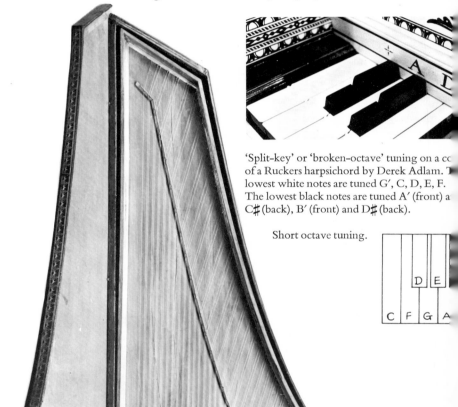

'Split-key' or 'broken-octave' tuning on a co of a Ruckers harpsichord by Derek Adlam. lowest white notes are tuned G′, C, D, E, F. The lowest black notes are tuned A′ (front) a C♯ (back), B′ (front) and D♯ (back).

Short octave tuning.

Harpsichord by Jerome of Bologna (1521). The instrument is inside its outer case. (Victoria and Albert Museum)

The same instrument photographed from above to show keyboard, two rows of jacks, soundboard, and curved bridge. Notice the rose (of varnished leather), a feature which early harpsichords inherited from the psaltery.

nuals were tuned to the same pitch so ey could be coupled together or used for tonal contrast or to avoid awkward rossing on the same keyboard. It should hasized, however, that the *typical* chord of the Renaissance was a single-l instrument with one basic sound only.

lavicytherium

ea of an upright version of the harpsichord o have been developed as early as 1460[49] e oldest surviving instrument – probably

ytherium from Virdung's *getutscht.*

– is now in the Royal College of Music.[50] gh the fact that the strings were vertical he mechanism more complicated since the ave to be *pulled* back instead of just back by their own weight, the instrument e up a lot less space, an advantage made it quite popular in the eighteenth y. The usual name for the instrument, *therium,* is first used by Virdung (1511) ys that the instrument is newly invented s strings of gut.[51] Although gut strings nlikely, Raymond Russell points out that *therium* means *keyed lyre* and a lyre had gut by definition.[52] During the Renaissance right harpsichord does not seem to have articularly popular, however, and as late 5 Mersenne still calls the clavicytherium form of spinet in use in Italy'.[53]

laviorganum

rliest reference to a sort of upright chord seems to have been in combination positive organ,[54] and during the ance a number of experimental instru- were built amalgamating different types d and string keyboards. The most on alignment was organ plus harpsichord, trument being known as the *claviorganum* h *clavecin organisé,* German *Orgelklavier,*

Italian *claviorgano).* The tuning problem of such instruments can be fairly intractable, and the simultaneous effect of two such different sounds is a delightful novelty which soon palls. Pepys put it rather nicely when he described the *claviorganum* which he heard in 1677 as 'but a bauble with a virginal joining on to it'.[54] As a two-in-one continuo instrument it was potenti- ally very useful during the baroque period but even then it continued to be thought of as the latest invention. In 1650 Kircher illustrates a claviorganum in his *Musurgia* and considers the idea new and unheard of. Other amalgamations of the Renaissance included the *épinette organisée* (probably spinet/organ) referred to by Rabelais,[54] and a spinet-regal, an example of which survives from 1587,[55] whilst a Dresden inventory of 1593 even lists two combinations of organ with clavichord.[54] Some of the early claviorgana such as those listed in Henry VIII's Inventory[30] may have been two separate instruments without any coupling device.

The virginals

In spite of the English use of the word as a generic term for all types of plucked keyboard

instruments, *virginal(s)* also designated a specific type. It is first mentioned by Paulus Paulirinus of Prague in *c.*1460[56] and the name was used in France and Germany as well as England. The origin of the word is not English nor has it anything to do with Queen Elizabeth I as has been often stated, although she certainly did play the instrument.[57] Virdung (1511) mentions the virginals but says that he knows nothing of its origin or invention.[58] Although Curt Sachs derives the name from the Latin *virga* meaning a rod (diminutive *virgula*) because of the virginals' jacks,[59] and Sibyl Marcuse from the fact that the frame drum of ancient East Mediterranean culture was traditionally played by women,[56] the most widely accepted view is that the name is related to the young ladies who are so regularly depicted playing the virginals.[60] There was certainly a standing joke on the

subject during the Renaissance which ranged from the fairly decorous, as on the title-page of *Parthenia* (1611), to the downright ribald as in Ben Johnson's *The Alchemist* where Face says to Dol:

Sweet Dol
You must go tune your virginal.[61]

The main differences between the harpsichord and virginals lie in the shape of the soundbox, the placing of the strings, and the existence of two bridges on the latter instrument. The typical virginals is oblong with the strings run- ning parallel to the keyboard instead of at right-angles to it. With the exception of the double virginals already mentioned, there was only one set of strings and no change of timbre was possible. Praetorius, however, mentions the *Arpichordum* as a type of virginals on which 'a

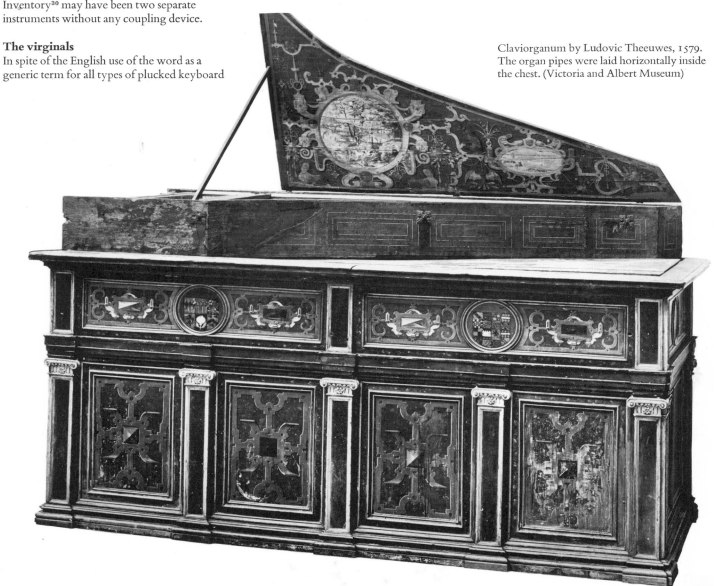

Claviorganum by Ludovic Theeuwes, 1579. The organ pipes were laid horizontally inside the chest. (Victoria and Albert Museum)

harp-like sound is produced by means of a special stop which governs metal jacks under the strings'.[62] This is evidently a special effect similar to the buzzing or rattling produced by the 'bray'-pins of the harp which Praetorius described as *harfenierend* (see chapter 4 page 22).

The placing of the keyboard on virginals varied; on Flemish instruments it was set either to the right or left and in 1699 Klaas Douwes explains that the name *muselar* was used for the former type of instrument and (confusingly) *spinet* for the latter.[63] Different placings of the keyboard involved different placings of the jacks in relation to the strings and the tone varies considerably according to where the

Title page from *Parthenia,* published in 1612 or 1613. In *Parthenia-in-violata* (*c.*1614) the title page shows a harpsichord instead of a virginals. (British Library; reproduced by permission of the Trustees)

strings are plucked. Writing in 1739 another Dutchman, Quirinus van Blankenburg, relates: 'of the virginals we will say in passing that those whose keyboard stands towards the left are even and playable ... but those which have the keyboard on the right-hand side are good in the right-hand, but grunt in the bass like young pigs.'[64] The compass of the virginals built by the Ruckers family was the same as that of their single-manual harpsichords, four octaves from C, with short-octave tuning in the bass.

The spinet
On the spinet the strings either run diagonally in front of the player or more or less parallel to

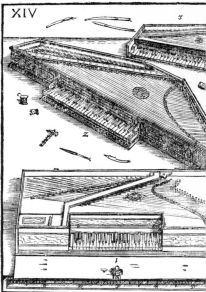

ABOVE .
Page from Praetorius' *Syntagma Musicum,* showing virginals (bottom) with centrally p[...] keyboard, spinet (middle), and octavina (top[...] Various accessories are scattered about: at th[...] several pieces of quill, on the left, two spools [...] wire, the tuning hammer, a quill-knife, and [...] hook for making eyes in the strings, and on [...] right a small vice or clamp.
LEFT
A Young Woman standing at the Virginals, by [...] Vermeer of Delft; second half of the sevente[...] century. A faithful representation of a Rucke[...] virginals, decorated with the printed papers [...] used by the family. (Windsor Castle)
LEFT BELOW ·
Virginals. Copy by Derek Adlam of an instrument made by Andreas Ruckers now i[...] the Vleeshuis Museum, Antwerp. (Collectio[...] Christopher Hogwood)

the keyboard as on the virginals. The typic[...] spinet form is an uneven six-sided shape wi[...] the longest side containing the keyboard. Normally there was one set of strings and a[...] four-octave compass. The French word *ép[...] and the Italian *spinetta* were applied fairly indiscriminately to all types of plucked key[...] board instruments, rather in the same way [...] *virginals* was used in England. Various expl[...] tions have been given for the origin of the [...] which occurs as early as 1496.[65] The Italian composer Banchieri made the suggestion i[...] *Conclusioni* (1609) that the spinet was name[...] after Giovanni Spina, the maker of an instr[...] ment dated 1501 which Banchieri had seen[...] Another theory is that the derivation is fro[...] the spinet's thorn-like plectra, *spinetta* bein[...] diminutive of the Italian *spina,* a thorn. As [...] Sybil Marcuse says, neither the etymology [...] the early history of the instrument is at all [...] clear.[65]

Praetorius[66] and others suggest that the s[...]

8 Brass

small instrument, tuned a fifth or an ⏑ higher than normal. On some double ⏑ als the second keyboard was tuned an ⏑ higher and the production of such 4-foot ⏑nents led to the use of the name *spinetta* ⏑ a or simply *ottavina*.

eigenwerk

⏑4 Praetorius entered the service of the ⏑of Brunswick and was very impressed by a ⏑strument which the Duke had recently ⏑ed. This was the *Geigenwerk*, invented in ⏑1570 by Hans Baiden of Nuremberg and ⏑oped by him over the next thirty years. ⏑rius devotes a disproportionate amount ⏑ce to the invention in his *Syntagma* ⏑um and quotes approvingly from Baiden's ⏑vritings on the subject.[67] The Geigenwerk ⏑ essence a super-mechanized version of ⏑rdy-gurdy, with brass and steel strings ⏑ted by five or six parchment-covered ⏑s set in motion by a treadle. Perhaps the ⏑remarkable feature was its ability to ⏑ *piano* and *forte*: the harder a key was ⏑ down the louder the sound became. ⏑d made at least twenty-three such ⏑ments[68] though none of them seems to have ⏑ed. A Spanish imitation of the Geigen- ⏑ dated 1625, is preserved in the Brussels ⏑um of Musical Instruments.[69] Samuel ⏑ heard a similar kind of instrument called ⏑rched Viall* at a meeting of the Royal ⏑ty in 1664. His verdict was: 'it will never ⏑ut after three hours stay it could not be ⏑in tune and so they were fain to go to ⏑other musique of instruments.'[70]

nwerk from Praetorius' *Syntagma Musicum*.

Whilst their medieval predecessors had enjoyed a fairly restricted musical usefulness, brass instruments found an entirely new lease of life during the Renaissance. The developments which took place during the second half of the fifteenth century were little short of revolutionary, and for the high standard of brass playing which undoubtedly existed during the sixteenth century much of the credit must go to the craftsmanship of the makers. The art of instrument-making in general achieved a new delicacy and finesse during the Renaissance. But whereas the improvements on strings and woodwind lay mainly in the *details* of construction, on the brass instruments the changes were fundamental and opened up new horizons of performing technique. By about the year 1500 the cornett had developed the various forms which remained unchanged throughout its career, the natural trumpet had established the shape it was to maintain for three hundred years, whilst the slide principle of the sackbut has never been improved upon and the modern trombone still adheres to the same basic design.

Besides their obvious exterior features the trumpet and sackbut also benefited from the tremendous improvements in metal-working which took place during the Renaissance.[1] Bending a thin-walled copper tube through a 180° curve without distorting the bore is a tricky process, but new alloys, precision tools, and new techniques in casting produced brass instruments which set a new standard in matters of intonation and tone quality. Many of them, especially the ceremonial trumpets, were often gorgeously decorated and engraved and deserve to be considered as works of art in their own right. One particularly important acoustical development was the exponential bell[2] which projects sound more effectively than a simple funnel of cone shape.[3] The great European centre for making brass instruments was the city of Nuremberg and Don Smithers lists the names of over sixty individual makers who worked there between 1500 and 1800.[4] Many of them operated family businesses which flourished for several generations and in the early period the leading name is unquestionably that of Neuschel. In his *General History of the Science and Practice of Music*, Sir John Hawkins says: 'The trumpet is said by Vincentio Galilei . . . to have been invented at Nuremberg; and there is extant a memoir which shews that trumpets were made to great perfection by an artist in that city, who was also an admired performer on that instrument, it is as follows; "Hans Meuschel [*sic*] of Nuremberg, for his accuracy in making trumpets, as also for his skill in playing on the same alone, and in the accompanyment with the voice, was of so great renown, that he was frequently sent for to the palaces of princes the distance of several

ABOVE
Copy by Boosey & Hawkes of a sackbut by Jörg Neuschel, dated 1557. The original instrument is in the collection of Anthony Baines. The water key on the slide is a modern addition.

BELOW
Unusually coiled trumpet by Anton Schnitzer the younger, dated 1598. (Kunsthistorisches Museum, Vienna)

hundred miles. Pope Leo X, for whom he had made sundry trumpets of silver, sent for him to Rome, and after having been delighted with his exquisite performance, dismissed him with a munificent reward." '[5] Whilst Don Smithers considers it doubtful whether Nuremberg produced the first true trumpets,[6] the Neuschel family achieved a high reputation for their skill during the Renaissance, and made a significant contribution to the development of both the trumpet and sackbut.

In spite of the transformation in construction and appearance, brass instruments retained their old associations and specific functions. Mention is made below of the use of the trumpet as a watchman's instrument, but the great glory of the renaissance brass family was the ceremonial music which it could provide for every important occasion, state or civic. As Mersenne says of the trumpet: 'they serve in time of peace and war for all sorts of public celebrations as is seen in marriages, banquets, tragedies and carrousels'.[7] Brass instruments regularly contributed to the pageantry of a royal procession or added to the glamour of civic ceremony. The Italian Vizani, writing in 1602, describes the public appearances of the dignitaries of the city of Bologna as follows: 'When they appear in public, these "Signori" are dressed in rich robes of silk, and during the winter they are muffled up with very precious furs as well. They are accompanied by a very respectable household of eight trumpeters, with a drummer or player of the nakers, who with these trumpets plays certain Moorish drums. To both the drums and the trumpets are attached banners with the arms of liberty; also eight

Trumpets and sackbuts from *The Triumph of Maximilian I* (1526).

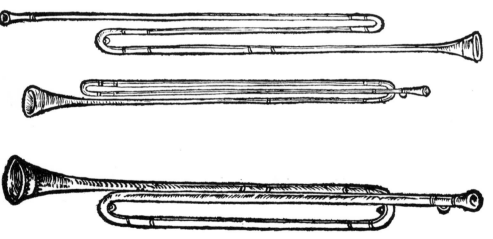

Three types of trumpet from Virdung's *Musica getutscht* (1511): *Thurner Horn*, *Clareta*, and *Felttrummet*.

excellent musicians with trombones and cornettos; a herald; a "spenditore"; nine pages dressed in scarlet cloaks and stockings in the livery of the city – white and red . . .'[8]

Other sources tell a similar story. In the grand cortège of musicians included in the *Triumph of Maximilian I*,[9] designed to honour the Holy Roman Emperor, pride of place is given to trumpets and sackbuts along with shawms and rauschpfeifen. A study of the English royal household accounts from the reign of Henry VIII to Elizabeth I reveal that at any given time there were more trumpeters on the payroll than any other type of instrumentalist.[10] At the coronation of Elizabeth in 1558 there were seventeen trumpeters, six 'sackebutts', and other

'musicians' who may well have included cornett players.[11]

The trumpet

In his *Musica getutscht* (1511) Virdung makes some interesting distinctions between different shapes and types of trumpet. He illustrates the *Thurner Horn* (a true trumpet in spite of its name) which displays the old-fashioned S shape frequently illustrated during the fifteenth century. It was from this S-shaped form of *buisine* that the slide trumpet had developed (see chapter 3, page 20). The name *Thurner Horn* means tower-horn, *ie* the instrument with which tower watchmen were equipped in order to raise the alarm in case of attack, fire,

or some civil disturbance. In Amsterdam and Hamburg in the seventeenth century it was noted that: 'When a Fire happens by Night, the Trumpets plac'd upon the Towers shall sound an Alarm, and hang out two Lanthorns to the Quarter, where the Fire is, and one on the other side.'[12] The tradition was of long standing: the 1452 fire regulations of Cologne state that when a fire is detected the watchers on the town-hall tower shall first sound their trumpets and then strike the fire bell.[13] As early as 1372 there were restrictions on trumpet-playing to avoid giving a false alarm: in that year in Paris unofficial trumpet-playing after the hour of curfew was made a crime, except at weddings.[14] All the same it is difficult to see why the old-fashioned S-shaped instrument should have been preferred for tower duties. As Philip Bate suggests,[15] it may be just that the military trumpeters, who were already forming themselves into unofficial guilds, liked to keep the more up-to-date instruments to themselves.

Virdung calls his other two trumpets the *Clareta* (from the same root as *clarion*) and the *Felttrummet* (field-trumpet). Both show the twice-folded oblong form of the natural trumpet. At this time a change in terminology seems to have been taking place. In 1519 the historian William Horman stated that 'A trumpette is streyght; but a clarion is wounde: in and out with an hope [*ie* hoop]'[16] and a distinction between the two was made as early as 1346 when the English army at the battle of Crécy was heralded by clarions as well as trumpets.[17] At that stage, however, nomenclature was anything but standardized. It seems likely that the clarion was associated with playing in the upper register (Virdung's

Clareta appears to have a narrow bore which would favour the production of the higher harmonics). This would certainly explain the use of the word *clarino* during the baroque period for the trumpet's brilliant upper register. The foundation for the virtuoso lip technique which baroque trumpeters displayed must have been laid during the late Renaissance though it does not become apparent until the beginning of the seventeenth century.

Praetorius (1619) and Mersenne (1635) both illustrate the standard natural trumpet: clearly the different transitional types of Virdung's time have merged into one. Praetorius tells us 'The trumpet . . . is a magnificent instrument. It is remarkable that in its higher register the instrument affords conjunctly almost all the diatonic notes and various chromatic notes as well.'[18] By this time we have the first surviving example of the sort of elaborate polyphonic fanfare which the trumpet bands of the late

NORMAL RANGE

*these notes are naturally out of tune

Range of the natural trumpet in C. In practice the fundamental was not used and trumpeters divided the rest of the compass between them. Praetorius gives g'' as the highest normal note but 'falsetto' notes as high as the f''' above. It seems likely that this is a misprint for d'''.

et 'clarino'

et 'quinta'

et 'alto e basso'

...sed in the 1st, 2nd, and 3rd trumpet parts
...occata from Monteverdi's *Orfeo*.

...ance must have played. This is the
...from Monteverdi's first opera *Orfeo*,[19]
...ed in Mantua in 1607, and the scoring
...he sort of division of labour which
...characteristic in baroque trumpet
... The top part, labelled *clarino*, lies in the
...ster between c″ and a″ (employing the
...o the thirteenth harmonics). The second
...olves only four notes of the common
...f C (c′, e′, g′, c″) whilst the third lies
... till (g, c′, e′). Baroque trumpeters
...arily specialized in one register only and
...id according to how high they went.
...day, with the facility of the modern
...rumpet, players who specialize in the
...mpet parts of Bach and Handel would
...deserve something very like danger

...teverdi's instruction for the performance
...Toccata is interesting because he mentions
...ct of mutes. 'Si fa un Tuono piu alto
...o sonar le trombe con le sordine'[19] (those
...g to play the trumpets with mutes make
...e higher). Early trumpet mutes were
...different in shape from modern ones,
...senne's illustration shows, and they not
...duced the tone and volume drastically
...ed as a transposing device as well. They
...aserted so far into the bell of the instru-
...hat they raised the pitch by a whole tone.
...can be little doubt that the Toccata which
...Orfeo should sound in D major, not in C
...ten, and thus match the D minor of the
...g ritornello.[20]

...ording to Praetorius, military trumpets
...ormally pitched in D which had been
...ndard key for all trumpets to be built in.
...ver, he tells us that court trumpeters had
...y taken to using crooks to lengthen the
...ad lower the pitch to C or even B flat.[21]
...rius also illustrates two other types of
...et: a straight wooden one, virtually
...al to that still used by Scandinavian
...rds (see chapter 3 page 19) and a *Jäger*
...er or hunting trumpet which shows the
...form adopted by some later German
...s. Some of the secrets of trumpet-playing
...the first time revealed in the *Modo per*
...re a sonare di tromba published by
...mo Fantini in 1638.[22] This is the first

printed tutor for the trumpet and includes
tonguing exercises, battle calls, and some pieces
for one and two trumpets with continuo. By
this time the words *trompette* (French), *tromba*
(Italian), and *Trompete* (German) had come into
general use to describe the natural trumpet,
though the French word *trompe* signified horn,
as the Spanish *trompa* still does to this day.

The horn
In a paper written in 1775 entitled 'Of the Horn
as a Charter or Instrument of Conveyance'
Samuel Pegge describes horns as being of four
sorts: drinking horns, hunting horns, horns for
blowing, or horns for drinking, a stopper being
provided for the last-named purpose.[23] If we
may borrow his classification for the sixteenth
century, it neatly epitomizes the horn's
backward state of development and limited
musical function. Nevertheless the horn began
to be regularly made of metal during the late
Renaissance, and makers experimented with

Two natural trumpets with additional tuning
crooks. Made by Michael Laird, based on various
originals.

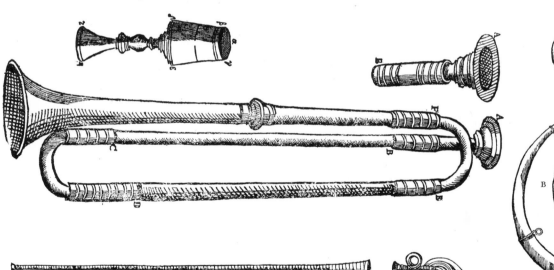

TOP
Trumpet with separate mouthpiece and mute
from Mersenne's *Harmonie Universelle* (1635).

BOTTOM
Straight wooden trumpet and coiled *Jäger
Trommer*, from Praetorius' *Syntagma Musicum*
(1619).

Different types of horn, from Mersenne's
Harmonie Universelle.

different types of curvature and coiling as can
be seen from Mersenne's illustrations. The
seventeenth-century *cor de chasse* developed
from a combination of two of the types he
shows: the tightly coiled *helical* horn (labelled
A) with the slender crescent-shaped horn
(labelled B) with one coil in the middle. It is
interesting that Mersenne mentions the playing
of *part* music on horns. 'If the hunters wish to
have the pleasure of performing some concerts
in four or more parts with their horns, it is
rather easy, provided they know how to make
their notes exact and they so proportion the

length and thickness of their *trompes* [ie horns]
that they maintain the same ratios as organ
pipes.'[24] And Mersenne goes on to explain the
necessary sizes for a horn consort. The first
surviving horn fanfare comes in Cavalli's opera
Le nozze di Teti e di Peleo (1639).[25] Although
written in five parts it consists of a simple
reiteration of the chord of C major and may
well to some extent represent earlier practice.
From the sixteenth century we have only
isolated hunting calls, though the sound of
horns was occasionally imitated in polyphonic
music. Edward Piers' madrigal *Hey, trola, there

boys there* (1614)[26] contains an elaborate imitation of hunting calls and it has even been
suggested that the tenor and bass parts of
Gombert's programme-chanson *La Chasse
de Lièvre* could be played on horns in F.[27]

The sackbut
The origin of the word 'sackbut' remains
uncertain. According to Galpin[28] it derives from
the fourteenth-century Spanish *sacabuche*
meaning literally 'draw-pipe'. Sachs[29] thinks
that a more likely derivation is from the French
saquer (to pull) and *bouter* (to push): the word

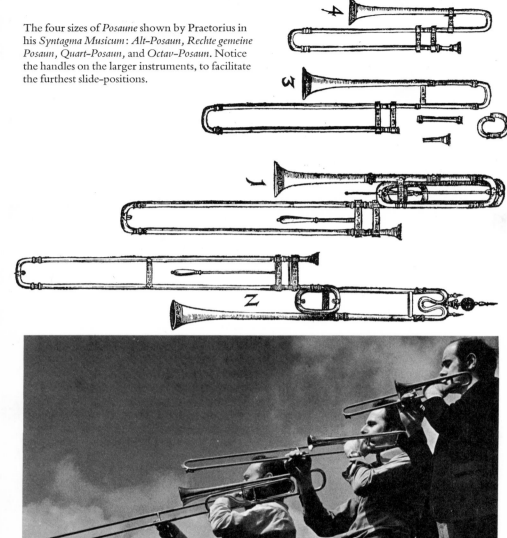

The four sizes of *Posaune* shown by Praetorius in his *Syntagma Musicum*: *Alt-Posaun*, *Rechte gemeine Posaun*, *Quart-Posaun*, and *Octav-Posaun*. Notice the handles on the larger instruments, to facilitate the furthest slide-positions.

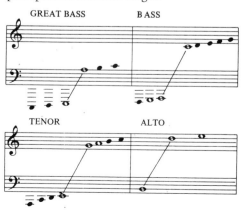

Tenor, alto, and soprano sackbuts. The water-keys are a modern addition. Tenor: Neuschel copy mentioned above. Alto: adapted from an undated alto trombone by Peerless. Soprano: made by Finke, based on various originals.

saqueboute is used from 1466 onwards, often in the form *trompette saqueboute*.[30] Whatever the origin, this foreign name certainly puzzled the English keepers of royal records and household accounts and from 1495 onwards references include: *shakbusshes*,[31] *seykebuds, sakbuds, shakebuttes, shagbutts*,[32] and even *shagbolt*.[33] The other basic names for the instrument emphasize its relation to the trumpet: *trombone* (in French and Italian as well as English) derived from *tromba*, and the German *Posaune*

derived from *buisine*. Virdung uses an intermediate spelling *Busaun*. Less common names included *tromba spezzata, trompette brisée,* and *trompette harmonique,* this last being used by Mersenne.

Equally uncertain is the date of the sackbut's first appearance. There is an interesting account of the manner in which English prelates were received on their entry into the Council of Constance (1414–18): 'die pusauner pusaunoten über einnander mit dreyen stymmen, als man

sunst gerwonlichen singet' (the trombonists tromboned together in three parts as one is otherwise accustomed to sing).[34] At this stage *pusauner* might have referred to some kind of slide trumpet or even still meant the old *buisine,* though it is difficult to imagine three buisines playing in parts 'as one is accustomed to sing'. By a curious coincidence two three-part pieces survive from the beginning of the fifteenth century which have a suggested instrumentation involving some kind of trumpet. They are *Virgo dulcis* by Henricus de Libero Castro, with its tenor marked 'Laudate eum in sono tube' and contratenor marked 'Tube', and the anonymous *Tuba gallicalis,* which is in the nature of a fanfare.[35] The source of both pieces is the lost Strasbourg manuscript and the restricted range of parts is almost identical in both (c–g' overall). Both pieces contain the note d, however, outside the compass of the slide trumpet, and it is possible, as with the contratenor *Trompette* by Dufay (see chapter 3, page 20), that the pieces were designed for an early form of sackbut.

It must be admitted, however, that evidence for the practical employment of the sackbut is scanty before the last years of the fifteenth century; yet it represented such a useful addition in the brass family that one imagines its use spreading rapidly. Writing in about 1487, Tinctoris gives us this valuable piece of information. 'However for the lowest contratenor parts, and often for any contratenor part, to the shawm players one adds brass players who play, very harmoniously, upon the kind of tuba which is called ... *trompone* in Italy and *sacque-boute* in France. When all these instruments are employed together, it is called the loud music'.[36] From 1500 onwards the sackbut is illustrated and mentioned regularly and the Neuschel family produced sackbuts as well as trumpets (see page 65). However, really detailed information is not available until the early seventeenth century. Praetorius gives four principal sizes with their ranges.

GREAT BASS   BASS

TENOR   ALTO

Sackbut ranges from Praetorius' *Syntagma Musicum*.

He makes it clear that the most useful size tenor in B♭ (the *Gemeine Rechte Posaun*) can cope with alto, tenor, or bass parts. was the standard instrument used by the players of the time and Praetorius singles two virtuosi for special mention. The 'fa master', Phileno of Munich, could manag range of D–e'' 'without any difficulty' w Erhardus Borussus whom Praetorius hear Dresden was apparently capable of quite astonishing feats unrivalled even today. only had a range of nearly four octaves fr low A' to high g'' but 'was able to execut coloraturas and jumps on his instrument is done on the *viola bastarda* and the corne Praetorius stresses that a tremendous adva enjoyed by all sackbuts was their adaptab to the various different pitches of the day changes could be made by slide or embou larger changes by the addition or subtract of crooks or other sections of tube. Praeto also mentions an alternative size of bass sa (a *Quint Posaun* in E♭) and there may wel been an alto in E♭ too, paving the way fo later orchestral alto trombone in the same

Mersenne (1635) adds two other particu interesting pieces of information.[38] In the of sound production the player should im the cornett, rather than the trumpet, presu to obtain flexibility and expressiveness of Mersenne also emphasizes the importance the sackbut's crooks and explains how the joining adjacent sections of parallel tube detachable so that the instrument could be conveniently dismantled. On the Neusche sackbut of 1557 (see page 65) the bell stay fixed, whilst those at the top of the slide a the mouthpipe are movable.[39] Apart from the only important feature which distingu a modern trombone from its predecessor greatly increased flare of the bell. It is stra that despite its considerable range of dyna wide chromatic compass, and secure inton the trombone did not become a regular m of the orchestra long before the early nine century. Part of the reason may lie in the trombone's use as a 'special effects' instrum Monteverdi uses a consort of *tromboni* in A of *Orfeo* to create the awesome mystery of Underworld. Coupled with the sinister so of the regal the effect is spine-chilling, and Mozart introduced trombones into the las of *Don Giovanni* he was drawing on an old association.

Although Praetorius calls the smallest si sackbut *alt* or *discant* there was, in fact, no trombone small enough to cope with real parts during the Renaissance. For outdoor the proper treble instrument for a consort sackbuts was the shawm; for more sophist indoor music and especially for doubling voices in church the cornett provided the

by Christopher Monk, based on a
...enth-century original.

the voices in cathedrals or in chapels.)[44]

The cornett emerged in its various renaissance forms towards the end of the fifteenth century, although the word is mentioned as early as about 1400.[45] The spelling with a double 't' was by no means standard in English, but is generally used today to avoid confusion with the nineteenth-century band instrument. The name means 'little horn', being a diminutive of the Latin *cornu*, hence the Spanish *corneta* and the Italian *cornetto* and *cornettino* (the latter a double diminutive). The French developed the name *cornet à bouqin* (cornett with a mouthpiece) whilst the typical German word was *Zink*.

Here is the Italian Bottrigari writing in 1594:

'Cornetts and trombones are played with such grace, taste and sure precision of the notes, that they are held the most excellent of the wind instruments in the profession. Their divisions are neither scrappy nor so wild that they spoil the underlying melody and the composer's design: but are introduced at such moments and with such vivacity and charm that they give the music the greatest beauty and spirit.'[46]

The secret of cornett playing clearly lies in the embouchure. Most professional cornettists today are also trumpet players and use a

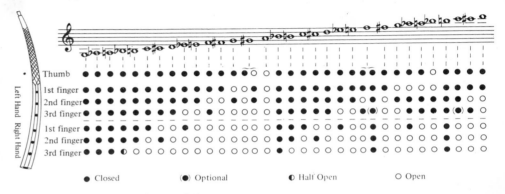

Fingering chart by Christopher Monk for a cornett in G.

● Closed   (●) Optional   ◑ Half Open   ○ Open

. One or two pieces were written for this ... combination including the *Sonata Pian' e* ...d other canzonas in Giovanni Gabrieli's *Symphoniae,* published in 1597,[40] as well ...thew Locke's *Music for His Majesty's* ...s and *Cornetts* of 1661.[41] During the ...enth century the sackbut even developed ... solo repertoire, mainly from composers ...ted with the Viennese court of the Holy ... Emperor Leopold I. No doubt the ...ce of virtuosi such as those mentioned by ...rius, coupled with the high standard of ...n-made instruments, encouraged ...sers such as Heinrich Biber and Johann ...lzer to include the sackbut along with ...lin and cornett in some of their sonatas, ... write the same kind of scales, trills, and ...tions as they did for the more naturally ...reble instruments. The end of the ...enth century, however, witnessed a ... in the playing of both shawm and ...t and this was probably the reason for the ...pment of the soprano sackbut, pitched in ...octave above the tenor, in order to ...ete the family. The earliest instruments ...size seem to have been made in Germany ...eden.[42]

...ornett

...ost versatile wind instrument of the ...sance was undoubtedly the cornett.

During its heyday – roughly 1500 to 1650 – cornetts were in demand for music of all kinds: indoors and outdoors, in serious music and dance music, in church and chamber, in the town bands and royal households. The highly individual qualities of the cornett stem from the fact that the instrument is a compromise: a hybrid form which combines the cup-mouthpiece technique of the brass with the finger technique of the woodwind. Hence its astonishing versatility: in the hands of a skilled player the cornett can sound as loud as the trumpet or blend with a recorder; it can outshine the violin in brilliant divisions or sing like a human voice. No other instrument had such a vocal quality; when, in 1742, Roger North reminisced about the depleted state of choirs after the Commonwealth he said: 'To say the truth nothing comes so near, or rather imitates so much, an excellent voice as a cornet pipe.'[43] Earlier he had expressed himself more succinctly: 'One might mistake it for a choice eunuch.'[43] Perhaps the most poetic and evocative description of the cornett's unique tone quality comes from Mersenne: 'Il est semble à l'esclat d'un rayon de Soleil, qui paroit dans l'ombre ou dans les tenebres, lors qu'on l'entend parmi les voix dans les Eglises Cathedrales, ou dans les Chapelles.' (It seems like the brilliance of a shaft of sunlight appearing in the shadow or in darkness, when one hears it among

Whatever their shape or method of construction all cornetts have some kind of cup-mouthpiece and seven holes, usually six finger-holes and a thumb-hole or in the case of some French instruments seven finger-holes and no thumb-hole. In spite of the absence of a seventh hole for the little finger, players were expected to be able to produce the missing note by slackening their embouchure or 'lipping down'. For the standard cornett in G, for example, the same fingering (all holes covered) is used for g, a♭, and a – see fingering chart. On the large tenor cornett a seventh finger-hole plus open-standing key was sometimes provided to give a firm bottom C. Nor is the rest of the cornett's fingering system quite as straightforward as that of woodwind instruments, and in any case the player still has to 'make' the notes with his lips: the finger-holes make them possible rather than probable. Altogether the cornett offers formidable difficulties of technique: a playing position which can quickly tire the fingers, an embouchure which can quickly tire the lips, and enormous problems of intonation and smoothing out the basic inequalities of the tone between 'covered' and 'open' notes. The more holes there are uncovered, the more difficult it is to achieve a good sound.

Yet renaissance players seem to have solved all the problems and there are many accounts of the cornett's agility as well as beauty of tone.

trumpet-style mouthpiece placed in a central position on the lips. Renaissance players favoured the smaller acorn-shaped mouthpiece often placed at the side of the mouth where the lips are thinner. Such an embouchure, whilst incompatible with modern brass techniques, must have made softer sustained playing easier. Mersenne tells us that two special attributes of the cornett are its ability to play as softly as the flute and the way it uses up very little breath. He mentions one of the French royal musicians, M. Quiclet, who could play for eighty measures without breathing ('which surpasses all credence') and the even more redoubtable M. Sourin of Avignon who could manage a hundred measures in one breath.[47]

Memoirs and reminiscences by professional instrumentalists are notably lacking from renaissance times but we do have a first-hand account from one cornett player, that true child of the time Benvenuto Cellini. He was born in 1500, and although his father made him play the flute, which he loathed, he also took up the cornett. Shortly after he set himself up in Rome in 1519 as a jeweller and goldsmith he took on a young apprentice called Paulino to whom he became rather attached. Cellini tells us in his autobiography: 'I loved him so passionately that I was always playing music for him in order to see his lovely face, which was normally rather sad and serious, brighten up when he

Detail of cornett player, showing side embouchure, from the *Procession of the Forty-eight Guilds and Corporations,* by Denis van Ansloot (*c.*1570–1628), painter of the archdukes of Brussels. (Prado, Madrid)

Two monks playing what appear to be straight cornetts. Their fingering and embouchure suggest a certain lack of expertise. From a fifteenth-century breviary. (National Museum, Stockholm)

Different sizes and types of cornett mouthpiece. The acorn-cup type is that preferred by renaissance players.

A, B, C, D for tenor cornett
E, F, H, I, for ordinary cornett
G, J, for cornettino

heard it. Whenever I took up the cornett, such a frank, beautiful smile came over his face that I am not at all surprised at those silly stories the Greeks wrote about their gods . . . He had a sister called Faustina who was even more beautiful, I think, than the Faustina the ancient books are always babbling about. Sometimes I used to visit their vineyard and from what I could judge it appeared to me that Paulino's father, a thoroughly worthy man, would have liked me as son-in-law. All this made me play a great deal more than usual.'[48]

According to Benvenuto Cellini it was his mastery of the cornett which brought him into contact with Pope Clement VII. One of the Pope's musicians sent a message to Cellini 'asking me if I would help them at the Pope's August festival in some very beautiful motets they had chosen, by playing the soprano part on my cornett. Although I was burning to finish my wonderful vase, as music is a marvellous business anyway, and to give my father some satisfaction, I was quite ready to join them. We spent a week before the festival practising together two hours a day. On the day itself we went along to the Belvedere, and while Pope Clement was having dinner we played the motets we had rehearsed so well that he had to admit he had never heard music played more exquisitely or more harmoniously.'[49]

And Cellini goes on to say that the Pope offered him a job on the spot. During the years 1523 to 1540 Benvenuto Cellini certainly served Clement VII and his successor Paul III

not only as artist and craftsman, but as soldier and gunner as well.

It would be interesting to know what type of cornett Benvenuto Cellini played, though unfortunately he gives us no details. By his time there were basically three varieties – curved, straight, and mute – all made in different sizes. The earliest to develop was probably the straight cornett (*cornetto diritto, gerader Zink*) which is the only type shown by Virdung in his *Musica getutscht* (1511). This was usually turned on a lathe instead of being made in two halves (see below). Because of the finger stretches involved it was impossible to make straight cornetts in sizes larger than the alto. In any case the curved form was obviously regarded as more comfortable and largely superseded the *diritti* during the course of the century. Straight cornetts continued to be made up to the nineteenth century, however.[50] The mute cornett (*cornetto muto, stiller Zink*) was also straight, but instead of having a separate detachable mouthpiece, a conical recess was cut into the top of the instrument itself, as on the *tuohitorvi* (see chapter 3, page 20). The formation of this mouthpiece, in particular the very wide throat, combined with a narrower bore, made the mute cornett an exquisitely soft instrument, ideal for playing with the recorder, lute, or viol.[51]

The favourite form of cornett was the *cornetto curvo* or *krumme Zink,* sometimes also described as *nero* or *schwarz* because of the black leather covering. The bore of the instrument is made in

two gouged-out halves, like the tuohitorvi. Then the inside is smoothed off and the two halves glued together. The outside is planed to a very beautiful eight-sided shape and finally the leather is glued round the outside in a single piece. This is mainly to seal any leaks which might develop along the bore. For similar reasons, cornetts were sometimes decorated with silver rings to strengthen the instrument at judicious points.[52] In one of the more spectacular performances of the Monteverdi *Vespers* (1610) in recent times, one cornett did literally come unstuck. Whether it was the high notes it had been playing, the cold temperature in the chapel, or a glue weakened after 300 years, the two halves of the cornett just came apart in the player's hands. In fairness it must be said that the taxing solo parts in the Vespers, particularly the *Sonata sopra Sancta Maria* and the obbligato in the *Deposuit* (which takes both instruments up to top d''), are enough to make any cornett want to fall apart. But this was the way composers treated the cornett: as a virtuoso instrument. Monteverdi's *Orfeo* (1607) also features the cornett, and a common inscription for early seventeenth-century instrumental parts was 'per cornetto overo violino', showing that the cornett was in every way as proficient as the violin.

TENOR CORNETT   CORNETT   CORNETTINO

Cornett ranges from Praetorius' *Syntagma Musicum.*

The standard size of cornett (straight, curved, or mute) was pitched in G giving a comfortable range of two octaves, extended by exceptionally proficient players as Praetorius shows. The *cornettino,* pitched a fourth or fifth higher in C or D, was a useful instrument for high parts, like those of Monteverdi, though it seems to have been much less common. There were also

alto cornetts in F, a tone below the standar[d] cornett: a mute cornett of this size was pro[bably] in use at Kassel when Schütz was a boy ch[orister] there. The tenor cornett in C was so large [it] necessitated two curves in the tube instead [of] one; hence an English name *lysarden* or *liza[rd.]* Praetorius, who tells us that it was also call[ed] *Cornon,* is fairly disparaging about the ton[e,] describing it as 'unlovely and horn-like'[53] [in its] lower register. Because of its wider bore th[e] tenor cornett is really more like the serpen[t;] the sound makes a good blend with voices [but] lacks the individual timbre of the higher cornetts and consequently was not much u[sed] for solo work. It was used in consort, how[ever,] and Anthony Baines[54] points out that the [ricercars] or canons by Johann Walther, published i[n 1542] and marked 'especially for cornetts', requi[re the] tenor cornett for the bottom part.[55]

During the baroque period the cornett w[as] gradually eclipsed not only by the baroqu[e] trumpet with its *clarino* technique, but by [the] baroque oboe too, which was easier to pla[y in] tune. Although Bach scored for the cornet[t in] eleven of his cantatas it was always in a supporting rather than a solo role. But it is remarkable just how long the tradition of cornett playing survived. For a century aft[er] the cornett had fallen into disuse one or tw[o] German town bands kept the tradition go[ing.] As late as 1840, the French composer and historian Kastner actually heard the sound [of] cornetts and trombones coming from the church tower in Stuttgart: a town band st[ill] playing their daily chorales in the old Ger[man] manner.[56] A few years later came the begin[ning] of our modern interest in the sounds and [in] the instruments of the past. But it came jus[t] too late – there were no cornett players lef[t;] the secrets of their art were buried togeth[er] with a fascinating link with the playing traditions of the Renaissance.

The serpent

'But the true bass of the cornett is perform[ed] with the serpent, so that one can say that o[ne] without the other is a body without soul.' So writes Mersenne,[57] though he does not

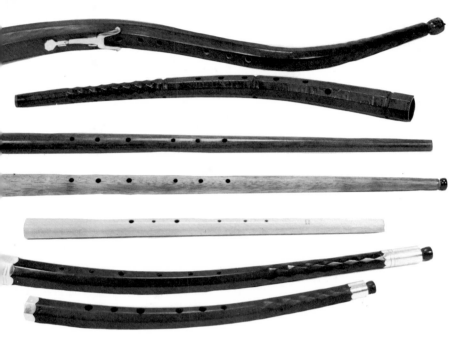

Different sizes and types of cornett:

1. Tenor cornett in C. Copy by Christopher Monk of an instrument *c*.1600, formerly in Canon Galpin's collection.

2. Alto cornett in F. Formerly in the Nettlefold collection, date uncertain, maker unknown.

3. Mute cornett in F. Copy by Christopher Monk of an instrument in the Karl Marx University Museum, Leipzig, thought to have been used at Kassel when Schütz was a choirboy there.

4. Straight cornett in F by Christopher Monk.

5. Mute cornett in C by Steinkopf/Moeck.

6. Standard cornett in G by Christopher Monk, based on a seventeenth-century original.

7. Cornettino in D by Christopher Monk, based on an instrument dated 1518 in the collection of Anthony Baines. (All but No 5, collection of Christopher Monk; No 5, author's collection)

to double men's voices. When it is well played, the serpent blends perfectly with a choir, losing its own individual timbre altogether, whilst giving an extra depth and fullness to the vocal sound. The serpent is not mentioned by Praetorius and its popularity spread only gradually during the seventeenth century. During the next two hundred years it enjoyed a flourishing career as a military band instrument and serpents were still in use in some of the English church bands of the late nineteenth century.

The *serpent d'église* as described by Mersenne was a keyless instrument with six finger-holes and a fundamental of E. It consisted of a conical tube over six feet long with a more widely expanding bore than any type of cornett (later serpents were rather larger and pitched in D or C). It was usually made in two halves which were glued together and bound with leather and it had an elbow-shaped brass crook to adjust the mouthpiece to a comfortable position. The serpentine contours of the instrument,

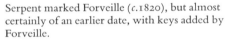

tenor cornett. Copy by Christopher of an instrument *c*.1600, formerly in Galpin's collection.

Serpent marked Forveille (*c*.1820), but almost certainly of an earlier date, with keys added by Forveille.

Serpent; typical keyless *serpent d'église* model with separate crook and mouthpieces, from Mersenne's *Harmonie Universelle*.

w the instrument's origin, merely telling
the sackbut is believed to be 'more
'. The serpent is thought to have been
ed in about 1590 by a canon of Auxerre,
mé Guillaume.[58] Whilst this remains a
point, the earliest use of the instrument
em to have been confined to France
it was an ecclesiastical instrument used

necessary to bring the holes and mouthpiece within reach of the player, seems to have given rise to similar names in every language: *Serpent* in German, *serpentone* in Italian, and *serpentón* in Spanish. Mersenne makes the surprising statement that 'it is so easy to play that a child of fifteen can sound it as easily as a man of thirty'.[59] In practice, great skill and musicianship are required, since every note depends on the player's embouchure and sense of pitch. The capricious nature of the instrument is shown by the various fingering charts published during the eighteenth and nineteenth centuries, no two of which agree about details of fingering or compass.[60] Certain notes can be lowered a fourth or more by slackening the embouchure and a favourite trick of some serpent players today is to play an *upward* scale whilst fingering a *downward* one. Nevertheless, the published tutors for the instrument[60] do prescribe a range of over three octaves and a degree of virtuosity which was perhaps not so common in the early days when the serpent's duty was to be seen rather than heard.

9 Strings

There can be no doubt of the pre-eminence of stringed instruments during the Renaissance, both in theory and in practice. Through a largely imagined inheritance from the instruments of the Ancients they were endowed with an allegorical and symbolic significance, faithfully represented in countless books and paintings. As a result of their wide compass and innate ability to match the human voice, they were indispensable to virtually all forms of indoor music-making, from dance music to church music. In the hands of the renaissance makers stringed instruments attained a new perfection of form and design which attracted amateurs and professionals alike. It was principally for strings that the various purely instrumental forms of ensemble music developed such as the fantasy, canzona, *in nomine*, and the new dance types. Like keyboard instruments, the strings developed a vast solo repertory with their own idiomatic forms of the prelude, ricercar, and *tastar de corde*. The amount of music specifically written for stringed instruments during the sixteenth century is enormous. A glance at Howard Mayer Brown's *Instrumental Music printed before 1600*[1] reveals the overwhelming proportion of publications devoted to string music, with the lute taking the lion's share. Yet this is merely the tip of the iceberg: the manuscript sources, particularly those for the lute or viol families, contain a vast repertoire which has not yet been fully explored in modern times.

Considering the daunting amount of material to be assimilated it is perhaps not surprising that the definitive account of most sixteenth-century stringed instruments remains to be written.[2] It is an area in which much research has been done in recent years and one in which exciting discoveries are still being made, amongst them the *Board Lute Book,*[3] unearthed by Robert Spencer, which contains over 188 pieces, a hundred of which are unique in some way, and the broken-consort lessons which came to light in the North Humberside County Record Office, Beverley.[4] The fruits of recent research are to be found in the various periodicals regularly mentioned in this book, particularly the *Lute Society Journal* and the *Journal of the Lute Society of America*. Both these journals deal regularly with other plucked instruments besides the lute and occasionally with bowed instruments as well.

Amongst the very varied repertoire for mixed string ensemble it is not mere chauvinism which leads one to single out Thomas Morley's *First Book of Consort Lessons*[5] of 1599 as a most remarkable and rewarding collection. The question of the flute/recorder part has already been mentioned in chapter 6, as has Praetorius' enthusiastic description of the novel and extraordinary effect of the English broken consort.[6] It is worth adding that the very careful scoring for the stringed instruments (viols, lute, bandora, and cittern) particularly in the pieces by Richard Allison, gives us a fascinating insight into contemporary habits of chordal accompaniment, making divisions, and ensemble playing. The roles of each instrument are so distinct, the arrangements so carefully worked out, and each part so perfectly suited to the instrument that Morley's book clearly represents a culminating point rather than the beginning of a tradition. The broken consort had a particular association with the private theatres. At Blackfriars, where the boys of the Chapel Royal acted, a foreigner wrote in 1602: 'For a whole hour preceding the play one listens to a delightful entertainment on organs, lutes, pandoras, mandoras, viols and pipes.'[7] The broken consort must have provided some of the incidental music to the plays themselves too. No better combination of soft instruments could be found for that tricky theatrical situation, music under dialogue, such as that commanded by Lorenzo in the last scene of *The Merchant of Venice* or implied by Orsino's famous opening line in *Twelfth Night*. Indeed, details of stringed instruments and their technique are woven throughout the whole fabric of Elizabethan and Jacobean literature.[8] Hamlet's remarks, to Rosencrantz and Guildenstern, 'you would pluck out the heart of my mystery' and 'though you can fret me you cannot play upon me'[9] are typical of many references of the period.

Playing stringed instruments was a recognized – and recommended – aristocratic pastime. As Henry Peacham says in *The Compleat Gentleman,* first published in 1622: 'I desire no more in you than to sing your part sure and at the first sight, withal to play the same upon your viol, or the exercise of the lute privately to yourself.'[10] Peacham's book represents an English counterpart to Castiglione's famous account of the ideal courtier, *Il Cortegiano* (1528), which takes the form of discussions held at the Ducal Palace in Urbino in 1507. The English translation of *Il Cortegiano* by Sir Thomas Hoby (1561) is interesting because of the way Hoby avoids translating some of the instruments mentioned by Castiglione literally, preferring to use the most appropriate English equivalent of his day. Thus *viola,* almost certainly used by Castiglione to mean *lira da braccio,* an instrument depicted several times in the Ducal Palace,[11] is rendered as 'lute' and 'Il cantare alla viola' as 'singing to the lute', whilst 'tutti gli instrumenti di tasti' (all keyboard instruments) becomes 'all instruments with frets'.[12] The following extract shows how Castiglione emphasizes the place of music and stringed instruments in renaissance society.

'But singing to the lute with the ditty (methink) is more pleasant than the rest, for it addeth to the words with such grace and strength that it is a great wonder. Also all instruments with frets are full of harmony, because the tunes of them are very perfect ... And the music of a set of viols doth no less delight a man, for it is very sweet and artificial. A man's breast giveth a great ornament and grace to these instruments, in the which I will have it sufficient that our Courtier have an understanding ... Now as touching the time and season when these sorts of music are to be practised, I believe at all times when a man is in familiar and loving company, having nothing else ado. But especially they are meet to be practised in the company of women, because those sights sweeten the minds of the hearers and make them more apt to be pierced with the pleasantness of music . . .'[13]

The plucked instruments

Apart from the harp, all the instruments in this section are linked by their use of frets. For the basic distinctions between the various types of construction the reader is referred back to chapter 4, page 24. During the Middle Ages fretting had been inconsistent; virtually every instrument with a fingerboard, including rebecs and fiddles, had been fretted at some stage, if only occasionally; during the Renaissance the application of frets was more standardized. Whilst on all fixed-fret instruments, such as the cittern, the fretting the job of the maker, on the movable-fret instruments, such as the lute, the responsibility was very much that of the player. Movable frets were made of gut and some idea of the mathematical complexities involved in setting them correctly can be gleaned from a study of John Dowland's instructions in the *Varietie of Lute-Lessons* (1610).[14] The number of frets inevitably varied to some extent and in any case the highest fret did not necessarily represent the upward limit of the instrument's compass. In the *Regola Rubertina* of 1542/3 Sylvestro Ganassi mentions fingering 'beyond the frets' as a part of advanced viol technique: 'It is necessary to give you a rule for playing above the frets (which is especially important for playing divisions) and up to the end of the fingerboard, as do those highly skilled players Alfonso da Ferrara, Joan-Battista Siciliano also Francesca da Milano and Rubertino Mantuano. I have seen them perform the impossible on their instruments. They are certainly the most famous players today and deserve great admiration. I have seen them above the frets as well and as agilely as if they were frets for every note.'[15] The upper reach

Still life with musical instruments, by Evaristo Baschensis (1617–77). (Accademia Carrara, Bergamo)

e fingerboard were clearly not regarded as
f bounds to a skilled player. During the
nth century and early sixteenth century
se of the plectrum was gradually aban-
d, and players developed a more subtle
r-technique. The exception here was the
n, the major plectrum instrument of the
issance.
e materials for string-making remained
a as they had been in the Middle Ages.[16]
trings were spun from sheep gut, metal
s were made of soft-tempered steel or
. Sometimes both types of metal string
used on the same instrument, steel being
rred for the higher strings, brass for the
r. The use of covered strings – those on
h a central core is wound round or
spun', usually with brass, in order to
ove the tone on low notes – did not
ne a regular practice until after the
seventeenth century. Before then the use
covered gut strings imposed a downward
in pitch on plucked instruments: on the
he sound of the lowest three strings was to
extent unsatisfactory (see below, p 77)
n the largest member of the family, the
rone, metal strings were frequently used.
e majority of plucked instruments, strings
arranged in pairs or 'courses', rather than
y: thus the four-course English cittern
ly had eight strings. On small wire-strung
uments, such as the cittern, it was customary
e lowest strings to be made of 'twisted'
s, ie two strands of brass wire twisted
her.[17] The question of stringing is a vexed
however: an instrument might have some
lower courses tuned in octaves, instead of
ns; it might have a double course in the
or one or two triple courses in the bass,
ditional unstopped bass courses which
single. Contemporary accounts do not
s make such things clear; when they do,
idence is sometimes conflicting.
the fretted instruments developed their
idiomatic system of tuning. During the
nth century some maintained a single basic
g, as the lute did: others, like the cittern
uitar, were more variable. Within the
of this book, the aim will be to give the
commonly used tunings rather than a
lete list. Associated with each tuning
n was a method of notation known as
ure. Although this may look rather
licated to the layman, for the performer it
eat deal easier to read than ordinary staff
ion since it actually shows him where to
is fingers. Each line of the stave represents
ourse of strings and a letter or number
tes which fret to use. The rhythm of the
is shown separately above the stave. One
advantage of tablature was the way it
ed the uncertainties of *musica ficta*, the rules

Apollo and the Muses, by Martin De Vos (1532–1605). Notice the mixture of actual renaissance instruments and imaginary classical reconstructions. In the centre is Apollo with his lyre or *kithara.* (Musées Royaux des Beaux-Arts de Belgique, Brussels)

by which certain notes were regularly sharpened or flattened. Another advantage lay in the fact that the notation was based on interval not pitch. A piece of lute music could be played on any size of lute providing that the tuning conformed to the correct series of intervals (it is, of course, essential to know on what tuning the tablature is based). A shortcoming of tablature is that it does not show the duration of notes accurately, but with plucked instruments the sound dies quickly anyway and the general rule was to sustain notes as much as possible, particularly in contrapuntal music. The earliest printed tablature is Francesco Spinacino's *Intabulatura de Lauto Libro Primo*[18] published by Petrucci in 1507, though the tradition clearly goes back long before that. Different countries adopted their own systems of tablature; in 1511 Virdung explained the rather different German tablature system, crediting Conrad Paumann with its invention.[19] For more details the reader is referred to the excellent summaries by

Gerald Hayes[20] and Diana Poulton.[21]

It is evident that professional players of plucked instruments were not restricted to reading from tablature. In Volume II of his *Syntagma Musicum* Praetorius describes situations where the players must have been able to read fluently from staff notation and improvise on the given part as well. He describes the care which must be taken 'when the lute, harp, *chitarron,* and theorbo are used as continuo instruments accompanying one or more voices; for they must at all times produce a firm, full-sounding, and continuous harmony which, as it were, carries the human voices, and they must play now intimately and softly, now strongly and freshly, according to the quality and number of the voices, and also according to the layout and location of the ensemble'.[22]

Ensemble music offered plucked instruments another quite different role too. 'If, however, the lute, theorbo, harp, *chitarron,* etc., are used as obbligato-instruments, then they, as well as

the other obbligato-instruments (which are interchanged and mixed with the voices to no other end than to ornament and embellish these, and, as it were, to flavour and spice them) must make themselves heard in a different manner, and . . . decorate and embellish the melody with variations and alterations of beautiful counterpoints according to the quality of the instrument.'[23]

Praetorius gives a tantalizing example of how plucked instruments could be used together in a grand ensemble. 'Thus I once performed the appealing, immoderately beautiful 7-part motet "Egressus Jesus", by the excellent composer, Giaches de Wert [1535–96], with 2 theorbos, 3 lutes, 2 citterns, 4 harpsichords and virginals, 7 viols, 2 transverse flutes, 2 boys, 1 alto, and *einer grossen Violen (Bass–Geig),* without organ or regal: which gave forth an excellently splendid, lordly resonance, so that, because of the sound of the great number of strings, almost everything in the church vibrated.'[24]

'Gothic' harp, from Glareanus' *Dodecachordon* (1547).

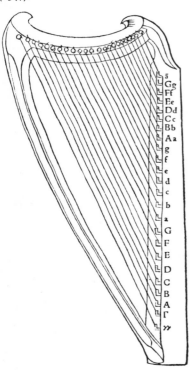

The harp

During the sixteenth century the harp lost its old supremacy among the plucked instruments. This was partly due to the tremendous progress made in construction and playing techniques of the rival lute and keyboard families and partly due to the harp's own limitations as a diatonic instrument, discussed in chapter 4.[25] Whilst it has been suggested[26] that players produced the missing chromatic notes by stopping the strings against the cross bar, this would certainly have damped the resonance of the string and produced a marked contrast in tone, alien to renaissance taste. As with the theory that harpists re-tuned quickly as they went along, it imposed another restriction, playing with one hand only; yet virtually all iconographical evidence from the fifteenth and sixteenth centuries confirms that players used two hands, the right for the upper strings, the left for the lower ones or vice versa.[27]

Two distinct varieties of harp emerged at the end of the Middle Ages – the Gothic and the Irish – and renaissance writers describe them both. Glareanus illustrates the Gothic type in his *Dodecachordon* (1547): he shows an instrument with 24 strings tuned diatonically from F to a″.[28] Praetorius confirms this range, indicating that some harps go no higher than c″.[29] Glareanus' harp is fitted with the traditional 'bray pins', whose buzzing effect evidently went out of fashion during the next hundred years, for Mersenne tells us: 'But it must be observed

that the strings do not touch the pegs at the exit of their holes, as they do when one uses *harpions*, or crooked pegs, which make them nasal. Their use has been abandoned to avoid this imperfection.'[30]

Whilst this type of harp was most often strung with gut,[31] the Irish harp was metal strung. According to Praetorius: 'The Irish harp, *harpa Irlandica* . . . has rather thick brass strings, forty-three in number, and a particularly lovely tone.'[32] The tone of the Irish harp was also praised by Francis Bacon in his *Sylva Sylvarum* published posthumously in 1627: 'No harp hath the sound so melting and prolonged as the Irish harp.'[33] Bacon also noted when writing about 'broken Musick or Consort Musick' that the Irish harp and bass viol sounded well together.[34]

Although Praetorius gives a most improbable tuning for the instrument it does seem likely, as Joan Rimmer has suggested, that by this stage some Irish harps were tuned partially chromatically. A diatonic harp with forty-three strings would otherwise have a range of six octaves, unusual at the time even on keyboard instruments.[35] The typical range of the Irish harp was similar to that of the Gothic instrument, as Vincenzo Galilei tells us in his *Dialogo della musica antica e della moderna* (1581):

'Among the stringed instruments now played in Italy there is first of all the Harp, which is none other than the ancient Cithara with many strings . . . It contains from the lowest note to the highest note more than three octaves.

'This most ancient instrument was brought to us (as Dante commented) from Ireland, where it is excellently made and in great quantities. The people of that island play it a great deal and have done so for many centuries, also it is the special emblem of the realm, where it is depicted and sculptured on public buildings and on coins . . . The harps in use among that people are somewhat bigger than ordinary ones. They have generally strings of brass, with a few of steel in the top register, like the Harpsichord. The players keep the fingernails of both hands rather long, shaping them carefully like the quills of the jacks which strike the strings of the Spinet . . . A few months ago (through the offices of a most courteous Irish gentleman) I carefully examined the stringing of that kind of harp. I find it to be the same as that which, with double the number of strings, was introduced into Italy a few years ago.'[36]

The instrument to which Galilei is referring in that last sentence is the big chromatic harp with two ranks of strings which was introduced into Italy, probably from Flanders, in the middle of the sixteenth century.[37] The demands of renaissance music made a fully chromatic compass desirable, yet with only a single set of

strings a chromatic or semi-chromatic tuning created considerable technical problems for the player. The first answer was to construct an instrument with two parallel rows of strings, one a primary diatonic row, the other a secondary row which included the chromatic notes. Later on in his *Dialogo* Galilei gives a stringing plan for a large harp with fifty-eight strings arranged in two ranks[38] and he describes it as being a common instrument in Italy.[39] The second and in many ways more successful answer was a triple-strung harp on which there were three sets of strings. Joan Rimmer has defined it as follows: 'The two outer ranks are identically tuned to a diatonic scale, the centre rank is tuned to the intervening chromatic notes plus two in each octave identical with the outer ranks. From the beginning its compass has been not less than four octaves and a fifth.'[40]

The triple-strung harp was devised in Italy at the end of the sixteenth century. According to Mersenne: 'I have also been advised that the harp with three courses was invented thirty or forty years ago by Mr Luc Anthoine Eustache, Neapolitan gentleman and high officer of Pope Paul V, and that Mr Orazio Michi has brought this instrument to its perfection, which he plays very excellently.'[41] To both double-strung and triple-strung harp the name *arpa doppia* was given,[42] probably because of the increased size and compass rather than in the sense of being double-strung.

Freed from the centuries-old restriction of

diatonicism the new double harp became a useful continuo instrument and was include[d] the ensembles which played for the court entertainments and *intermedii*, though with nothing like the regularity of the other pluc[ked] or keyboard instruments. Amongst the mo[st] lavish of all the *intermedii* were those which took place in Florence in 1589, to celebrate [the] wedding of Ferdinand de Medici and Chris[tine] of Lorraine. The continuo instruments incl[uded] double harps as well as various sizes of lutes[,] chitarrone, and organ.[43] Monteverdi not on[ly] included *Un Arpa doppia* in his score of *Orfe[o]* (1607) but entrusted it with one of the brilli[ant] series of obbligati which embroider Orfeo'[s] famous 'Possente spirto' in Act III. This bea[utiful] and expressive solo part, with its fully writt[en] out ornaments, gives some idea of contemp[orary] extemporized practice and the virtuosity of which the double harp was capable. It expl[oits] an exceptionally wide compass from G′ to [...]

Amongst the fairly scanty repertoire for various sixteenth- and seventeenth-century harps, the following may be mentioned:
1. The solo *tiento* for harp or organ by Alon[so] Mudarra, published in his *Tres Libros* (1546[).]
2. The Robert ap Huw Manuscript *c.*1613, [a] cross-section of Welsh harp music written [in] tablature.[46]
3. The *Mottects or Grave Chamber Musique* [...] by Martin Peerson, in which the title page includes the Irish harp as an alternative 'for [...] want of organs' along with the virginals,

Irish harp, from Praetorius' *Syntagma Musicum*.

Triple harp, from Mersenne's *Harmonie Universelle*. Only two sets of strings are visib[le]

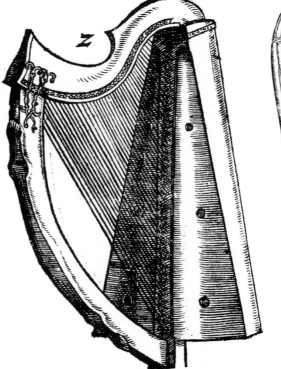

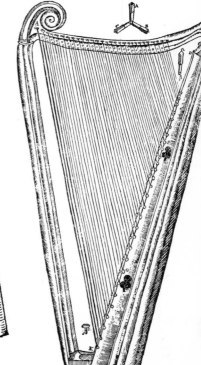

lute, and bandora.[47]

he consorts of William Lawes, for the
uisite combination of violin, viol, theorbo,
harp.[48]

st as earlier Irish harps survived as a folk
ument both in Ireland and (as the clarsach)
otland, so from the end of the seventeenth
ury the history of the triple harp belongs
ost exclusively to Wales.[49]

lute

lst all the lute's regular names in European
uages are derived from the Arabic *al 'ud*
, *Laute, lauto, láud,* etc.), some theorists
raetorius) use the Latin word *testudo*
rtoise), which was originally applied to
ncient Greek lyre with a tortoise-shell
ator. During the Renaissance the lute
estionably occupied a special place of
ur, second only to the human voice. It was
ourtly instrument *par excellence* and its
toire was enormous, only a tiny proportion
regularly heard today. The replacement
e old plectrum technique by the use of the
rs, coupled with the craftsmanship of the
ssance lute-makers, made possible a new
acy and expressiveness in playing, a breadth
hnique, and a range of nuances never
ble before. The renaissance lute became
rincipal instrument for all kinds of what
ight properly term chamber music. Its
ds were soft, intimate, and exquisite: it was
eal partner for the human voice, a perfect
h for other soft instruments, and the most
ent of all solo instruments. The importance
e lute in renaissance music is reflected by
ther arts. Philosophers discussed it,
ists endowed it with the power of Apollo's
poets praised it, and painters never ceased
delight in depicting it in a wide variety of
– the angel concerts of the fifteenth
ry,[50] the homely scenes of domestic
c-making of the Flemish School, the
tuous canvases of Titian, Tintoretto, and
ns, and the narcissistic portraits of
vaggio. In literature the lute became the
dary instrument of Orpheus, with which
armed all Nature and attempted to lead
dice out of Hell: its noble classical associa-
are often invoked at moments of high
dy. In the last act of Thomas Heywood's
oman killed with Kindness the heroine says:

w the lute. Oft have I sung to thee:
re both out of tune, both out of time . . .
reak this lute upon my coach's wheel
e last music that I e'er shall make;
s my husband's gift, but my farewell
earth's joy . . .[51]

ually the lute had a role in comedy; its
ous associations (often displayed in
ings as well) can be detected in Thomas

Dekker's *The Honest Whore* and John Marston's
The Dutch Courtesan, both of whose heroines
are professional lutenists of a certain kind. In
Shakespeare's *The Taming of the Shrew* both
Katharina and Bianca take lute lessons: the
disastrous progress of Katharina's lesson is
ruefully described by Hortensio:

I did but tell her she mistook her frets,
And bowed her hand to teach her fingering;
When, with a most impatient, devilish spirit,
'Frets, call you these?' quoth she, 'I'll fume
    with them.'
And with that word she struck me on the head,
And through the instrument my pate made way,
And there I stood amazed for a while,
As on a pillory, looking through the lute;
While she did call me rascal fiddler
And twangling Jack, with twenty such vile
    terms,
As had she studied to misuse me so.[52]

It is hardly surprising that the lute is so
commonly referred to in Elizabethan and
Jacobean literature since it was England which
saw the finest flowering of lute music and
produced the greatest lutenist composer, John
Dowland (1563–1626). His strange melancholic
genius was perfectly suited to the medium of
lute songs and solos and as both composer and
performer he was celebrated at home and
abroad. According to Richard Barnfield's
sonnet 'If music and sweet poetry agree':

Dowland to thee is dear; whose heavenly touch
Upon the lute, doth ravish human sense.[53]

Much of Dowland's early career was spent on
the continent. He played at the courts of the
Duke of Brunswick, the Landgrave of Hesse,
and the Grand Duke of Tuscany. From 1598 to
1606 he was intermittently in the service of the
King of Denmark, at an unheard-of rate of pay,
and in 1612 he became one of James I's lutenists.
Although Dowland initiated a whole series of
song publications starting with the *First Book of
Songs* in 1597,[54] surprisingly little of his solo lute
music appeared in print during his lifetime.
Thanks to the work of Diana Poulton we now
have not only a full-length account of
Dowland's life and music[55] but a complete
edition of his solo compositions as well.[56]

TOP RIGHT
*The Ambassadors Jean de Dinteville and Georges
de Selve,* by Hans Holbein (1477–1543). The
picture shows two renaissance noblemen, with
various books and instruments symbolic of
renaissance humanism and learning. Naturally
the lute takes pride of place. (National Gallery,
London)
RIGHT
The lute player, by Caravaggio (1573–1610).
(The Hermitage, Leningrad)

The work of Dowland and his numerous English contemporaries marks the zenith of lute music composition, often referred to as The Golden Age. But as with the English madrigal, the development was late and comparatively short-lived. For the beginnings of the tradition

Giovanni Antonio Terzi,[59] published in 1593 and 1599, while the French predilection for the *air de cour* (graceful song with lute accompaniment) is first shown by Adrian le Roy's publication of 1571. As Michael Prynne has pointed out,[60] the interchange between

Concert with chitarrone and lute (1624), by Gerard van Honthorst. The lute is often found in the hands of courtesans: this painting certainly emphasizes the instrument's seductive qualities. (The Louvre, Paris)

Lute solo: *Orlando Sleepeth,* by John Dowland. Modern edition by Diana Poulton and Basil Lam (Faber, 1974), showing transcription in modern staff notation (above) and original tablature (below).

we must look to Italy, where Petrucci issued the first printed books of lute music in Venice in 1507–8. One of them, the *Intabulatura de Lauto* (1508)[57] by Joan Ambrosio Dalza, consists mostly of dances, some of them arranged in suites. There are duets as well as solos and a number of free improvisatory pieces called either *tastar de corde* or *recercar*. Italy remained the most fruitful source of lute music for the first half of the sixteenth century and the work of Francesco da Milano[58] is outstanding. It is noteworthy that at this stage over half the printed music consisted of arrangements of vocal pieces; later on, more idiomatic forms such as the prelude and fantasy became more important. By the end of the century the lute repertory had become thoroughly international and was dominated by the three main schools: Italian, French, and English. The Italian solo style is well represented by the lute books of

countries is illustrated by the Hungarian-Polish lutenist Valentin Bakfark (Greff). His books were published at Lyons (1553), Paris (1564), Cracow (1565), and Antwerp (1569). The collection published by J. B. Besard in 1603 and entitled *Thesaurus harmonicus*[61] is a splendid compendium containing over 400 pieces and representing most of the leading lutenist composers. There were individual schools of lute-making too,[62] although their styles were much less distinct than those of the contemporary keyboard instrument makers. The best known makers worked in Italy, though surprisingly most of them were German. One of the first cities to acquire fame for its lutes was Bologna, with the work of Laux and Sigismond Maler and Hans Frei. Later in the century the lead shifted to Padua and Venice, where the name of Tieffenbrucker is pre-eminent. Members of this family worked in both cities and more surviving

lutes are ascribed to the Paduan Wendelin Tieffenbrucker than to any other old maker. However, not all of these may be genuine;[63] precious few sixteenth-century lutes have survived in their original playing condition and a number of forgeries are known to exist. The Kunsthistorisches Museum, Vienna, houses a particularly fine collection of old lutes.

The delicacy and expressiveness of renaissance lute music is allied to the incredibly light construction of the instrument. The flat table, or belly, is usually made of pine, planed to as little as one sixteenth of an inch in thickness. Its most obvious feature is the carved circular sound-hole or 'rose', though equally important acoustically are the wooden bars (six or more in number) glued underneath the table to strengthen it and increase the resonance; much of the lute-maker's skill lies in the barring and in the finish of the table. The pear-shaped back

is built up of a series of ribs, shaped and ben over a mould, and then glued together edge edge. Usually made of sycamore (though c yew, and cypress are used as well), the ribs a incredibly thin, often no more than one thi second of an inch in thickness. A well made is so sensitive that it literally trembles in resp to the touch.[64] Of necessity the stringing m be light too, since the delicate body is unabl withstand the strain of a dozen or more stri at any kind of high tension. With the exige of modern concert giving in mind, some of today's lutes are rather more heavily built a tightly strung. Such instruments can produ wide range of dynamics and project their so well in a large hall. They demand a rather aggressive finger technique, however, more that of the modern Spanish guitar than the renaissance lute, and the high string-tension makes some of the intricacies of sixteenth- a

teenth-century ornamentation well-nigh
ssible. The old writers make clear that the
ing or 'striking' action involved the soft
f the tip of the thumb or fingers, not the
and the movements of both hands,
er stopping or striking, should be as small
sible. To this end the little finger should
ghtly on the belly or near the treble end
bridge, discouraging any grand sweep of
nd across the strings. A most important
e of lute playing was to allow the strings
onate freely after they had been struck
avoid unnecessary damping. According
*Necessary Observations belonging to the Lute
te playing* by Jean-Baptiste Besard, in the
ation by either Robert or John Dowland
Varietie of Lute-Lessons (1610): '... nothing
re sweet, then when those parts . . . are
y combined, which cannot be if the
s be suddenly taken from the strings: for
oice perisheth suddenly, when the
ing thereof is ended . . . Therefore keep
fingers in what strings soever you strike
ially when you strike the bass) whilst the
fingers are stopping other stops, and
ve them not till another note come,
doth immediately fall upon another
or some other part.'[65]

the time of the first lute publications at
ginning of the sixteenth century the lute
had become fairly standardized in
ing and tuning. Virdung,[66] followed by
s of other writers in the next hundred
[67] explains the typical stringing in pairs
urses' tuned G, c, f, a, d', g'. This tuning
ne known as the 'old' tuning or *vieil*
; it is sometimes given a tone higher.
ng's illustration shows that the top course
gle, not double, and this is confirmed as
1596 by William Barley in his *New
of Tabliture*[68]. From Thomas Robinson's
le of Musicke*[69] (1603) and Robert
and's *Varietie of Lute-Lessons*[14] (1610),
ver, we may infer that the treble course
ometimes double-strung in England in the
years of the seventeenth century. John
and's *Other Necessary Observations . . .*
he contributed to his son's book include
struction: 'First set on your Trebles which
be strained neither too stiff nor too slack,
such a reasonable height, that they may
r a pleasant sound.'[70]

is method of tuning the top course of the
high as it will go and then adjusting the
strings in accordance with it, rather than
g to tune the instrument to a specific
was a very practical one. The treble string
vn as a 'minikin') required particularly
ut and was very liable to break: nowadays
players use the more durable nylon for all
rings. Whilst the standard lutes were G
lutes, with the pitch roughly equivalent

to that given in the tuning given above, there
were a number of smaller and larger sizes all
tuned to the same series of intervals. Praetorius[71]
explains that an ensemble of lutes can offer as
many as seven different pitches. He lists them
as follows, giving the note to which the treble
string should be tuned in each case.

1. small octave lute   d'' or c''
2. small descant lute   b'
3. descant lute   a'
4. usual choir or alto lute   g'
5. tenor lute   e'
6. bass lute   d'
7. large octave bass lute   g

Since *covered* gut strings were not developed
until the later seventeenth century the bass
strings were rather dull and muddy in quality,
and in the sixteenth century it was customary
to tune the lowest three courses in octaves rather
than unisons. Thus, the most typical sixteenth-
century lute tuning was as follows (the roman
numerals designate the courses):

I   II   III   IV   V   VI

Typical lute tuning.

Dowland and other later players abandoned
the octave tuning although it appears not to
have entirely died out.[72]

From the many published instructions for
playing the lute[73] two German authors emerge
as being particularly significant. The Nuremberg lute maker and player Hans Gerle
included two tutors (1532 and 1533) amongst his
series of publications whilst Hans Newsidler's
Ein Newgeordnet Künstlich Lautenbuch[74] (1536) is
interesting for its series of graded pieces. Both
Gerle and Newsidler seem to have provided
the material for later books of instruction.
From the theoretical as well as practical point of
view Vincenzo Galilei's *Il Fronimo*,[75] first
published in 1568 and revised and re-issued in
1584, is particularly valuable. Galilei was a
member of the Camerata, the courtly circle of
poets and musicians who met regularly at the
house of Count Bardi in Florence in the 1580s
and 90s. *Il Fronimo*, besides emphasizing the
classical background of renaissance musical
thought, makes satirical reference to the contemporary additions to the lute which Galilei
says will soon require as large a hand as
Artaxerxes'.[76]

Eumatio: Dite per fede vostra quello rispose.
Fronimo: Mi disse esser si ritrouate, per hauere
nel Liuto come nell organo, il pedale.
Eumatio: Ha, ha, ha![77]

(*Eumatio*: Tell me, by your faith, what he replied.
Fronimo: He said he had discovered a way to
have a pedal on the lute, as on the organ.
Eumatio: Ha, ha, ha!)

Whilst Virdung makes clear that the six-
course lute was standard, he also mentions the
existence of five and seven courses. As the
century progressed a seventh course became
more common: it was usually tuned to D, a
fourth below the bass course (sometimes a tone
or a fifth below). From the end of the sixteenth
century onwards three extra courses of bass

The Lutenist: engraving by Ludwig Büsinck
(1630). Notice that here the lute's top course is
double-strung. (Rijksmuseum, Amsterdam)

strings are found, tuned to C or D, E or E♭, and
F. By 1630 eight courses were common. Such
developments are symptomatic of the lute's
struggle to keep pace with the new developments in music, particularly the demands of
continuo. Alternative tunings to the *vieil accord*
proliferated in equal measure. The *Trésor
d'Orphée*[77] published by the French lutenist
Francisque in 1600 contains several pieces
marked 'à cordes avallées' (literally 'with
lowered strings'). The new tunings seem to have
originated in France and they include a 'Sharp
Tune' of G c f a c' e', a 'Flat Tune' of G c f
a♭' c' e♭', and an *accord nouveau* or *extraordinaire*
A d f a d' f'.[78] Mattheson's complaint[79] that a
lutenist spent most of his life tuning rather than
actually playing reflects the inconvenient
necessity of regular re-tunings, which upset the
stability of the instrument. During the seventeenth century the lute's status was gradually

Lute with nine courses by Wendelio Venere,
Padua (1584). (Collection of Robert Spencer)

Lute with extra bass strings ascribed to Wendelin
Tieffenbrucker, Padua (c.1600). (Music-Historical
Museum, Stockholm)

undermined, and it was eventually ousted in all its various roles by the baroque keyboard instruments, which could cope more easily with continuo and more brilliantly with the new solo style.

One of the best known seventeenth-century books of instruction is Thomas Mace's *Musick's Monument*[80] (1676). Mace, a great enthusiast for his instrument, resisted the lute's inevitable decline, and demands:

What is the cause, my Dear-Renowned Lute
That art of late so Silent and so Mute?

To which his lute replies:

The World is grown so Slight, full of New
    Fangles
And takes their chief Delight in Jingle-Jangles.[81]

Yet the lute which Mace advocates is already well removed from that of Dowland's time, being the so-called 'French lute', with two peg-boxes and a total of twelve courses tuned to the 'Flat Tune'.

Theorbo and chitarrone

Dissatisfaction with the sound produced by the lowest courses of the lute and the desire to improve and extend its bass register are evident as early as the mid-sixteenth century. The larger *theorbo* and still larger *chitarrone* were developed specifically as *accompanying* instruments: both have a particularly resonant lower register, made possible by the longer fingerboard and greater string length. There are two pegboxes, one for the stopped strings, the other for the extra basses which extend the range downwards diatonically. The wider spacing of the frets on the fingerboard meant that neither instrument was so well suited to the rapid fingerwork and changes of position typical of solo lute music. Praetorius writes about both instruments under the name 'theorbo'; whilst we make a specific distinction between them today, early seventeenth-century writers regarded them as interchangeable. 'Like the *viola bastarda* the theorbo is used as an accompanying instrument for sopranos and tenors, for no coloraturas and ornamentations can be executed on it because of its wide size and fretting; and thus quite a simple finger technique must be used on it. The theorbo is also very lovely to hear together with other instruments in full ensemble and whenever else it is used together with bass instruments or in their stead.'[82]

An important feature of tuning distinguishes both theorbo and chitarrone from the lute. Because of the string length it was necessary to tune the top one or two courses an octave *lower* than the corresponding lute tuning. Whilst this is no disadvantage in accompanying, it deprives both instruments of the lute's bright treble register. Nevertheless an interesting solo

repertoire did develop for both instruments, exploiting their special characteristics; despite Praetorius' assertion there is an extensive use of 'coloraturas and ornamentations'. Duets were common too and include Bellerophon Castaldi's *Capricci* (1622) for two theorbos of different sizes. Kapsberger, a German nobleman, produced an impressive series of solo publications for the chitarrone which span a period of nearly forty years, starting with the *Libro Primo d'Intavolatura di chitaroni* (1604). Equally significant are the works of Alessandro Piccinini.[83] He provides some interesting information[84] about playing technique on both lute and chitarrone, describing how to arpeggiate an accompaniment, how to obtain 'sweeter sounds' by plucking half-way between the rose and the bridge (*ie* moving the hand from the standard playing position), and even recommending the use of fingernails.

Of the two instruments, the theorbo appears to have developed first; what is perhaps the earliest mention of the name (as *una tiorba*)

Detail from *The presentation in the Temple*, by Carpaccio (*c.*1455–1526). (Galleria Accademia, Venice)

occurs in an inventory of the Accademia Filamonica, Verona, in 1544.[85] The name (French, *théorbe, tuorbe*; German, *Theorb*; Italian, *tiorba, tuorba*) may derive from the Arabic *tarab*.[86] Its origins in Europe are obscure, the invention having having been ascribed to a number of people including Antonio Naldi, who served the Medici family, and a Signor Tiorba about 1600.[86] It seems fairly likely that the initial development took place in Italy. In *Il fronimo* (1584) Vincenzo Galilei described the additional strings on the lute and theorbo as a novelty to which he was opposed.[86] If we are to judge by the account of the seventeenth-century Dr Plume, the arrival of the theorbo in England

Lute and theorbo from Mersenne's *Harmonie Universelle*.

in the midst of the threat of Popish conspiracies was not without incident. 'Inigo Jones first brought the theorbo in England *c. ann.* 1605. At Dover it was thought some engine brought from Popish countries to destroy the King, and he and it sent up to Council Table.'[87] However the portrait of Lady Mary Sidney (*d.* 1586) at Penshurst Place[88] suggests that though Inigo Jones' instrument may have caused a stir, it was not the first of its kind to reach England.

On the theorbo there were normally between fourteen and sixteen courses tuned to the *viel accord,* plus the extra bass strings. Thus Mersenne gives the tuning F', G', A', B', C, D, E, F/, G, c, f, a, d, g, or the same intervals a

tone higher.[88] The strings were normally of gut and both peg-boxes were usually set in the same plane as the fingerboard, instead of being angled back, as on the lute: a mixture of single and double courses was common.[89] Mersenne's illustration shows double stringing through[out] except for the treble course. As a continuo instrument the theorbo proved useful throughout the baroque period. It is regularly mentioned as a alternative to the organ and harpsichord in English song books of the late seventeenth century and Handel scored for *Esther* (1732) and *Athalia* (1733).

Besides the standard theorbo there was a smaller version, the *tiorbino*, of which two les have survived.[90] More important was ...lication of the second peg-box to the ...lf to help cope with the additional bass ...a development which took place ...the seventeenth century. Nomenclature ...s rather confused at this point, but ...temporary names theorbo-lute, *luth* ...and *theorbierte Laute* describe an ...ent which retains the basic tuning of the ...employs the twin peg-box of the theorbo to carry the increased number of bass strings. It was customary to modify old lutes in this way, although surviving examples are comparatively rare.[91]

The largest member of the lute family is usually referred to today as the *chitarrone*;

Chitarrone by Hans Jordan, Markneukirchen (left), showing the curved, ribbed back, and ceterone by Robert Hadaway, Gayton, Norfolk (right), showing the flat back.

...1648), by Laurent de la Hire (1606–56). ...rrone is shown being tuned. (Metropolitan ...m, New York)

confusingly the name is an augmentation of *chitarra*, Italian for guitar. The word *archlute* (French, *archiluth*; German, *Erzlaute*; Italian, *arciliuto*), commonly applied to it today, appears however to have been normally used for the extended lute.[92] Praetorius refers to it as a *Roman theorbo* as well as a chitarrone.[97] Once again the origins of the instrument would appear to lie in Italy, and its use for vocal accompaniment was highly favoured by Italian composers.[93] In his *Le Nuove Musiche* (1602) Caccini stated that 'the chitarrone is better fitted to accompany the voice than any other instrument' and Monteverdi calls for 'Duoi chitaroni' in *L'Orfeo* (1607).[94]

The earliest surviving examples of the chitarrone date from the second half of the sixteenth century, amongst them the magnificent instruments made by Magno Tieffenbrucker in Venice.[95] To avoid inordinate length the bass peg-box is usually doubled back on itself in the form known as a 'swan-head', and as with some of the larger sizes of lute there was often a triple rose instead of a single one. The stringing was variable, though the most common system was six double courses plus eight single basses. Metal was preferred for the basses, though gut as well as metal was used for the fingered courses.[96] For his 'Roman theorbo' Praetorius[97] gives the *vieil accord* with the top two courses down the octave (G, c, f, a, d, g) plus eight basses (F′, G′, A′, B′, C, D, E, F), and this arrangement would seem to be fairly typical.

Mandora, pandurina, colascione, and angélique

Four other members of the lute family should be included here. With the exception of the pandurina they are described in some detail in James Talbot's manuscript[98] and photographs of extant examples are included in Anthony Baines' *European and American Musical Instruments*.[99] Of the four, the mandora is by far the most significant, with a history stretching back at least to the twelfth century. As the reader will remember from chapter 4 (page 25) the mandora is basically a small lute; hence the Latin name sometimes given to it, *testudo minor*. In English the French spelling *mandore* is sometimes used in preference to the Italian *mandora*.[100] According to Trichet the mandora originally had no frets but later acquired nine: formerly four single strings had been common but in his day players had added a fifth or sixth string to produce what was in effect a miniature lute, or *mandore luthée*.[101] Talbot describes an *arch mandore*, a miniature archlute with seven extra basses.[102] Mersenne illustrates an instrument with four single strings, whilst Praetorius gives two tunings for a five-course instrument: c, g, c′, g′, c″ and c, f, c′, f′, c″, though many variants existed. He also mentions a smaller size, the *pandurina,* with four strings tuned to g, d′, g′, d″. He says: 'Some pandurinas have five pairs of strings and can easily be carried inside a coat. In France these instruments are said to be very common, and some musicians are so skilled on them that they can play courantes, voltes, and other French dances and songs of the like . . .'[103] He goes on to say that the pandurina could be played either with the fingers or with a plectrum.

The mandora was normally played with a plectrum and was basically an instrument of popular music-making, ideal for the treble parts of dance music. It was much used in

seventeenth-century Italy and is the ancestor of the later mandolin. Trichet mentions a tutor published by Adrian Le Roy in 1585, though this has unfortunately been lost, together with a volume of mandora tablature by Pierre Brunet (1578).[104] An example of the 'classic' mandora style of the period is provided by the *Tablature de Mandore* (1626), a collection of court dances published by François, Sieur de Chancy, for his employer Cardinal Richelieu.

The *colascione* (French, *colachon*) was a European offshoot of the Eastern long-necked lute.[105] There were two or three single or

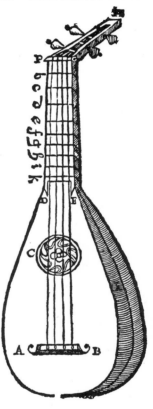

Mandora, from Mersenne's *Harmonie Universelle*.

double courses normally of metal, although gut seems also to have been employed.[106] The disproportionately long neck allowed for as many as 24 movable frets[105] and Mersenne[107] tells us that the belly was sometimes made half of wood and half of parchment, a method of construction still common in the East today. An early example of the colascione, made in Naples, dates from 1535.[108]

The *angélique*, *angelica*, or angel-lute was an archlute with a long neck, sixteen or seventeen single gut strings and two peg-boxes. Its principal feature was that it was tuned diatonically: this supposedly made it easier to play and recommended it to amateurs.[109] Praetorius

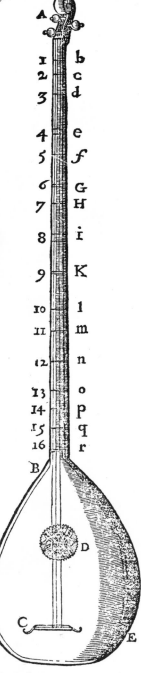

Colascione, from Mersenne's *Harmonie Universelle*.

quite rightly regarded it as no more than a minor novelty though a splendidly decorated *angélique* by Tielke has survived.[110]

The cittern
Although the lute was far and away the most widely used plucked instrument of the Renaissance, the cittern came next to it in popularity. There was an extensive solo repertoire for the instrument, both published and in manuscript,[111] the cittern was frequently depicted by artists,[112] and in Italy at least it was held in as high esteem as the lute.[113] Cittern

music, like lute music, explores a wide range from simple dance tunes and ballad settings to elaborate polyphony; the technique required is every bit as demanding as that of the lute. Moreover, whilst the sixteenth-century lute was largely standardized the cittern was not: the courses varied from four to six in number and there were several 'standard' tunings. The usefulness of the cittern and the respect with which it was regarded can be seen from the number of cittern offspring which proliferated in the second half of the sixteenth century. The ceterone, orpharion, bandora, penorcon, and other more obscure relatives all share essential features of the cittern – robust construction, flat back, metal strings, and fixed frets – and they added considerably to the variety of plucked sounds available. The gut-strung lute and guitar were rather less prodigal in this respect.

It is curious that the cittern's true place in renaissance music has so often been mis-represented. Praetorius describes the four-course cittern as 'a rather ignoble kind of instrument played by cobblers and barbers'[114] and other writers ever since have been content to repeat a similarly one-sided view. It is quite true that in England especially citterns were found in barber's shops to amuse the waiting customers and the instrument's easy availability became a standing joke. Hence Thomas Dekker's jibe in *The Honest Whore*:

'Is she a whore?'
'A barber's cittern for every serving-man to play upon.'[115]

In *The Silent Woman*, Ben Jonson is equally derisive: 'That cursed barber . . . I have married his cittern that's common to all men.'[116] But, as we have already observed, the lute did not entirely escape this sort of association either, and in any case regarding the cittern merely as a barber's shop instrument is rather like thinking of the piano as an instrument only found in public houses. Thanks to recent research the cittern is once more beginning to recover its rightful place amongst the principal plucked instruments of the Renaissance. I am most indebted to James Tyler for allowing me to use material from his forthcoming book on the cittern and its music in this chapter.

As we have seen[117] the cittern first appeared in Italy in medieval times, and throughout its long career it retained a special association with the country of its origin. From the earliest literary references in the Middle Ages it was known as *cetra*, derived from the Greek *kithara*: hence also *cistra* (French), *Cister* (German), *cithren* and other English variants. Emmanuel Winternitz[118] has shown the extent to which the cittern became a classical symbol in both the visual arts and literature: it was regarded as a

revival of the kithara itself, the lyre of classical times. Whilst the early history of the cittern is obscure, information from the sixteenth century is plentiful. In his *Scintille di Musica* of 1533 Lanfranco gives the fundamental tuning for all Italian and English music.

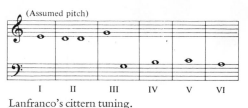

Lanfranco's cittern tuning.

The mixture of single and double courses and the octave tuning for III are unusual, and were later discarded in favour of straightforward unison pairs. Four or five-course citterns used the same tuning, minus the lowest one or two courses. It is interesting that taken in the order III, VI, IV, V, II, I the courses describe a hexachord, the standard scale unit for all western music. Praetorius calls it the 'Old Italian' tuning,[119] though music continued to be written for it as late as 1602. The most curious feature of the cittern of Lanfranco's time (fully allowed for in the tablature) was that the fretting was *diatonic*, not chromatic as on the lute or any other fretted instrument. Tablature for this type of cittern is found as late as the eighteenth century.

Perhaps the most archaic feature of the renaissance cittern was that it retained the old plectrum technique of the Middle Ages. No source before Playford's *Musick's Delight on the Cithren* of 1666 prescribes that the strings should be plucked with the fingers as on the lute. Most instruction books, starting with the earliest surviving cittern tutor, the *Brève et facile Instruction* (c. 1565) of Adrian le Roy, make it clear that the strings should be plucked with a quill plectrum. By the time of Adrian le Roy's publication the cittern had become standardized as a four-course instrument in France and Northern Europe. This is what Praetorius calls the 'French' cittern[120] and the tuning was as follows with triple stringing in the lowest two courses. The fretting however, was still partly diatonic.

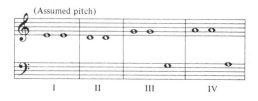

Adrian le Roy's cittern tuning.

In 1574 Paolo Virchi published his *Il Primo Libro . . . Di Citthara* which initiated what amounted to a cittern revival in Italy. The

book's dedication reads: 'The citthara has always stood in some consideration amon[g] people because, being played with a quill[,] a lively and pleasant tone and because it h[as] well-ordered proportion and differs little [from] such instruments as the lute and the harps[ichord] which have already attained perfection. [It] is only now that the citthara begins to del[ight] such noble personages as the Duke of Bav[aria] and the Archduke Ferdinand of the Tyro[l].

Virchi's aim was to elevate the cittern t[o a] new level of artistic appreciation. His mu[sic is] predominantly of a serious nature, deman[ding a] technique of the highest order. The instr[ument] for which he wrote was a six-course instr[ument].

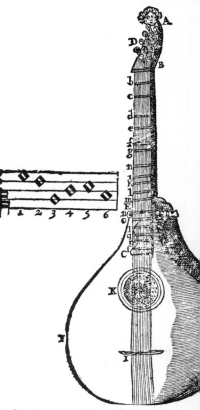

Italian six-course cittern, from Mersenne's *Harmonie Universelle*.

English-style four-course cittern by Richar[d] Margulies, New York.

ly chromatic fretting on which the
wo courses were true bass strings. The
s as follows:

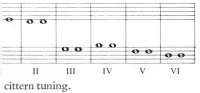

| | II | III | IV | V | VI |

cittern tuning.

ed seventh course (tuned to G) is also
ned. By a great stroke of fortune a
cent six-course cittern made by Virchi's
Girolamo has been preserved in perfect
on and is now in the Kunsthistorisches
m, Vienna. It was made for Archduke
nd in 1574, the very year in which *Il
ibro* was published. Since Girolamo
was one of the leading makers of the
n school, along with Gasparo da Salò
ovanni Paolo Maggini, it is hardly
ng that his craftsmanship is exquisite,
ng the perfect vehicle for his son's music.
the older style citterns, which were
out of the solid, this instrument was a
redesigned and 'modernized' multi-
l construction.[121] The scrolls at the

made by Girolamo Virchi, Brescia
Kunsthistorisches Museum, Vienna)

shoulders, though less pronounced than in
earlier instruments, are still a reminder of the
Greek kithara, with its arms and yoke. This
refined version of the cittern evidently caught on
rapidly; according to Vincenzo Galilei, writing
in 1581: 'Today, those citterns made in
Brescia are supposed to be of the highest
repute. They are much used and appreciated
among the nobility and, so it is said by their
makers, perhaps a revival of the antique
kithara.'[122]

Whilst Paolo Virchi's book is arguably the
greatest collection of cittern music, it is closely
rivalled by a number of English publications[123]
in spite of the barber's-shop tradition. Although

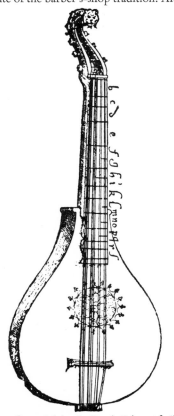

Cittern from Adrian Le Roy's *Brève et facile
instruction*, Paris (1565). Notice the triple stringing
in the bottom two courses.

he wrote for the more restricted four-course
cittern (in the tuning inherited from Lanfranco)
Anthony Holborne (*The Cittharn Schoole,
1597*[124]) provides an eloquent testimonial to the
skill of English cittern players. As in Virchi's
music there are some wide leaps and awkward
stretches for the left hand, which has to ascend
to the dizzy heights of the eighteenth fret.
Some of Holborne's pieces have a separate
bass part (probably intended for a bass viol)
which complements the cittern part and avoids
the chord inversions which occur with the
four-course cittern's re-entrant tuning.

Galliard for cittern and bass by Anthony
Holborne. Modern edition by Masakata
Kanazawa (Harvard UP, 1973), showing original
tablature (above) and transcription in modern
staff notation, together with separate bass part
(below).

as early as 1524 when the Duke of Mantua ordered several *citaroni*,[126] but there is no firm evidence before the end of the sixteenth century. Agazzari (1607)[127] mentions the ceterone as a useful instrument for a continuo ensemble, and in the 1615 edition of *Orfeo* Monteverdi lists 'duoi ceteroni' as well as 'duoi chitaroni'. Praetorius mentions 'die grosse cither/Italis ceterone' in *Syntagma Musicum* Volume III.[128] In Volume II he describes a twelve-course cittern which 'produced a strong and magnificent sound like a harpsichord'.[129] He gives the tuning as: e♭, B♭, f, c, g, d, a, e, / b, g, d', e'. There were a number of alternative methods, mostly using the traditional re-entrant tuning. The extent to which courses were single or double is uncertain.

Bandora and orpharion

'In the fourth year of Queen Elizabeth, John Rose, dwelling in Bridewell, devised and made an instrument with wire strings, commonly called the Bandora, and left a son, far excelling himself in making Bandores, Voyall de Gamboes, and other instruments.'[130]

like a lute, but it is tuned differently and the top strings of the lute.'

The bandora was in fact a bass instrument with a sonorous quality which perfectly complements the bright tone of the citte the broken consort. It was regularly used accompanying the voice, as in Anthony Munday's *A Banquet of Daintie Conceits* (published to be sung 'either to the lute, b virginalles or anie other instrument' or N Peerson's *Mottects, or Grave Chamber Mu* (1630) 'which for want of organs, may b performed on virginals, base-lute, bando Irish harpe'. There is a quantity of solo ba music too,[133] always distinguishable by it individual system of tuning. Whilst the v question of octave doubling remains unsettled,[134] the normal tuning was C, D, G for a six-course instrument. In practice, it well to tune the lowest pairs of strings in octaves as shown below.

By the end of the sixteenth century a s course was added in the bass, tuned to G'. bandora had fifteen frets and a characteris gently scalloped silhouette. The origin of

Ceterone by Robert Hadaway, Gayton, Norfolk; copy of the instrument by Gironimo Campi, in the Museo Bardini, Florence.

Bandora by Donald Gill, Fleet, Hants. For convenience of tuning the instrument has been fitted with machine-heads (like those of the modern guitar) instead of pegs.

Besides its solo repertoire and its role in the broken consort, the cittern was also used as a melodic instrument, as an alternative to the treble violin or viol. In his *Del sonare sopra il basso* (1607) Agostino Agazzari said that the cittern was harmonically incomplete, but best suited for *melodic* ornamentation.[125] With its plectrum to help etch out a solo line, the cittern was one of the last plucked instruments to preserve its old medieval function as a monophonic instrument.

The ceterone

Because of the inconsistency of spelling in renaissance times it was customary until recently to identify the *ceterone* with the *chitarrone*. However, the ceterone is in fact a true bass cittern, with a flat back and robust construction: an excellent example by Gironimo Campi is preserved in the Museo Bardini, Florence. Like the chitarrone, the ceterone has a number of additional unstopped bass strings and is particularly suitable for continuo. It may date from

Thus the birth of the bandora is chronicled in Stow's *Annals*, the date firmly fixed as 1561. Four years later *bandores* were among the instruments used in the interludes to a production of Gascoignes's play *Jocasta*,[131] whilst in 1572 it was proposed that there should be a teacher of music 'to play the lute, the bandora and the cittern' in the projected Queen Elizabeth's Academy.[132] Praetorius confirms that the bandora was an English invention and adds: 'It has six and sometimes seven courses

Typical bandora tuning.

name is uncertain: Donald Gill has sugges that it may derive from the Spanish *bandu* flat-backed instrument mentioned as early the fourteenth century (as *mandurria*[136]). Ir time of Juan Bermudo[137] (1555) the *bandu*

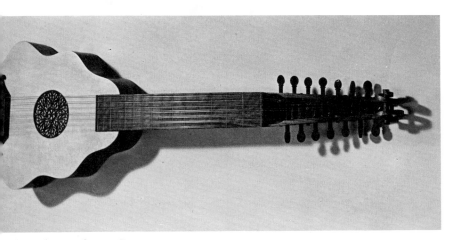

on by Robert Hadaway, Gayton,
, based on the measurements of the
on by John Rose. (Collection of Anthony

nes had five strings and fifteen frets, and
ssibly have been the starting point for
lish instrument.

ugh no English bandora has survived,
arion by John Rose is extant,[138] long
d at Helmingham as a gift of Queen
h I. This remarkable instrument
ohn Rose as a persuasive advocate of
ung instruments: he thoroughly
od the advantages of wire stringing
e more temperamental gut, and the way
n the sturdier flat-backed construction
ithstand the tension of wire strings. His
ents went far beyond the stage of mere
nentation. The bandora and orpharion
tioned as alternative or obligatory
ents in nineteen music books published
n 1588 and 1630;[139] in thirty-two house-
ventories made between 1565 and 1648
dora and orpharion occur as frequently
te.[140] The instruments were regularly
ogether; Drayton mentions them in a
f 1590[141] and in his New Booke of
e (1596) William Barley describes the
ouch required by the orpharion and
a, differing from that of the lute. The
must be 'easily drawn over the strings,
suddenly gripped, or sharply stroken
te is: for if ye should do so, then the
ings would clash or jarre together the
inst the other ... Therefore it is meet
observe the difference of the stroke.'[142]
orpharion and bandora have a basically
shape and structure, both having fifteen
d an ingenious method of string
nent. The bridge is fixed, not movable
e cittern, and the strings run over a
etal saddle set into the bridge and are
d to little metal pegs driven into the
de of the bridge. The main difference
n the two instruments lies in their size

and tuning. The smaller orpharion was the
wire-strung equivalent of the lute and was
tuned in exactly the same way. Initially it had
six courses and a tuning of G, c, f, a, d', g', but
by 1600 a seventh course had been added and
thereafter the orpharion's tuning became as
variable as that of the lute. Since the lute and
orpharion share the same tuning they also share
the same tablature. Consequently, whilst there
is no specific solo repertory for the orpharion,
as there is for the bandora, virtually the whole
of the lute repertoire is available and appropriate to it. No less than twelve books of lute
tablature published between 1579 and 1622
specify the orpharion as an alternative and as
Donald Gill says: 'On the evidence of these
printed music books it is clear that we are no
longer justified in thinking of the vast bulk of
surviving MS tablatures solely in terms of the
gut-strung lute. We must think of it as much in
terms of the wire-strung orpharion with its very
different tonal qualities and general characteristics.'[143]

The lute and orpharion make particularly
effective partners in the extensive lute duet
repertoire. The contrast in timbre gives an
additional spice to the music and helps to make
the details of imitation clear to the listener. The
'stately' orpharion, as Barley calls it, is a superb
solo instrument in its own right and deserves
much wider recognition. An ingenious feature
is the way the bridge, frets, and nut were sometimes set obliquely so as to shorten the treble
strings but give extra length in the bass. This
experimental feature was also applied to the
bandora.

The development of the bandora and
orpharion is basically an English phenomenon.
However at the end of the sixteenth century
in France there are a number of references to
the *pandore*[144] (this seems to have been the

usual French word) and the Trichet MS (c. 1640)
contains a section devoted to 'La Pandore et
l'Orpharion'. Both instruments were known to
Praetorius, almost certainly at first hand, and
they turn up sporadically on the continent (as
in England) for a century or more after their
invention.

Penorcon, poliphant, and stump

Brief mention may be made here of three
rather obscure relatives of the cittern of which
no specimens have survived. The *penorcon* is
mentioned only by Praetorius and is apparently
somewhere in between an orpharion and a
bandora. 'The Penorcon is an instrument of
almost the same kind [as the bandora] only its
body is a little broader than that of the bandora,
and its fingerboard is quite broad, so that nine
courses of strings can be strung over it. In
length it is somewhat shorter than the bandora
and longer than an orpharion.'[146]

According to John Playford[147] the *poliphant*
(or *polyphone*) and *stump* were invented c.1600 by
Daniel Farrant. In the *Introduction to the Skill
of Music* (1683) Playford says: 'I have been

Bandora (1), Orpharion (2), and Penorcon (3)
from Praetorius' *Syntagma Musicum*.
BELOW RIGHT
Instrument resembling the description of a
poliphant, by Wendelin Tieffenbrucker, Padua
(c.1590). (Kunsthistorisches Museum, Vienna)

informed by an ancient Musician and her
Servant that Queen Elizabeth did often recreate
herself on an Excellent Instrument called the
Poliphant, not much unlike a Lute, but strung
with wire ...'[148]

Whilst Donald Gill believes that the instrument referred to here is more likely to have been
an orpharion,[149] the poliphant certainly did
exist. It seems to have been an attempt to
produce some kind of cross between the
bandora and the harp, and accounts by James
Talbot, Randle Holme, and Francis Prujeane
agree on a total of about forty strings.[150] Its
range would appear to have been almost
entirely diatonic.[151] The so-called 'bandora' by
Wendelin Tieffenbrucker now in the
Kunsthistorisches Museum, Vienna, corresponds to the various surviving descriptions of
the poliphant. It has three sets of strings. On the
bass side a curving harp-like frame supports
twenty basses, while on the treble side across
the left side of the belly are fifteen diatonic
strings.[152]

Of the stump there are no surviving examples
or descriptions though the name does suggest
a small instrument. One piece of stump music
is extant, however, entitled *Alman R. Johnson
to the stump by F. P.*[153] It demands seven fingered
courses, tuned to the old lute tuning, plus
eight open basses, giving the impression that
the stump was a wire-strung equivalent of
the theorbo.[154] James Talbot does mention a

variety of orpharion which 'like the English Theorbo' carries '5 . . . rankes of open Basses'.[155] As Donald Gill says, there is nothing to suggest that the stump was a curiosity like the poliphant.[155]

Vihuela and guitar

The sixteenth-century ancestors of the guitar differ significantly from the modern 'classical' or Spanish guitar and certain features link them closely with the other fretted instruments of the Renaissance. Instead of fixed metal frets and single strings the early guitar and vihuela had tied-on gut frets and lightly strung double courses of gut strings which produced a tone nearer to that of the lute than the modern guitar. Players read from tablature just as lutenists did and had a wide and varied repertoire to draw on. Whilst the vihuela was a sophisticated instrument of courtly society, the guitar belongs to the more popular realms of music-making and between them the two instruments covered the gamut of sixteenth-century instrumental forms. One or two contemporary writers emphasize the fact that the vihuela and guitar share the same basic design, the chief difference being the stringing. In 1544 Miguel de Fuenllana wrote of the 'vihuela a cuatro ordenes que dizen guitarra' (the four-course vihuela called guitar)[156] whilst in the following year Juan Bermudo stated that it was only necessary to remove the top and bottom courses of a vihuela in order to transform it into a guitar.[156] He does also say, however, that the guitar was shorter (*mas corto*)[157] and the difference of size does seem to have been pronounced, the vihuela being generally much larger than the guitar. In any case the careers of the two instruments were so distinct that they are best dealt with separately.

The Spanish word *vihuela*, like the Italian *viola*, was a generic term for all stringed instruments, whether plucked or bowed, and the different types were distinguished by various qualifications, thus:

vihuela de arco for the bowed types
vihuela de peñola (or *de péndola*) for the plectrum-plucked types
vihuela de mano for the finger-plucked types.[158]

It was this last name (often shortened simply to *vihuela*) which came to refer specifically to the type of six-course guitar discussed here. The career of the vihuela was unique among renaissance instruments. Whilst its use was restricted entirely to Spain and to a certain extent Southern Italy, and to a relatively short period of time, in its heyday it enjoyed a prestige and a popularity accorded elsewhere only to the lute. During the years 1536 to 1576 seven major publications of vihuela music appeared in Spain,[159] representing nearly all the

Orpheus playing the vihuela, from Luis de Milàn's *El Maestro*.
RIGHT
Guitar by Belchoir Diaz (1581). (Royal College of Music)

principal Spanish composers. They show that the vihuela excelled both as a virtuoso soloist and an elegant accompanist, with a repertoire embracing elaborate fantasias and intabulations of ensemble music as well as numerous *villancicos*, *romances*, and *canciones*, many of which rank amongst the finest songs of the age. The vihuela was even accorded the lute's classical attributes; Juan Bermudo tells it was invented by Mercury,[160] Luis de Milán shows it in the hands of Orpheus,[161] and the fact that the lute is referred to as the *vihuela de Flandes*[162] (Flemish vihuela) suggests that to some extent the Spaniards regarded the lute as a foreign instrument.

It is fitting that the first, and in many ways the best, of the vihuela publications should have come from the hands of a nobleman. Luis de Milán[168] (*c.*1500–*c.*1562) grew up in Valencia at the court of Germaine de Foix, niece of Louis XII and the second wife of Ferdinand of Aragon. His interest in current aristocratic pastimes is reflected in his first published work, the *Libro de motes de damas y cavalleros* (1535); this consists of instructions for a courtly party game of an amorous nature involving mottos and forfeits. Milán also produced a Spanish version of Castiglione's famous book, issued in 1561 as *El Cortesano*. His one musical publication, the *Libro de música de vihuela de mano intitulado El Maestro*[164] (1536) contains the first solo songs ever printed in Spain and was one of the most helpful and instructive of all renaissance instrumental tutors. The title *El Maestro* means

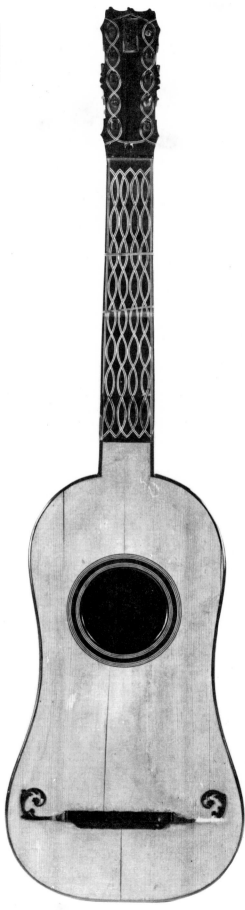

literally 'The Teacher', and the book is arranged for a beginner on the vihuela, has to master twenty-two fantasies and pavans before attempting to accompany first song. Amongst various suggestions performance, Milán includes the first in of tempo in the history of music.

The standard tuning for the vihuela corresponds to that of the lute: the *vieil* of G, c, f, a, d', g'. Milán and other write make it clear that the vihuela varied in si that consequently there was no fixed pit the instrument. In *El Maestro*[165] Milán d how to select strings appropriate to the s the instrument and then start by tuning treble course to the pitch which suited it Whilst the treble course could be either or double, the lower courses were all do ones, unisons or octaves, like the lower courses on the lute.[166] Milán's instructio for a vihuela with ten frets. It is curious only one vihuela has been preserved fro Renaissance[167] and that vihuelas are illus comparatively rarely. As a result it is dif be sure what the most common size was though clearly it was larger than the typ four-course guitar. Both Milán and Ber show instruments of about the same size modern guitar whilst the one surviving is larger still. This very beautiful instrun has a flat back, shallow sides about half t depth of a modern guitar, a gently incur waist, and a belly decorated with five ro

By the end of the sixteenth century th vihuela was already on the wane, and du the following century its history gradua merges with that of the guitar. By the ye the guitar had achieved an extraordinary of popularity throughout Europe. As Ja Tyler has pointed out,[170] the extent to w the renaissance guitar and its music are n today is altogether surprising considerin immense vogue which exists for the late 'classical' instrument. Whilst most of the contents of the seven vihuela books are a today in one form or another,[159] the twe publications for four-course guitar[171] wh appeared during the sixteenth century ha been virtually ignored. A certain amoun confusion has arisen through the various which were applied to the guitar, mostly stemming from the Greek *kithara*. The It *chitarra,* the Spanish *guitarra,* and the Fre *guiterre* are the most commonly found na from the latter comes the anglicized *gitte* The sixteenth-century gittern, however, mentioned as *gitteron* as early as 1547 in Henry VIII's Inventory,[173] is quite a diffe instrument from the medieval gittern an name refers, like the other names mentio above, to the small four-course guitar. Pl still uses the name in his *A Booke of New*

Cithern and Gittern (1652). Praetorius, altogether less reliable about plucked instruments than about other types, is very [confusi]ng on the subject of guitars. He uses the [name q]uintern for the four-course guitar,[174] a [am]biguous name also used for the gittern, [citte]rn and lute.[175]

[As w]ith the vihuela, our knowledge of the [gu]itar is limited by a shortage of specimens. [No in]struments have survived from the [sixteent]h century,[176] both with vaulted backs [mad]e out of a series of ribs, the method of [constru]ction used on the lute. It seems likely, [howev]er, that both flat and vaulted construction [was u]sed in the sixteenth century for both [guitar a]nd vihuela.[177] The Diaz guitar in the [collecti]on of the Royal College of Music is an [amazin]gly light, delicate instrument about half [the size] of a modern 'classical' guitar. As with [the surv]iving vihuela, the sides are quite [deep]. One of the most informative sources [on b]oth vihuela and guitar is the Declaraciòn [de Instr]umentos Musicales (1555) of Juan Bermudo [in whic]h he gives the following common

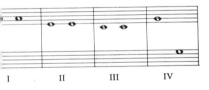

[Bermu]do's guitar tuning.

[The su]ccession of intervals – fourth, third, [fourth] – corresponds to the inner courses of the [lute]. The necessity for octave tuning in the [top] a note as high as g gives some idea of the [st]ring length (on the Diaz guitar roughly [2 fee]t). Bermudo also gives an alternative [tuning] with the bass tuned a tone lower. [The] four-course guitar was especially [popula]r in France, where it appears to have [been fa]voured by King Henri II himself[178] and [after 1]550 there are a succession of French [publica]tions for the instrument, notably by [Guilla]ume Morlaye and Adrian le Roy. The [reperto]ire was generally light – arrangements [of chan]sons, dances, and so on – though there [are a nu]mber of more extended fantasies too.[179] [Thro]ughout the sixteenth century the guitar [was const]antly linked with the cittern. As early as [1487]Tinctoris[180] mentioned the guitarra and [cittur]la side by side as instruments of the [comm]on people. The first published book for [citt]ern is an appendix to Guillaume [Morlay]e's Quatriesme Livre . . . De Guiterre [1552] and Thomas Wythorne wrote that in [t]he year 1549 he 'learned to play upon [the citt]ern and cittern, which two instruments [were th]en strange in England and therefore the

more desired and esteemed'.[181] Wythorne, incidentally, took a particular fancy to the gittern; in his autobiography he relates how a young girl once left an amorous verse addressed to him placed beneath the strings of his gittern.[182]

The close association of guitar and cittern, which continues up to Playford's 1652 publication mentioned above, is emphasized by the re-entrant tuning for the guitar given to Scipione Cerreto in his Della Prattica Musica of 1601. It will be observed that, apart from IV

Scipione Cerreto's guitar tuning.

being unison rather than octave, the intervals are the same as in the alternative tuning of Bermudo mentioned above.

At this point it should be admitted that the early history of the guitar family is rather more involved than the foregoing analysis might suggest, with a certain amount of interrelation between the vihuela and guitar types. Bermudo describes a vihuela with seven courses[183] and Fuenllana gives music for a five-course 'vihuela'.[184] The latter instrument was, in fact, the five-course guitar which began to appear from the 1550s onwards and as the chitarra spagnola or Spanish guitar became the most popular member of the family after 1600. The regular tuning is that given by Juan Carlos y Amat in 1586,[185] though re-entrant systems of tuning were occasionally called for as well.

Carlos y Amat's guitar tuning.

Finally, mention should be made of a number of specialized varieties of guitar which may be conveniently listed as follows:
bandurria: according to Bermudo this was a small three-course instrument shaped like a rebec tuned to a fourth and fifth (or vice versa) and played with a plectrum. Four- and five-course instruments were also known.[186]
chitarriglia: a smaller, higher-pitched version of the Spanish guitar.[187]
chitarrino: the seventeenth-century name for the small four-course guitar.[188]
chitarra battente: a five-course metal-strung guitar, played with a plectrum. Unlike the other

Viole da gamba and da braccio. Detail from a spinet lid painted in 1619 by Friedrich von Falckenberg. (Germanisches Museum, Nuremberg)

members of the guitar family it has fixed metal frets.[189]
mandola: this ambiguous name was sometimes applied to a number of small types of guitar.[190]

The bowed instruments

There are two long-standing misconceptions about early bowed instruments which have still not entirely vanished. One is that the viol is a medieval as well as a renaissance instrument,

and the other is that the violin family somehow or other developed from it. In fact, both viol and violin families emerged within less than a century of each other – they belong to the same rather than to different generations of early music – whilst their status, technique, construction, and repertoire are quite distinct. The confusion about the period to which the viol belongs comes from the ambiguity of medieval words such as vielle or viella which are often mis-translated as 'viol'.[191] As for the distinctions between the two instruments, their typical physical characteristics c.1600 may be distinguished as shown in the table below.[192]

VIOL	VIOLIN
6 strings	4 strings
Tuning in fourths with one third in the middle	Tuning in fifths
Long tailpiece	Shorter tailpiece
Wide fretted fingerboard	Narrower unfretted fingerboard
Flat back and sloping shoulders	Rounded back and shoulders
Deep sides	Shallow sides
No purfling round edges	Purfling round edges
Reinforcing crossbars inside	A reinforcing longitudinal bassbar inside
C-shaped or 'flame' sound-holes	f-shaped sound-holes
Pegbox surmounted by a carved head	Pegbox surmounted by a scroll

Overhand grip for the violin bow.

Underhand grip for the treble viol bow.

Detail from *The Marriage at Cana,* by Paolo Veronese (1563). The viol player in the foreground is a self-portrait. Notice the transitional playing position. (The Louvre, Paris)

Venice 1542–3, the three standard sizes of and their tunings are clearly set out.

Viol tunings from Ganassi's *Regola Rubertin*

The wide range of each size of viol made existence of an alto viol unnecessary. In th seventeenth century a few large treble vio were made, however, tuned a tone lower the treble (starting on c) and designated 'a The tenor viol was sometimes tuned a ton higher (starting on A): this was part of wl Mersenne[206] called 'tuning in the Italian manner'.

Ganassi's *Regola Rubertina* shows that a advanced standard of viol playing had bee developed before the middle of the sixteer century. As in his companion tutor for the recorder, the *Fontegara,* Ganassi gives prec details of technique: much of the informa about holding the instrument, fingering, bowing, and making divisions is most valu and the range he explores is impressive, co

In general terms the violin is of more robust construction than the viol. On the latter instrument the wood is thinner throughout and the strings are lighter, longer, and less tense.[193] The playing positions involved were equally distinct. All the viols were played in a sitting position, the player holding the instrument vertically on or between his knees, whilst the smaller members of the violin family were played under the chin or on the shoulder, resting more or less horizontally on the arm. Hence the qualifications *viola da gamba* (leg-fiddle) and *viola da braccio* (arm-fiddle). The bow grip was different also, the viol bow being held underhand with the fingers controlling the tension of the horse-hair whilst the violin bow was held overhand, albeit with a quite different grip from that used today. The bow itself presented one common feature, on whatever instrument it was used: the inward camber found on modern bows did not appear until the mid-eighteenth century.[194]

The viol

From the details already given the reader will have observed the many similarities (tuning, fretting, light construction and stringing, etc.) between the viol and the plucked instruments of the Renaissance. It may be added that throughout the sixteenth and seventeenth centuries it was customary to write certain types of viol music in tablature. Whilst its precise origins remain obscure, there is little doubt that the viol came into being just as the earliest bowed instruments did: by the application of the bow to a pre-existing plucked instrument. One or two renaissance paintings clearly illustrate the transition: players are shown seated, holding the instrument guitar-style across the knees, whilst the right hand desperately tries to find some comfortable way of bowing.

It was natural that the position of the instrument should change from the horizontal to the vertical, with the bottom end gripped by the knees. The most widely accepted theory[196] is that the viol developed in Spain during the second half of the fifteenth century. Several Italian renaissance writers hint at this,[196] and the most obvious plucked equivalent to the viol is certainly the vihuela whose shape, size, and tuning correspond with that of the tenor viol. Viol-making and playing first seem to have caught on in Italy, however.[197] In Germany a common early sixteenth-century name for the viol was *welsche Geige,* literally 'foreign fiddle' (the word *Geige* was used, like the Italian *viola* and the Spanish *vihuela,* as a generic term). In England a consort of viols first makes an appearance in the records of the King's Music for 1540: six of the players are Italians, from Cremona, Milan, and Venice.[198]

One thing is certain: the outward appearance of the viol varied enormously during the first hundred years or so of its existence and only became standardized after 1600. What we tend to think of as the typical viol design was only one amongst the many shapes and sizes of the sixteenth century.[199] A particularly interesting transitional shape is that shown by Virdung in his *Musica getutscht:* it has the bent-back pegbox of the lute together with the central rose and fixed bridge common to the lute and guitar. The omission of a movable bridge – an essential feature unless all the strings are to be sounded at once – seems altogether curious. Gerald Hayes regarded the omission as a mistake,[200] though if that is the case it was a mistake cheerfully repeated by Agricola in his *Musica instrumentalis deudtsch* in the editions of both 1528 and 1545. Since Virdung and Agricola show the bridges quite clearly on the rebecs which they illustrate, one cannot avoid the suspicion that the *Gross*

Geigen or *dreierley Geigen* were chordal instruments on which all the strings *were* sounded simultaneously. The existence of nine strings on Virdung's instrument is difficult to credit otherwise. Instruments of this shape certainly existed: one or two surviving sixteenth-century instruments do have the same narrow waist and sharply incurving sides.[201] though not in conjunction with the sharply angled peg-box. Stringing was variable too. Five-string viols are found at every period[202] and Agricola tells us that his discant, altus, and tenor instruments have five strings, even though his illustrations show only four.[203] In his *Epitome musical* (1556) Philibert Jambe de Fer says that viols in France had five strings tuned in a series of fourths whereas Italy had viols with six strings.[204] During the baroque period a seventh string was sometimes added to the bass viol to extend the range downwards.

Virdung omits the tuning of the viols which he describes and so the first account we have is that of Agricola in 1528.[203] Although the nomenclature of different sizes does not correspond with later practice (Agricola's 'bass' being equivalent to the normal tenor) the lowest tuning he gives corresponds to the lute or vihuela: G, c, f, a, d', g'. In Sylvestro Ganassi's *Regola Rubertina,*[205] published in

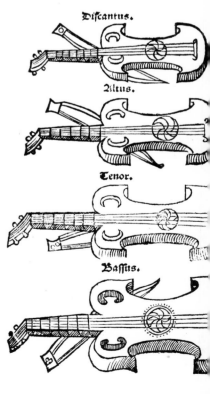

Grossen Geigen, from Agricola's *Musica instrumentalis deudtsch.*

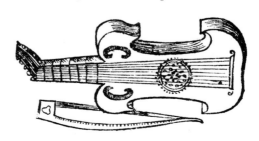

Gross Geigen, from Virdung's *Musica getutscht.*

bes nearly four octaves.[208] Ganassi explains
he viols could be used, like the lute, to
pany singing: as an illustration he gives
rigal, *Io vorei Dio d'amor,* arranged for
ice to sing one part and two (occasionally
other parts to be played on the viol. This
method of self-accompaniment, Ganassi
, which had been vigorously explored in
y, and he mentions two notable men who
ed at it, Juliano Tiburtino and Lodovico
nino, both of Florence.[209] He compares
ordal use of the viol with that of the *lira*
cio and notes that the differences between
truments necessitates a considerable
nce in treatment.[210] Nevertheless, as often
ns with renaissance theorists, sound
on sense is found side by side with
te nonsense. Ganassi is at pains to establish
classical pedigree for his instrument and
point he refers to ancient statues as the
of information for bowed instruments
quity. He uses the word 'violone' for
ol.

tice how the violone is made with six
. I often wondered which was more
t, the lute or the violone, when I wanted
cribe its origin. Having discussed the
on with various people, I recalled having
nong the antiquities of Rome . . . one
who had in his hands a bowed viola
c to those mentioned above. There I
diately recognized that the violone was
ancient than the lute, on the evidence of
ry of Orpheus, who is not mentioned as
he lute, but rather the instrument with
and bow that is the lira, which with its
and its bow is like the violone. But as to
e, it was lira or lirone, although most
call it violone. But it is more correct to
irone, and, in the plural, lironi, rather
iolone, or violoni; our evidence is based
pheus and his lyre . . .'[211]

urd as it sounds today, all this was taken
sly and, as mentioned earlier on, the
ared the aristocratic attributes of the
d was cultivated amongst courtly society
ter by gentleman amateurs. Perhaps it was
onally cultivated a little too seriously, for
land the viol became a regular subject
amongst the dramatists, having the
tation of an affected ass. Sir Andrew
heek 'plays o' the viol de gamboys', Sir
Belch tells us,[212] and in Ben Jonson's
Man out of his Humour Sir Fastidious Brisk
Saviolina whilst scraping away on the
ol and puffing tobacco.[213] Perhaps the
musing reference is that in Thomas
eton's *A Trick to Catch the old One* where
phorus Hoard takes pride in his niece's
plishments as follows: 'The voice
en her lips, and the viol between her legs,

she'll be fit for a consort very speedily.'[214]

By the beginning of the seventeenth century
there was certainly every encouragement for
amateur and professional alike to learn to play
the viol, since the repertoire for the instrument
was considerable, and embraced some of the
finest music of the age. A consort of viols
provided the perfect instrumental combination
for renaissance polyphony: sonorous, flexible,
and sustained, viols can make clear every detail
of a complex five- or six-part texture. The
in nomines, pavans, and fantasies by composers
such as Byrd, Coperario, Ferrabosco, Gibbons,
Lupo, Tomkins, and many others form an
exquisite chamber music repertory which, in
the case of many of the lesser known composers,
has still not been fully explored.[215] The tradition
continued through the seventeenth century
with the work of Jenkins and Locke to the
wonderful set of fantasies by Purcell[216] which
form the culminating point in the development
of viol consort music. Consort songs were
popular too;[217] viols provide an ideal
accompaniment to a solo voice, particularly
in laments such as 'Pandolpho' by Robert
Parsons[218] or William Byrd's 'Ye Sacred Muses',
an elegy on the death of Thomas Tallis (1585).[219]

Whilst the English developed a particular
predilection for viol playing and consort music,
there was plenty of activity on the continent
too. Praetorius makes it clear that the use of a
consort of viols was an everyday matter[220]
though he suggests a rather different performance practice. The standard combination of viols
for seventeenth-century English music would
have been that set out by Thomas Mace in;
1676: 'Your *Best Provision* (and *most Compleat*)
will be, a *Good Chest of Viols; Six,* in *Number;*
viz. 2 *Basses, 2 Tenors* and 2 *Trebles:* All Truly,
and *Proportionably Suited.*'[221]

Praetorius says that when the English play
their viols, the tuning is somewhat higher than
that to which he is accustomed.[222] His chief
tunings are: bass G', C, F, A, d, g; tenor D, G,
c, e, a, d'; treble G, c, f, a, d', g'. Thus the bass
and treble are a fifth lower, and the tenor a
fourth lower, than the standard tunings quoted
from Ganassi above. Similar low pitches are
confirmed by other writers, including Zacconi
(1592) and Banchieri (1609).[223] The discrepancy
is all the more puzzling since it cannot just be
one of pitch; Mace's chest of viols tuned as
Praetorius suggests would make a miserable
noise, since the stringing would be too low for
the instruments. Praetorius can only mean that
he is used to a viol consort of *larger* instruments,
with (in English terminology) tenors for the top
parts, basses for the middle parts and extra
large basses for the lowest parts. Yet if such a
deep-pitched consort existed what did it play,
since consort repertoire descending to G' is
conspicuously lacking? An answer has recently

TOP
Concert before King Louis XIII, Anon, 1630.
A consort of the larger sizes of viols, similar to
that described by Gerle. (Musée des Beaux Arts,
Troyes)

BOTTOM
A modern viol consort: treble, tenor, two basses.

been provided by Michael Morrow in a
stimulating article[224] chiefly concerned with
two publications by Hans Gerle: *Musica Teusch*
(1532) and *Musica und Tabulatur* (1546). 'Gerle
states that the normal four-part viol consort
consists of a tenor in A, two basses in D and a
contrabass in A (the latter, however, lacking the
bottom A string).'[225] Gerle's music for viol
consort,[226] the earliest to be printed, employs
an apparently normal compass descending to F.
Since it was printed in tablature, however, Gerle
was able to make clear that each instrument
was to be used in its upper register, ascending
as high as the fifth – or even seventh – fret on
the top string.[227] The effect of a consort of viols
used in this way would certainly be totally
different from the accepted 'English' sound:

the evidence of Praetorius and the other writers
mentioned above suggests that such a practice
may have been quite widespread.

The violone

From the mid-sixteenth to the mid-seventeenth
century the viol family was complemented by
some kind of double bass instrument, usually
referred to today as the *violone,* of which a few
rare examples have survived.[228] As Francis
Baines has pointed out,[229] the name is somewhat
ambiguous as far as early usage is concerned.
Ganassi uses 'violone' to refer to the normal
bass viol, Ortiz uses it to refer to all the viols,
whilst in the baroque period both Corelli
and Handel used it for the cello.[230] In his
Musikalische Exequien Schütz uses 'violone' for

the *gross Bassgeige,* an instrument a little larger than the cello.[231] Further confusion arises from the fact that up to the eighteenth century the name 'violone' was regularly used for the double bass, a much more common instrument than the true violone. As a result it has often been stated that the modern double bass belongs to the viol family, not the violin family, although this idea has been effectively challenged by Eric Halfpenny.[232] Nevertheless, the double bass itself was the least standardized member of the violin family; during the seventeenth and eighteenth centuries it was commonly built with five strings, provided with a fretted fingerboard, and bowed underhand,[233] all of which has naturally led to confusion with the violone.

Even when we restrict the term 'violone' to members of the viol family, an element of uncertainty remains. It was clearly a six-string instrument, more lightly constructed than the double bass, and fretted and tuned like a viol. But what was it tuned to? Banchieri[234] describes a *violone in contrabasso* tuned an octave below the bass viol, *ie* D', G', C, E, A, d. This is a true contrabass instrument, operating at 16-foot pitch. The violone illustrated by Praetorius is a 16-foot instrument too, and it is of huge proportions: according to the scale he gives it would stand nearly eight feet high.[235] Yet most of the surviving instruments are relatively small. Should they then be tuned an octave lower than the bass viol, or to some intermediate tuning such as mentioned by Gerle for his largest size of viol?

There is a great deal of evidence to suggest that the 'normal' violone tuning was not a full octave below the bass, and that the instrument was not a true 16-foot instrument at all. Banchieri also speaks of a *violone da gamba,* tuned G', C, F, A, d, g,[236] as the true bass of the consort[237] and there is corroboration from Gerle, Zacconi, Cerone, and Praetorius.[228] Rather than doubling the bass part at the octave, the most common function of the violone may well have been to provide the bass part of consort music on its own, such as in the set of fantasias a 3 'with the double-bass' by Orlando Gibbons.[239] Nevertheless, most violones played today are tuned an octave below the bass viol and are commonly used for octave doubling as the baroque double bass was.

Division viol, lyra viol, and viola bastarda

From the mid-sixteenth century the viol started to develop its own solo repertory. In his *Regola Rubertina* Ganassi provided players with a number of studies similar in character and purpose to the early lute ricercars, and employing double- and even triple-stopping. Ten years later the Spaniard Diego Ortiz issued his *Tratado de Glosas* (Rome 1553),[240] giving viol

players some splendid sets of divisions over popular basses such as the *Romanesca* or chansons such as *O felici occhi miei.*

For rapid solo work a slightly smaller version of the standard bass viol was developed, sometimes called the 'division' viol, a name immortalized in the title of Christopher Simpson's publication of 1665.[241] Simpson says: 'A Viol for Division, should be of something a lesser size than a Consort Bass; that so the Hand may better command it: more or less short, according to the reach of his fingers who is to use it . . . The sound should be quick and sprightly, like a Violin.'[242] Simpson goes on to

give a full account of the construction and playing of divisions: 'These several sorts of Divisions are used upon the Bass-Viol, very promiscuously, according to the Fancy of the Player or Composer . . .'[243]

Judging from his compositions, Simpson was a highly skilled performer: by his time England had become noted for its viol playing and English violists were much sought after, often being met with on the continent.[244] From about the year 1600 an idiomatic solo style had developed, known as 'playing the lyra way'. There is an extensive repertoire[245] for the so-called 'lyra viol' which may be regarded as a

parallel development to the solo lute reper of the seventeenth century, since it was wr in tablature and involved a variable system tuning to suit the nature of each piece. 'Pla the lyra way' explored the technical possil of the viol to the full: it made extensive us double- and triple-stopping and even emp special effects such as pizzicato. A selection the tunings required by lyra-viol music is opposite. The majority of them involve th use of fifths to widen the overall compass a facilitate the stopping of full chords.

Amongst the composers who wrote lyra viol music the eccentric personality of To

Violone from Praetorius' *Syntagma Musicum*

Hume[246] (d. *c.*1645) is outstanding. His *Th First Part of Ayres*[247] was issued in 1605 with punning title 'Musicall Humours' printed top of every page. The titles are fanciful su 'My Mistresse hath a pretty thing', 'Tickle quickly', and 'Hit in the middle', though Hume includes a number of expression ma and directions for interpretation including 'Drum this with the back of the bow' – the *col legno* in history. As did a number of oth composers, Hume wrote music for two an even three lyra-viols together as well as sol pieces.

Modern violone by Wolfgang Nebel, Celle.
The tuning screws are a modern addition for the convenience of the player.

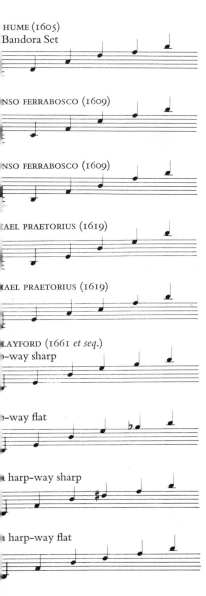

HUME (1605)
Bandora Set

NSO FERRABOSCO (1609)

NSO FERRABOSCO (1609)

AEL PRAETORIUS (1619)

AEL PRAETORIUS (1619)

LAYFORD (1661 *et seq.*)
-way sharp

-way flat

a harp-way sharp

a harp-way flat

ould be emphasized that any viol could
ed and played 'the lyra way' and it was
cessary to obtain a special instrument to
ra-viol music. One or two purpose-built
iols' have survived, however;[248] they are
y smaller in size than the division viol.
rius describes such an instrument ('its
s somewhat longer and larger than that
nor'[249]) calling it the *viola bastarda*.
ntions an unusual English version which
ition to the six gut strings had a set of
r more sympathetic metal strings laid
neath.[250] In *Musick's Recreation on the Viol,
Vay* (1661) the invention is attributed by
 ayford to the ingenious Daniel Farrant,
 it would seem to have enjoyed a fairly
 ived existence. Playford says: '. . . by the
g of those Strings above with the *Bow,*
 d was drawn from those of Wire
 neath, which made it very Harmonious.

Of this sort of *Viols* I have seen many, but *Time* and *Disuse* has set them aside.'[251]

However, Praetorius' statement that the *viola bastarda* was used mainly as an accompanying instrument, like the theorbo (see p. 78), seems to be mistaken. All the repertoire for it from Girolamo dalla Casa (1584)[252] onwards makes it clear that the *viola bastarda* was a virtuoso speciality, using a normal small bass viol in *normal tuning*, and is not in any way to be confused with the idiosyncrasies of the lyra viol. In other words, the *viola bastarda* was simply the continental equivalent of the English division viol. However, modern writers have regularly repeated Praetorius' assertions to the contrary.

The lirone
One relative of the viol was developed as an entirely chordal instrument. This was the *lirone* or *lira da gamba*, a marriage of the bass viol with the *lira da braccio* (see below). The typical features are found on the instrument made by the Paduan lute-maker Wendelin Tieffenbrucker *c.*1590, and now in the Kunsthistorisches Museum, Vienna: intricate outline, *S*-holes, broad neck, frontal pegs, flattish bridge, and drone strings set to the side of the fingerboard. A rather different type, named *lirone perfetto* in one source,[253] is preserved in the Brussels Museum of Musical Instruments: the outline is plainer, there is a rose as well as *f*-holes, and there are no drone strings.[254] Apart from the drone strings, the lirone had from nine to fourteen stopped strings, tuned in fourths, fifths, and octaves.[255] Cerreto, Praetorius, and Mersenne give various different tunings; of the three writers it is Cerreto who gives us the most detailed account of playing techniques.[256] He illustrates how to play accompaniments with chords of from four to six notes, and emphasizes that even in a solo part players should still use a chordal technique. Cerreto assures his students 'that if in the strokes they touch upon some other string, it will not matter provided the same concord is maintained. It is difficult, especially when playing on the middle strings, to avoid touching more than one string because the bridge is only slightly arched.'[257] The tuning he gives is as follows:

Lirone tuning given by Scipione Cerreto.

Writing about the lirone Mersenne says: 'Now the sound of the lyre is very languishing and suitable for exciting devotion and causing the spirit to commune with itself; it is used to accompany the voice and recitatives . . . There is no instrument which represents so well the

music of Orpheus and antiquity.'[258]

The lirone was mainly used in Italy *c.*1550–1650 in court entertainments, *intermedii,* and operas. Cerreto mentions the existence of no less than seven masters of the lirone in Naples in his day, and 'un lirone' appears several times in the *intermedii* of 1565 by Striggio and Corteccia.[259] In 1567, Cosimo Bartoli praised Alessandro Striggio (the elder) 'who is . . . even more than excellent in playing the "viola" [*ie* lirone], and he plays on it in four voices at one time with such elegance and fullness of tone that he amazes the listeners'.[260]

Renaissance fiddle and lira da braccio
We can now turn from the instruments held and played *da gamba* to the *da braccio* types. Before the advent of the violin family there were three main types of bowed instruments played on the arm: the rebec, already fully dealt with in chapter 4, the renaissance fiddle

Angel musician playing a renaissance fiddle. Panel from the Reliquary of St Ursula, by Hans Memling (*c.*1435–94). (Hôpital St Jean, Bruges)

Lira da gamba or lirone by Wendelin Tieffen-brucker, second half of the sixteenth century. (Kunsthistorisches Museum, Vienna)

Lira da braccio made in northern Italy, sixteenth century. (Musical Instrument Museum, Berlin)

(a matured version of the medieval fiddle), and the *lira da braccio* which may be regarded as an offshoot of the fiddle. The name *viola da braccio*, which first occurs in 1543, was first used as a generic term like the older *viola*, but gradually came to refer to the members of the new violin family.[261]

By 1500 the typical renaissance fiddle had five strings, one of which might be an unstopped drone. It had developed a multi-sectional construction with a separate neck, fingerboard, top, back, and connecting ribs. Although it was quite regularly fretted, the appearance of the fiddle closely foreshadowed that of the violin: both were treble instruments of a comparable size.[262] During the second half of the fifteenth century the *lira da braccio* had evolved as a distinct type. Its outline resembled that of the violin too, although it was larger, generally more like a modern viola in size. It had seven strings, two of them drone strings which ran off the fingerboard, and at least until after 1600, frets do not seem to have been used. Praetorius gives the following tuning, reminiscent of medieval fiddle tunings:

Tuning of the *lira da braccio* given in Praetorius' *Syntagma Musicum*.

The importance of the *lira da braccio* in Italian renaissance culture has been shown by Emanuel Winternitz.[263] Like the lirone, which developed from it, it was primarily a chordal instrument as Winternitz says, 'used by recitalists who improvised polyphonic accompaniments for their singing, and therefore one of the most characteristic implements of the intended rhapsodic art of the ancients'.[264] Many writers accepted the idea that the *lira da braccio* was, in fact, an ancient instrument. Like the classical lyre it had seven strings, two of them unstopped strings which always sounded for their full length like those of the lyre. Even the kithara's plectrum was credited with being some kind of fiddle bow. In mythological scenes both Apollo and Orpheus are found holding the instrument: equally, the *lira da braccio* is often shown hanging up by way of symbolic inspiration to some worthy humanistic scholar of the Renaissance.

The *lira da braccio* must not be regarded merely as a toy of theorists and dilettantes. It occupied a central position in the musical performances of Italian courtly life, particularly in the first part of the sixteenth century. At the courts of Ferrara and Milan virtuosi of the *lira da braccio* were employed.[265] In his discussion of the

musical interests of Leonardo, Vasari stresses his predilection for the instrument. Leonardo was a man 'who by nature possessed a spirit both lofty and full of grace which enabled him to improvise divinely in singing and playing the lira da braccio'.[266] According to Vasari, it was as a player of the lira da braccio that Leonardo was introduced to the Milanese court in 1494 and presented to the Duke.[267]

A poet with lira da braccio, from *Epithome Plutarchi* (1501).

The violin
Having reached the instrument which of all those dealt with in this book is the most universally familiar today, it is tempting to follow Praetorius and say: '. . . since everyone knows about the violin family, it is unnecessary to indicate or write anything further about it.'[268] Yet after a gap of three and a half centuries, the early history of the violin is far from clear. For a comprehensive survey of the instrument before 1600, the reader is referred to the first part of David Boyden's fascinating study *The History of Violin Playing*, which takes Praetorius' cryptic remark as its starting point. As David Boyden says,[269] what everyone knew then nobody knows now, and it is frustrating that whilst the *Syntagma Musicum* is a mine of information about such relative obscurities as the *Geigenwerk* and tromba marina, the family which was to become the most important in Western music is curtly dismissed.

Praetorius might well have been able to give a precise answer to the question which has fascinated many historians since his time: when, where, and by whom was the violin invented?[270] Today we must be content with placing the emergence of the violin as c.1550 in Italy, after

some twenty or thirty years of experimental designs. The earliest representations of the new instrument are found in paintings executed by Gaudenzio Ferrari (c.1480–1546) in the early 1530s.[271] At this early stage the three component members of the violin family are already clearly distinguished: treble, alto-tenor, and bass, equivalent to the three principal sizes of the viol family.[272] Whilst the instruments have most of the violin's features – typical outline, scro[ll] bulging back, *f*-holes, and overhand grip [of] bow – there are only three strings. On the three-string violin the tuning was g, d', a' corresponding to the lowest three strings o[f] fully developed instrument.[273] It is someti[mes] stated that since *violino* is a diminutive of *v[iola]* the viola must have been the first member the family to develop. But as David Boyde[n]

Lira da braccio. Detail from *The Parnassus*, by Raphael (1483–1520). (Vatican Museum)

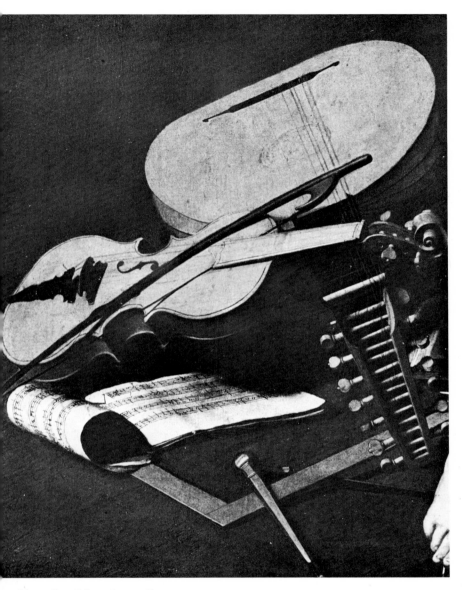

and bow. Detail from *Love as Conqueror*,
...ravaggio (1573–1610). (Staatliches
...um, Berlin)

...[274] all the evidence suggests that the
...emerged as a family: to start with, the
...*violin,* unqualified, might refer to a treble,
...enor, or bass instrument, and whilst it
...ally came to refer exclusively to the
...est member of the family, Venetian
...osers still used *violino* for the viola as well
...violin at the end of the sixteenth century.[275]
...nni Gabrieli wrote a part labelled *violino*
...*Sonata Pian' e Forte* (1597) which descends
... the violin's bottom string and is clearly
...ded for the viola.[276]
...e first positive evidence for the four-
...ed violin family comes in 1556 with the
...ne *Musical* of Philibert Jambe de Fer: 'The
...[*violon*] is very different from the viol
... First of all it has only four strings, which

are tuned in fifths . . . The form of the body is
smaller, flatter and in sound it is much harsher
[*rude*].'[277] Jambe de Fer gives the standard
modern tunings for the upper two members of
the family (*violon* and *haute contre-taille*), whilst
his *bas* is a tone lower than the modern cello, a
tradition which persists in France up to the time
of Mersenne.[278] Particularly interesting are the

1. BAS   2. HAUTECONTRE- 3. DESSUS
                    TAILLE

Tunings for the violin family given by
Philibert Jambe de Fer.

hints which Jambe de Fer drops about the
violin's musical status compared to the viol.

'Why do you call one type of instrument
viols and the other violins?'

'We call viols those with which gentleman
merchants and other virtuous people pass their
time . . . The other type is called violin; it is
commonly used for dancing, and with good
reason, for it is much easier to tune . . . It is also
easier to carry, a very necessary thing while
leading wedding processions or mummeries
. . . I have not illustrated the said violin because
you can think of it as resembling the viol, added
to which there are few persons who use it save
those who make a living from it through their
labour.'[279]

Throughout the second half of the sixteenth
century the violin was an exclusively *professional*
instrument, just as the shawm and cornett were,
and its principal repertoire was dance music.
It comes as no surprise that hardly any specific
repertoire for it survives for this period: the
violin is mentioned as an alternative to the viol
in one or two publications, such as Anthony
Holborne's *Pavans, Galliards, Almans and other
Short Aeirs*[280] of 1599, Morley's *First Book of
Consort Lessons*[281] of the same year, and
Dowland's *Lachrimae*[282] of 1605. The earliest
printed music for violin consists of two dances
which formed part of the *Ballet comique de la
reine* performed for a royal wedding festivity at
the French court in 1581.[283] Violins had been
popular there since the importation of an
Italian dance band of violins led by Balthasar
de Beaujoyeulx in about 1555. In Britain the
violin became a regular town bandsman's
instrument, though apparently it was not always
well played. When Mary Queen of Scots
arrived in Edinburgh in 1561, the French
chronicler Brantôme describes how 'In the
evening as she [the Queen] wished to sleep, five
or six hundred scoundrels [*marauts*] of the town
serenaded her with wretched violins and small
rebecs, of which there is no lack in this country;
and they began to sing psalms than which
nothing more badly sung or out of tune could
be imagined. Alas, what music and what repose
for her night!'[284]

In Italy the violin quickly became more
versatile and made its way into more elevated
company. We find it regularly amongst the
instruments required for the courtly *intermedii,*
such as those of Florence in 1589 which
celebrated the wedding of Ferdinand de Medici
to Christine of Lorraine. The Sinfonia by
Luca Marenzio which introduced the second
intermedio included a *violino* playing with lutes,
harp, chitarrone, two liras, *basso di viola,* and
viola bastarda.[285] Needless to say, the theorists
hastened to furnish the violin with an honourable
pedigree. According to Bernardi in his

Ragionamenti musicali of 1581: 'The violin was
invented by Orpheus, son of Apollo and
Calliope. The ancient poetess Sappho invented
the bow fitted with horse-hair, and was the first
to use the violin and the viola in the way they
are used today; and this happened 624 years
before the coming of our Lord Jesus Christ.'[286]

The violin's true pedigree was rather mixed
since it represented a fusion of the noble *lira da
braccio* with the renaissance fiddle and the much
less elevated rebec. Nonetheless, the violin
derived great strength and richness from its
triple parentage: the instrument which emerged
in the middle of the sixteenth century had an
outstanding potential for expressiveness, agility,
and sonority. And as everyone knows it had the
most incredible success story of any instrument
in the whole history of music. Within fifty
years it had conquered any initial doubts and
prejudices, within a hundred it had invaded
every sphere of musical life, church, chamber,
and opera house, it had laid the foundation of
the string section of the modern orchestra, it
had developed an enviable and already
prodigiously difficult solo repertoire, and as far
as any kind of instrumental ensemble was
concerned it had eclipsed all other instruments.

Of course, none of this would have been
possible without the artistry and craftsmanship
of the early violin-makers. And perhaps theirs
was the most remarkable achievement – to bring
a new instrument to the peak of perfection in
such a short period. The great school of makers
was centred in two Italian cities. At Brescia
there was Gasparo da Salò who died in 1609,
and Paolo Maggini who died about 1632. At
Cremona there was the Amati family, stretching
from Andrea, who died about 1580, to his
grandson, Nicola, who died in 1684. And in the
following century Cremona was the home of
the greatest violin-maker of all time, Antonio
Stradivari.

Violinist playing in French style. Lithograph of
an oil painting by Gerard Dou, dated 1665.

Chapter 1 Woodwind

1 Anthony Baines, *Woodwind Instruments and their History* (Faber, London 1957) p.229.
2 Curt Sachs, *The History of Musical Instruments* (Norton, New York 1940) p.120.
3 Gerald Hayes, 'Musical Instruments', *New Oxford History of Music*, III (O.U.P. London 1960) p.478.
4 Sybil Marcuse, *Musical Instruments: A Comprehensive Dictionary* (New York 1964) p.59.
5 Francis W. Galpin, *Old English Instruments of Music*, fourth edition revised by Thurston Dart (Methuen, London 1965) p.121.
6 See Barbara Seagrave and Wesley Thomas, *The Songs of the Minnesingers* (University of Illinois Press, Urbana 1966) pp.189–99.
7 See Richard Rastall, 'Minstrelsy, Church and Clergy in Medieval England', *Proceedings of the Royal Musical Association*, 97 (1971) pp.83–98.
8 See Emanuel Winternitz, *Musical Instruments and their Symbolism in Western Art* (Faber, London 1967) p.153.
9 Galpin, op. cit. p.127.
10 See Frank Harrison and Joan Rimmer, *European Musical Instruments* (Studio Vista, London 1964) plate 77.
11 Anthony Baines, *Bagpipes*, Pitt Rivers Museum Occasional Papers on Technology, 9 (Oxford 1960). Francis Collinson, *The Bagpipe* (Routledge and Kegan Paul, London and Boston 1975).
12 Sachs, op. cit. p.141.
13 The Italian *zampogna* is an exception.
14 For reproductions of the illustrations see José Guerrero Lovillo, *Las Cantigas: Estudio Arqueologico de sus Miniaturas* (Madrid 1949).
15 For a modern edition see Leo Schrade (ed.), *Polyphonic Music of the Fourteenth Century*, III (L'Oiseau Lyre, Monaco 1956) pp.122–3.
16 Gilbert Reaney, *Machaut* (O.U.P. London 1971) p.16.
17 Edmund A. Bowles, 'Instruments at the Court of Burgundy (1363–1467)', *Galpin Society Journal*, VI (1953) p.41.
18 Hayes, op. cit. p.499.
19 Anthony Baines, *Woodwind Instruments and their History* (Faber, London 1957) pp.217–18.
20 Hayes, op. cit. p.502.
21 Sachs, op. cit. p.288.
22 Hayes, op. cit. p.497.
23 Anthony Baines, *Woodwind Instruments and their History* (Faber, London 1957) p.235.
24 Anthony Baines, 'Fifteenth-century Instruments in Tinctoris's De Inventione et Usu Musicae', *Galpin Society Journal*, III (1950) p.20.
25 Sachs, op. cit. p.287.
26 Hayes, op. cit. p.496.
27 Ibid. p.493.
28 See Winternitz, op. cit. pp.79, 208–9.
29 See Galpin, op. cit. plate 43. See also Werner Bachmann, *The Origins of Bowing* (O.U.P. London 1969) plates 58 and 59.
30 Frederick Crane, *Extant Medieval Musical Instruments* (University of Iowa Press, Iowa City 1972) p.42.
31 Galpin, op. cit. p.103.
32 Sachs, op. cit. p.289.
33 Crane, op. cit. pp.27–43.
34 See table of early bone flutes in J. V. S. Megaw, 'A Medieval Bone Pipe from White Castle', *Galpin Society Journal*, XVI (1963) p.91.
35 For the complete song see Friedrich Gennrich, *Troubadours, Trouvères, Minnesang and Meistergesang* (Arno Volk Verlag, Cologne 1960) p.34.
36 Juvigny played his flageolet at wedding celebrations in the Louvre in 1581. See Christopher Welch, *Lectures on the Recorder* (London 1911, reprinted by O.U.P. London 1961) p.50.
37 Marin Mersenne, *Harmonie Universelle* (Paris 1635) translated by Roger E. Chapman (Martinus Nijhoff, The Hague 1957) pp.301–2.
38 For an interesting example of the *dvojnice's* music see W. S. Allen, 'The Double Pipes of the Adriatic', *Recorder and Music Magazine*, vol.1 no.4 (February 1964).
39 Crane, op. cit. p.40.
40 Hayes, op. cit. p.501.
41 Thomas Weelkes, *Airs or Fantastic Spirits of Three Voices* (1608) no. 28.
42 Edgar Hunt, *The Recorder and its Music* (Herbert Jenkins, London 1962).
43 Brian Trowell, 'King Henry IV, Recorder-Player', *Galpin Society Journal*, X (1957) pp.83–4.
44 Lawrence Wright, 'The Music of the Renaissance', *Recorder and Music Magazine*, vol. 1 no. 9 (May 1965) p.264.
45 Crane, op. cit. p.39.
46 For a description see Curt Sachs, 'Das Gemshorn', *Zeitschrift für Musikwissenschaft* (1918–19) I, pp.153–6.
47 For more details of evidence see Horace Fitzpatrick, 'The Gemshorn: A Reconstruction', *Proceedings of the Royal Musical Association*, 99 (1973) pp.1–14.

Chapter 2 Keyboard

1 Willi Apel, *The History of Keyboard Music to 1700*, translated and revised by Hans Tischler (Indiana University Press, Bloomington 1972) p.9.
2 Ibid. p.11.
3 Ibid. p.12.
4 Jean Perrot, *The Organ from its Invention in the Hellenistic Period to the end of the Thirteenth Century*, translated by Norma Deane (O.U.P. London 1971) p.230. Recently, doubts have been expressed about the extent to which this account is to be taken literally. See James W. McKinnon, 'The Tenth-Century Organ at Winchester', *The Organ Yearbook*, V (1974), pp. 4–19.
5 Sir Jack Westrup, *An Introduction to Musical History* (Hutchinson, London 1959) p.82.
6 See John Caldwell, 'The Organ in the Medieval Latin Liturgy, 800–1500', *Proceedings of the Royal Musical Association*, 93 (1967) pp.15–16.
7 Ethel Thurston, *The Works of Perotin* (Kalmus, New York 1970) p.131.
8 For a modern edition see Willi Apel (ed.), *Keyboard Music of the Fourteenth and Fifteenth Centuries* (American Institute of Musicology 1963).
9 For a modern edition see Dragan Plamenac (ed.), *Keyboard Music of the Late Middle Ages in Codex Faenza 117*, (American Institute of Musicology 1972). This collection presents certain puzzling features, however, suggesting that not all the pieces are intended for keyboard alone.
10 Gerald Hayes, 'Musical Instruments', *New Oxford History of Music*, III (O.U.P. London 1960) p.500.
11 Leonard Ellinwood, 'The Fourteenth Century in Italy', *New Oxford History of Music*, III (O.U.P. London 1960) p.78.
12 Ibid. p.36.
13 Perrot, op. cit. pp.271–2.
14 William Leslie Sumner, *The Organ*, fourth edition (Macdonald, London 1973) pp.52–3.
15 *Grove's Dictionary of Music and Musicians*, fifth edition (Macmillan, London 1966) vol. II p.60.
16 Sumner, op. cit. pp.161–3.
17 Werner Bachmann, *The Origins of Bowing*, translated by Norman Deane (O.U.P. London 1969) pp.105–7.
18 Ibid. p.108–9.
19 Marin Mersenne, *Harmonie Universelle*, Paris 1635, translated by Roger E. Chapman (Martinus Nijhoff, The Hague 1957) p.271.
20 For further information see Francis Baines, 'Introducing the hurdy-gurdy', *Early Music*, vol. 3 no. 1, (January 1975) pp.33–7.
21 Hans Neupert, *The Clavichord*, translated by Ann P. P. Feldberg (Bärenreiter, Kassel 1965) p.9.
22 Ibid. p.10.
23 The existence of a monochord with several strings is a moot point. See Walter Nef, 'The Polychord', *Galpin Society Journal*, IV (1951) pp.20–3.
24 Neupert, op. cit. p.12.
25 Ibid. p.14.
26 See Edmund M. Ripin, 'Towards an Identification of the Chekker', *Galpin Society Journal*, XXVIII, April 1975, pp.11–25.
27 For a complete description see Neupert, op. cit. p.27.
28 For a discussion of the advantages and disadvantages of the fretted clavichord see Edwin M. Ripin, 'A Reassessment of the Fretted Clavichord', *Galpin Society Journal*, XXIII (1970) pp.40–8.
29 For a modern edition see B. A. Wallner (ed.), *Das Buxheimer Orgelbuch*, Das Erbe Deutsche Musik, vols. XXXVII–IX (1958–9).
30 Thurston Dart, 'The Clavichord', *Musical Instruments Through the Ages* (Penguin, London 1961) p.7.

Chapter 3 Brass

1 For a modern edition see Heinrich Besseler (ed.), Guillaume Dufay, *Opera Omnia*, IV (American Institute of Musicology, Rome 1962) pp.79–80.
2 Francis W. Galpin, *Old English Instruments of Music*, fourth edition revised by Thurston Dart (Methuen, London 1965) p.148.
3 Ibid. p.147.
4 Sybil Marcuse, *Musical Instruments: A Comprehensive Dictionary* (New York 1964) p.375.
5 Alexander Buchner, *Musical Instruments: An Illustrated History* (Artia, Prague 1973; English edition Octopus Books, London 1973) pp.261–2.
6 Edmund A. Bowles, 'Instruments at the Court of Burgundy 1363–1467', *Galpin Society Journal*, VI (1953) p.42.
7 See Barbara Seagrave and Wesley Thomas, *The Songs of the Minnesingers* (University of Illinois Press, Urbana 1966) pp.189–99.
8 Francis W. Galpin, *A Textbook of European Musical Instruments* (London 1937) p.240. See also Francis W. Galpin, 'The Sackbut, its Evolution and History', *Proceedings of the Musical Association* (London 1906) pp.1–25.
9 For a full account see Don L. Smithers, *The Music and History of the Baroque Trumpet before 1721* (Dent, London 1973) pp.46–9.
10 For a modern edition see Heinrich Besseler (ed.), Guillaume Dufay, *Opera Omnia*, VI (American Institute of Musicology, Rome 1964) p.102.
11 Ibid., foreword p.XII.

Chapter 4 Strings

1 Werner Bachmann, *The Origins of Bowing*, translated by Norma Deane (O.U.P. London 1969) pp.20–21.
2 Ibid. pp.78–82. Bachmann gives a fascinating account of the methods of string manufacture.
3 Francis W. Galpin, *Old English Instruments of Music*, fourth edition revised by Thurston Dart (Methuen, London 1965) p.12.
4 Frank Harrison and Joan Rimmer, *European Musical Instruments* (Studio Vista, London 1964) p.21.
5 The Robert ap Huw Manuscript of *c.*1613 contains a cross-section of Welsh harp music written in tablature. Unfortunately it is too far removed from the Middle Ages for anything but general inferences to be drawn from it. See Thurston Dart, 'Robert ap Huw's manuscript', *Galpin Society Journal*, XXI (1968) pp.52–65.
6 See Joan Rimmer, *The Irish Harp* (Eire Cultural Relations Committee, Dublin 1969) pp.31–5.
7 Ibid. p.33.
8 Ibid. p.29.
9 Michael Praetorius, *Syntagma Musicum*, II, 'De Organographia' (Wolfenbüttel 1619), translated by Harold Blumenfeld (St Louis 1949) p.59.
10 See Joan Rimmer, op. cit. pp.13–27, and 'The Morphology of the Irish Harp', *Galpin Society Journal*, XVII (1964) pp.39–49.
11 In his poem *Dit de la harpe*. See Roslyn Rensch, *The Harp* (Duckworth, London 1969) p.90.
12 Ibid. p.70.
13 Curt Sachs, *The History of Musical Instruments* (Norton, New York 1940) p.264.
14 Rensch, op. cit. p.67.
15 Ibid. p.66.
16 For details of some surviving medieval lyres see Frederick Crane, *Extant Medieval Musical Instruments* (University of Iowa Press, Iowa City 1972) pp.10–14 and 78–9.
17 Galpin, op. cit. pp.1–2.
18 For further information see John Leach, 'The Psaltery', *The Consort*, 27 (1971) pp.39–49.
19 Galpin, op. cit. p.44. However, the *De Musica*, formerly attributed to Odo of Cluny, is now regarded as anonymous (see Huglo, *Les Tonaires*, Heugel, Paris 1971, p.184).
20 Further information see John Leach, 'The Dulcimer', *The Consort*, 25 (1969) pp.390–5, and David Kettlewell, 'First steps on the dulcimer', *Early Music*, vol. 2 no. 4 (October 1974) pp.247–53.
21 Galpin, op. cit. p.48.
22 Willi Apel, *Masters of the Keyboard* (Harvard University Press, Cambridge, Mass. 1947) p.18.
23 Sybil Marcuse, *Musical Instruments: A Comprehensive Dictionary* (New York 1964) pp.158–9. See also Cecil Clutton, 'Arnault's MS.', *Galpin Society Journal*, V (1952) pp.3–8.
24 Sachs, op. cit. p.82.
25 See Laurence Picken, 'The Origin of the Short Lute', *Galpin Society Journal*, VIII (1955) pp.32–42.
26 Op. cit.
27 For a useful summary of information about early renaissance lutes see Peter Danner, 'Before Petrucci: the Lute in the Fifteenth Century', *Journal of the Lute Society of America*, V (1972) pp.4–17.
28 Anthony Baines, 'Fifteenth-century Instruments in Tinctoris's De Inventione et Usu Musicae', *Galpin Society Journal*, III (1950) p.24.
29 Gerald Hayes, 'Musical Instruments', *New Oxford History of Music*, III (O.U.P. London 1960) p.483.
30 Danner, op. cit. pp.4–7.
31 Crane, op. cit. pp.15, 79.
32 Danner, op. cit. p.4.
33 See Ian Harwood, 'A fifteenth-century lute design', *Lute Society Journal*, II (1960) pp.3–8.
34 Hayes, op. cit. p.488.
35 Ibid. p.489.
36 Galpin, op. cit. p.29.
37 Praetorius, op. cit. p.53.
38 Mary Remnant, 'Rebec, Fiddle and Crowd in England', *Proceedings of the Royal Musical Association*, 95 (1969) p.20.
39 Sachs, op. cit. p.273.
40 Hayes, op. cit. p.490.
41 For reproductions of the illustrations see José Guerrero Lovillo, *Las Cantigas: Estudio Arquelogico de sus Miniaturas* (Madrid 1949).
42 Hayes, op. cit. p.491.
43 Sachs, op. cit. p.252.
44 Baines, op. cit. p.23.
45 See Mary Remnant, 'The Gittern in English Mediaeval Art', *Galpin Society Journal*, XVIII (1965) pp.104–9.
46 Hayes, op. cit. p.490.
47 Galpin, op. cit. p.16.
48 Lines 174 and 176.
49 In an as yet unpublished article. I am most grateful to Lawrence Wright for allowing me to mention it here.
50 Hayes, op. cit. p.489.
51 Marcuse, op. cit. p.103; Hayes, op. cit. p.489; Galpin, op. cit. p.16.
52 Baines, op. cit. p.23.
53 See next section, p.29.
54 See Emanuel Winternitz, *Musical Instruments and their Symbolism in Western Art* (Faber, London 1967) pp.57–65.
55 Galpin, op. cit. p.21.
56 I am indebted to James Tyler for drawing my attention to this important point.
57 Bachmann, op. cit. p.74.
58 They are regularly cited in the footnotes of this chapter.
59 Anthony Baines, 'Ancient and Folk Backgrounds', *Musical Instruments Through the Ages* (Penguin, London 1961) p.216.
60 Bachmann, op. cit. p.55.
61 Ibid. plate 22.
62 Mary Remnant, 'Rebec, Fiddle and Crowd in England', *Proceedings of the Royal Musical Association*, 95 (1969) p.15.
63 Ibid. p.19.
64 Marcuse, op. cit. p.437.
65 Bachmann, op. cit. p.131.
66 Mary Remnant, 'Rebec, Fiddle and Crowd in England', *Proceedings of the Royal Musical Association*, 95 (1969) p.20.
67 Mary Remnant, 'The use of Frets on Rebecs and Mediaeval Fiddles', *Galpin Society Journal*, XXI (1968) p.149.
68 Lines 142–6.
69 Anthony Baines, 'Fifteenth-century Instruments in Tinctoris's De Inventione et Usu Musicae', *Galpin Society Journal*, III (1950) pp.24–5.
70 Bachmann, op. cit. pp.120, 123.
71 Ibid. p.120.
72 Ibid. p.130.
73 Ibid. p.125.
74 Simon Maria Cserba, *Hieronymus de Moravia, Tractatus de Musica* (Regensburg 1935).
75 Bachmann, op. cit. p.80.
76 Mary Remnant, 'Rebec, Fiddle and Crowd in England: Some Further Observations', *Proceedings of the Royal Musical Association*, 96 (1970) pp.149–50.
77 Bachmann, op. cit. p.120.
78 Mary Remnant, 'Rebec, Fiddle and Crowd in England', *Proceedings of the Royal Musical Association*, 95 (1969) pp.16–17.
79 Bachmann, op. cit. pp.85–6.
80 Mary Remnant, 'The Use of Frets on Rebecs and Mediaeval Fiddles', *Galpin Society Journal*, XXI (1968) p.148.
81 Bachmann, op. cit. p.113.
82 Ibid. p.114.
83 Otto Andersson, *The Bowed Harp* (London 1930) pp.110–42.
84 Ibid. p.113.
85 Mary Remnant, 'Rebec, Fiddle and Crowd in England', *Proceedings of the Royal Musical Association*, 95 (1969) p.22.
86 Bachmann, op. cit. pp.114–15.
87 Mary Remnant, 'Rebec, Fiddle and Crowd in England', *Proceedings of the Royal Musical Association*, 95 (1969) p.23.
88 Sachs, op. cit. p.290.
89 Heinrich Glarean, *Dodecachordon* (1547), translated by Clement A. Miller (American Institute of Musicolog[y] 1965).
90 Ibid. pp.87–8.
91 Marcuse, op. cit. pp.542–3.
92 Galpin, op. cit. pp.72–4.

Chapter 5 Percussion

1 See Jeremy Montagu, 'On the Reconstruction of Mediaeval Instruments of Percussion', *Galpin Society Journal*, XXIII (1970) pp.104–14. See also Alan Mynett 'On the reconstruction of a mediaeval tabor', *Early Music*, vol. 1 no. 4 (October 1973) pp.223–7, and James Blades and Jeremy Montagu, 'Capriol's Revenge', *Early Music*, vol. 1 no. 2 (April 1973) pp.84–92.
2 Jeremy Montagu, op. cit. See also his article 'Early percussion techniques', *Early Music*, vol. 2 no. 1 (January 1974) pp.20–4.
3 Jeremy Montagu, 'On the Reconstruction of Mediaeval Instruments of Percussion', *Galpin Society Journal*, XXIII (1970) p.114.
4 Gerald Hayes, 'Musical Instruments', *New Oxford History of Music*, III (O.U.P. London 1960) p.493.
5 James Blades, *Percussion Instruments and their History* (Faber, London 1970) chapters 11 and 12.
6 Ibid., p.223.
7 Hayes, op. cit. p.492.
8 Richard Rastall, 'The Minstrels of the English Royal Households', *R.M.A. Research Chronicle No. 4* (1964) pp.1–41.
9 Francis W. Galpin, *Old English Instruments of Music*, fourth edition revised by Thurston Dart (Methuen, London 1965) p.179.
10 Ibid. p.183.
11 Blades, op. cit. p.226.
12 Ibid. p.227.

not Arbeau, *Orchésographie* (Langres 1588),
lated by Cyril W. Beaumont (London 1925),
blished Dance Horizons (New York, n.d.).
p.41.
l Marcuse, *Musical Instruments: A Comprehensive*
onary (New York 1964) p.508.
Blades, op. cit. plate 81.
. J. de Hen, 'Folk Instruments of Belgium:
I', *Galpin Society Journal*, XXV (1972) pp.105–10.
nits van Waesberghe, *Cymbala* (American Institute
lusicology, Rome 1951) pp.11–17.
iam Smoldon, 'The Music of the Mediaeval
rch Drama', *The Musical Quarterly*, vol. XLVIII
(October 1962) pp.493–4.
ard Rastall, 'Minstrelsy, Church and Clergy in
ieval England', *Proceedings of the Royal Musical*
ciation, 97 (1971) pp.95–8.
sberghe, op. cit. pp.17–18.
olt Schlick, *Spiegel der Orgelmacher und Organisten*
1; ed. P. Smets, Mainz 1937; modern German
on by Ernst Flade, Mainz 1932). See R. Kendall,
es on Arnold Schlick', *Acta musicologica*, XI (1939)
6.
in Mersenne, *Harmonie Universelle* (Paris 1635),
slated by Roger E. Chapman (Martinus Nijhoff,
Hague 1957) p.227.
: Sachs, *The History of Musical Instruments*
rton, New York 1940) p.439.
es, op. cit. p.192.
first medieval mention of the triangle is as an
ument without rings. See Blades, op. cit. p.191.
senne, op. cit. p.548.
. p.547.
idsummer Night's Dream, Act II Scene ii.
es, op. cit. p.193.
senne, op. cit. p.546.
len, op. cit. p.100.
erick Crane, 'The Jew's Harp as Aerophone',
in Society Journal, XXI (1968) pp.66–9.
hael Praetorius, *Syntagma Musicum*, II, 'De
anographia' (Wolfenbüttel 1619), translated by
old Blumenfeld (St Louis 1949) p.6.
senne, op. cit. p.548.
indebted to Miss Madeau Stewart for passing on
suggestion.
cuse, op. cit. pp.264–5.
more information about this fascinating
ument see John Wright, 'Another look into the
nology of the Jew's Harp', *Brussels Museum of*
ical Instruments Bulletin, II (1972) pp.51–9.

apter 6 Woodwind

L. Smithers *The Music and History of the*
que Trumpet before 1721 (Dent. London 1973) p.68.
hony Baines. *Woodwind Instruments and their*
ory (Faber, London 1957) pp.241–2.
Henry VIII's Inventory, 1547, in Francis W.
pin, *Old English Instruments of Music* (fourth
ion, revised by Thurston Dart; Methuen, London
5) pp.215–22.
ry Cart de Lafontaine, *The King's Musick*
vello, London 1909; reprinted Da Capo, New
k 1973) pp.1–42.
ald Hayes, 'Instruments and Instrumental
ation', *New Oxford History of Music*, IV (O.U.P.
don 1968) p.741.
hael Praetorius, *Syntagma Musicum*, II, 'De
anographia' (Wolfenbüttel 1619; translated by
old Blumenfeld, St Louis 1949) p.46.
man Susato, *Danserye* (Antwerp 1551; edited by
Giesbert, two volumes, Schott, Mainz 1936).
cted dances from Holborne's publications are
lable, arranged for recorder consort by various
ors, and published by Schott, London: RMS 496,
750, RMS 752, RMS 754, RMS 533, RMS 1330,
1148. A complete edition, arranged and
sposed for brass instruments, is available from
sica Rara, London.
Anthony Baines, 'Two Cassel Inventories',
pin Society Journal, IV (1951) pp.30–8, and
rcello Castellani, 'A 1593 Veronese Inventory',
pin Society Journal, XXVI (1973) pp.15–24.
pin, op. cit. pp.215–22.
hony Baines, *Woodwind Instruments and their*
ory (Faber, London 1957) p.239.
l. p.240.
also Howard Mayer Brown, *Sixteenth-Century*
rumentation: The Music for the Florentine Intermedii
nerican Institute of Musicology, 1973).
hony Baines, 'James Talbot's Manuscript I. Wind
ruments', *Galpin Society Journal*, I (1948) pp.9–26.
Anthony Baines, *Woodwind Instruments and their*
ory (Faber, London 1957) plate XXII.
l. pp.76–86.
il Marcuse, *Musical Instruments: A Comprehensive*
tionary (New York 1964) p.87.
etorius, op. cit. p.36.
rcuse, op. cit. p.238.
J. S. Manifold, *The Music in English Drama*
ckliff, London 1956) pp.55–63.
Walter L. Woodfill, *Musicians in English Society*
(Princeton University Press, 1953; reprinted Da Capo, New York 1969) p.72. Richard Rastall has suggested that 'wait' refers to a small size of shawm only; see Richard Rastall, 'The Minstrels of the English Royal Household', *RMA Research Chronicle No. 4* (1964) p.5.

22 Marcuse, op. cit. pp.584–5.
23 Ibid. p.411.
24 Woodfill, op. cit. p.235.
25 Anthony Baines, *Woodwind Instruments and their History* (Faber, London 1957) p.268.
26 See Anthony Baines, 'Shawms of the Sardana Coblas', *Galpin Society Journal*, V (1952) pp.9–16.
27 Anthony Baines, *Woodwind Instruments and their History* (Faber, London 1957) p.269.
28 Praetorius, op. cit. p.37.
29 Anthony Baines, *Woodwind Instruments and their History* (Faber, London 1957) p.271. See also Guy Oldham, 'Two Pieces for 5-part Shawm Band', *Music, Libraries and Instruments* (Hinrichsen, London 1961) pp.233–8.
30 Praetorius, op. cit. p.37.
31 Anthony Baines, *Woodwind Instruments and their History* (Faber, London 1957) p.269.
32 Curt Sachs, *The History of Musical Instruments* (Norton, N w York 1940) p.315.
33 Praetorius, op. cit. p.41.
34 Sachs, op. cit. p.315.
35 See Marcuse, op. cit. p.39, and Hayes, op. cit. p.741.
36 Praetorius, op. cit. p.41–2.
37 Lafontaine, op. cit. p.4.
38 Anthony Baines, *Woodwind Instruments and their History* (Faber, London 1957) p.263.
39 Galpin, op. cit. p.220.
40 Lyndesay G. Langwill, *The Bassoon and Contrabassoon* (Benn, London 1965) p.7.
41 Anthony Baines, *European and American Musical Instruments* (Batsford, London 1966) p.109.
42 Langwill, op. cit. p.9.
43 Ibid. p.9.
44 Brown, op. cit. p.126.
45 Langwill, op. cit. pp.7–8.
46 See Francis W. Galpin, 'The Romance of the Phagotum', *Proceedings of the Musical Association*, LXVII (London 1940–1).
47 See William A. Cocks, 'The Phagotum: An Attempt at Reconstruction', *Galpin Society Journal*, XII (1959) pp.49–57.
48 Langwill, op. cit. p.8.
49 Marcuse, op. cit. p.44.
50 See Anthony Baines, *European and American Musical Instruments* (Batsford, London 1966) plate 588.
51 Praetorius, op. cit. p.38.
52 Ibid. p.38 (see p.32 also for the first mention of Schreiber).
53 Langwill, op. cit. pp.31–2. See also Anthony Baines, *European and American Instruments* (Batsford, London 1966) plate 586.
54 H. Jean Hedlund, 'Ensemble Music for Small Bassoons', *Galpin Society Journal*, XI (1958) pp.78–84.
55 For a list of compositions see Langwill, op. cit. pp.72–7.
56 See Marin Mersenne, *Harmonie Universelle* (Paris 1635) pp.243–4.
57 Marcuse, op. cit. p.486.
58 Ibid. p.486.
59 Praetorius, op. cit. p.39.
60 Mersenne, op. cit. pp.372–5.
61 Marcuse, op. cit. p.433.
62 For a reproduction see Marc Pincherle, *An Illustrated History of Music* (Macmillan, London 1963) p.60.
63 For a list of surviving specimens see *Grove's Dictionary of Music and Musicians*, fifth edition (Macmillan, London 1966) vol. VII pp.5–6.
64 Praetorius, op. cit. p.40.
65 Ibid. p.40.
66 Anthony Baines, *European and American Musical Instruments* (Batsford, London 1966) p.98.
67 e.g. Sachs, op. cit. p.319.
68 *Grove's Dictionary of Music and Musicians*, fifth edition (Macmillan, London 1966) vol. VII p.6.
69 Sir John Hawkins, *A General History of the Science and Practice of Music* (1776; reprint of the Novello edition of 1853, Dover, New York 1963) vol. II p.611, footnote.
70 Anthony Baines, *European and American Musical Instruments* (Batsford, London 1966) p.99.
71 Peter Williams, *The European Organ 1450–1850* (Batsford, London 1966) p.274.
72 *Grove's Dictionary of Music and Musicians*, fifth edition (Macmillan, London 1966) vol. II p.547.
73 Anthony Baines, *European and American Musical Instruments* (Batsford, London 1966) p.97.
74 See Marcus Wells, 'The crumhorn: historical sources', *Early Music*, vol. 1 no. 3 (1973) pp.139–41.
75 See Bernard Thomas, 'An introduction to the crumhorn repertoire', *Early Music*, vol. 1 no. 3 (1973) p.142.
76 Ibid. pp.142–6.
77 For a modern edition see Andrew C. Minor and Bonner Mitchell, *A Renaissance Entertainment* (University of Missouri Press, Columbus, Missouri) pp.247–62.
78 Brown, op. cit. p.90.
79 Ibid. p.99.
80 Ibid. p.103.
81 Edited by Otto Gombosi in *Das Chorwerk*, no. 6 (Möseler, Wolfenbüttel 1931).
82 *Grove's Dictionary of Music and Musicians*, fifth edition (Macmillan, London 1966) vol. II p.548.
83 Edited by Günther Oberst, *Gesamtausgabe der Musikalischen Werke von Michael Praetorius*, XV (Möseler, Wolfenbüttel n.d.) pp.314–15.
84 Ibid. p.XI.
85 Brown, op. cit. p.69.
86 Edited by Bernard Thomas, London Pro Musica, LPM RB1 (London 1972).
87 Bernard Thomas, 'An introduction to the crumhorn repertoire', *Early Music*, vol. 1 no. 3 (1973) p.143.
88 Galpin, op. cit. pp.215–22.
89 Hayes, op. cit. p.741.
90 One *bransle* is printed in *Grove's Dictionary of Music and Musicians*, fifth edition (Macmillan, London 1966) vol. II p.548.
91 See Anthony Baines, *European and American Musical Instruments* (Batsford, London 1966) plate 520.
92 Praetorius, op. cit. p.41.
93 Ibid. p.41.
94 Frank Harrison and Joan Rimmer, *European Musical Instruments* (Studio Vista, London 1964) p.25.
95 Anthony Baines, *European and American Musical Instruments* (Batsford, London 1966) p.97.
96 Harrison and Rimmer, op. cit. p.25.
97 For an interesting discussion of the problem of the *dolzaina*, see Brown, op. cit. pp.70–2.
98 Ibid. p.72.
99 Praetorius, op. cit. p.39.
100 I have borrowed the conjectural singular form *doppione* from Marcuse, op. cit. p.150. The original sources mention the plural, *doppioni*, only.
101 Praetorius, op. cit. p.39.
102 Rainer Weber and J. H. van der Meer, 'Some Facts and Guesses concerning *Doppioni*', *Galpin Society Journal*, XXV (1972) pp.25–6.
103 Ibid. pp.22–9.
104 Marcuse, op. cit. p.436.
105 One instrument from each collection is illustrated in Anthony Baines, *European and American Musical Instruments* (Batsford, London 1966) plates 521–3. The Prague instruments are all illustrated in Alexander Buchner, *Musical Instruments: An Illustrated History* (Artia, Prague 1973; English edition published by Octopus Books, London 1973) plates 96, 98–100.
106 Mersenne, op. cit. pp.380–2.
107 Anthony Baines, *Woodwind Instruments and their History* (Faber, London 1957) p.258.
108 Sachs, op. cit. p.322.
109 Praetorius, op. cit. p.42.
110 Ibid. p.42.
111 Sachs, op. cit. p.323.
112 See chapter 1, p.10.
113 Galpin, op. cit. pp.215–22.
114 Woodfill, op. cit. p.299.
115 Francis Collinson, *The Bagpipe* (Routledge and Kegan Paul, London 1975) p.108.
116 Ibid. p.98.
117 Ibid. p.115.
118 Praetorius, op. cit. p.43.
119 Anthony Baines, *Bagpipes* (Pitt Rivers Museum, University of Oxford, Occasional Papers on Technology, 9, Oxford 1960), and Collinson, op. cit.
120 Praetorius, op. cit. p.33.
121 In his *Epitome Musical* (Lyon 1556). See Edgar Hunt, *The Recorder and its Music* (Herbert Jenkins, London 1962) p.37.
122 See Joscelyn Godwin, 'The Renaissance Flute', *The Consort*, Annual Journal of the Dolmetsch Foundation, 28 (1972) p.76.
123 Hunt, op. cit. p.29.
124 Galpin, op. cit. pp.215–22.
125 Lafontaine, op. cit. p.45.
126 Thomas Morley, *First Book of Consort Lessons* (edited by Sydney Beck, Peters, London 1959).
127 See Ian Harwood, 'Rosseter's *Lessons for Consort* of 1609', *Lute Society Journal* (1965) pp.15–23.
128 Although the term 'broken consort' properly belongs to the mid-seventeenth century, it has become common practice today to use it for the 6-part ensemble of Morley's *Consort Lessons*, particularly since Sydney Beck's use of it in his introduction to the edition cited above.
129 I am indebted to Ian Harwood for this information.
130 See Sydney Beck's introduction to Morley, op. cit. pp.23, 40.
131 Ibid. p.23.
132 See chapter 1, p.11.
133 First occurrence 1514. See Marcuse, op. cit. p.190.
134 Marcuse, op. cit. p.463.
135 Praetorius, op. cit. p.21.
136 Lawrence Wright, 'Renaissance recorder music', *Recorder and Music Magazine*, vol. 1 no. 9 (1965) p.265.
137 *Fleiten* and *schwieglen* must refer to flutes and recorders. Although *schwegel* often meant tabor-pipe, such a meaning is unlikely here.
138 For a modern edition of all the pieces involving recorder and flute from the second of the two collections see Bernard Thomas (ed.), *Pierre Attaingnant: fourteen chansons 1533* (London Pro Musica Edition, LPM PC1, London 1972).
139 See Bernard Thomas's introduction to his edition cited above, p.2.
140 Claudio Monteverdi, *Vesperae Beatae Mariae Virginis* (1610; edited by Gottfried Wolters, Möseler, Wolfenbüttel 1966).
141 The word *pifara*, found in the second part, is surely a mistake: no form of shawm could be intended here.
142 Jacob van Eyck, *Der Fluyten Lust-hof* (1646; edited by Gerrit Vellekoop, 3 vols.; Muziekuitgeverij Ixijzet, Amsterdam 1957).
143 Hunt, op. cit. p.37.
144 Godwin, op. cit. p.75.
145 Lawrence Wright, 'The Recorder Consort in the Renaissance', *Recorder and Music Magazine*, vol. 1 no. 6 (1964) p.179.
146 Godwin, op. cit. pp.70–81.
147 Bernard Thomas, 'The renaissance flute', *Early Music*, vol. 3 no. 1 (1975) pp.2–10.
148 Anthony Baines, 'Two Cassel Inventories', *Galpin Society Journal*, IV (1951) pp.30–8.
149 Mersenne, op. cit. p.312.
150 Godwin, op. cit. p.75.
151 Bernard Thomas, 'The renaissance flute', *Early Music*, vol. 3 no. 1 (1975) pp.6–8.
152 Ibid. pp.3–4.
153 Lawrence Wright, 'The Recorder Consort in the Renaissance', *Recorder and Music Magazine*, vol. 1 no. 6 (1964) p.179.
154 Godwin, op. cit. p.72.
155 Ibid. p.74.
156 Robert L. Weaver, 'Sixteenth-Century Instrumentation', *Musical Quarterly*, XLVII no. 3 (1961) p.373.
157 Minor and Mitchell, op. cit. p.276.
158 Weaver, op. cit. p.373.
159 Marcuse, op. cit. p.463.
160 Thoinot Arbeau, *Orchésographie* (Langres 1588; translated by Cyril W. Beaumont, London 1925; republished Dance Horizons, New York n.d.) p.42.
161 Stanley Applebaum (ed.), *The Triumph of Maximilian I* (Dover, New York 1964) p.2.
162 *Hamlet*, Act III Scene ii.
163 Sylvestro Ganassi, *Opera Intitulata Fontegara* (1535; edited by Hildemarie Peter, Robert Lienau, Berlin 1956; English translation by Dorothy Swainson).
164 Edgar Hunt, *The Recorder and its Music* (Herbert Jenkins, London 1972).
165 Praetorius, op. cit. p.34.
166 Hunt, op. cit. pp.41–2.
167 Mersenne, op. cit. p.307.
168 Lawrence Wright, 'The Recorder Consort in the Renaissance', *Recorder and Music Magazine*, vol. 1 no. 6 (1964) p.180.
169 Anthony Baines, *Woodwind Instruments and their History* (Faber, London 1957) p.248.
170 See Hunt, op. cit. plate V, for the instrument minus its keys and fontanelle. See Anthony Baines, *European and American Musical Instruments* (Batsford, London 1966) plate 414, for the instrument with fontanelle, keys, cap, and crook restored.
171 Or possibly D; the exact intended pitch of the instrument is uncertain.
172 See Charles Warren Fox, 'An early duet for recorder and lute', *The Guitar Review*, 9 (1949) pp.34–5.
173 Lawrence Wright, 'Renaissance recorder music', *Recorder and Music Magazine*, vol. 1 no. 9 (1965) p.266.
174 Robert Stevenson, *Spanish Cathedral Music in the Golden Age* (Berkeley and Los Angeles 1961) pp.152–67.
175 Robert Stevenson, 'European Music in 16th-century Guatemala', *Musical Quarterly*, vol. L no. 3 (1964) pp.341–52.
176 Lawrence Wright, 'Renaissance recorder music', *Recorder and Music Magazine*, vol. 1 no. 9 (1965) p.265.
177 Anthony Baines, 'Two Cassel Inventories', *Galpin Society Journal*, IV (1951) p.35.
178 Emanuel Winternitz, 'Keyboards for Wind instruments invented by Leonardo da Vinci', *Aspects of Mediaeval and Renaissance Music* (O.U.P. London 1967) pp.883–8.
179 Ibid. p.888.

Chapter 7 Keyboard

1 Philip James, *Early Keyboard Instruments* (Holland Press, London 1930) p.22.
2 See Howard Mayer Brown, *Instrumental Music printed before 1600* (Harvard University Press, Cambridge, Mass. 1965).
3 Denis Stevens (ed.), *The Mulliner Book*, Musica Britannica, vol. 1, second revised edition (London 1962).
4 J. A. Fuller Maitland and W. Barclay Squire (ed.), *The Fitzwilliam Virginal Book* (Breitkopf and Härtel 1899; reprinted Dover, New York 1963) 2 vols.
5 Stanley Applebaum (ed.), *The Triumph of*

Maximilian I (Dover, New York 1964).

6 Gilbert Chase, *The Music of Spain*, second revised edition (Dover, New York 1959) p.68.

7 Gerald Stares Bedbrook, *Keyboard Music from the Middle Ages to the beginning of the Baroque* (Macmillan, London 1949) pp.107–8.

8 Willi Apel, *Masters of the Keyboard* (Harvard University Press, Cambridge, Mass. 1947) p.55.

9 Howard Mayer Brown, *Sixteenth-Century Instrumentation: The Music for the Florentine Intermedii* (American Institute of Musicology, 1973) p.97.

10 Frank Harrison and Joan Rimmer, *European Musical Instruments* (Studio Vista, London 1964) p.25.

11 Arnolt Schlick, *Spiegel der Orgelmacher unt organisten* (1511), ed. P. Smets (Mainz 1937); modern German version by Ernst Flade (Mainz 1932). See R. Kendall, 'Notes on Arnold Schlick', *Acta musicologica*, XI (1939) pp.136–43.

12 *Grove's Dictionary of Music and Musicians*, fifth edition (Macmillan, London 1966) vol. VIII p.586.

13 Frank Hubbard, *Three Centuries of Harpsichord Making* (Harvard University Press, Cambridge, Mass. 1965) pp.32–3.

14 Michael Praetorius, *Syntagma Musicum*, II, 'De Organographia' (Wolfenbüttel 1619), translated by Harold Blumenfeld (St Louis 1949) pp.63–5.

15 Oliver Strunk, *Source Readings in Music History* (Norton, New York 1950) p.297.

16 William Leslie Sumner, *The Organ*, fourth edition (Macdonald, London 1973) p.53.

17 For a list see Willi Apel, *The History of Keyboard Music to 1700*, translated and revised by Hans Tischler (Indiana University Press, Bloomington 1972) pp.33–4.

18 B. A. Wallner (ed.), *Das Buxheimer Orgelbuch*, Das Erbe Deutsche Musik, vols. XXXVII–IX (1958–9).

19 Double pedalling occurs as early as the *Tablature of Adam of Ileborgh* (1448). See Willi Apel, *The History of Keyboard Music to 1700* (translated and revised by Hans Tischler, Indiana University Press, Bloomington 1972) pp.59–60.

20 Ibid. p.48.

21 For a complete description see Sumner, op. cit. pp.59–60 and 66–7.

22 Willi Apel, *Masters of the Keyboard* (Harvard University Press, Cambridge, Mass. 1947) p.11.

23 Sumner, op. cit. pp.65–6.

24 Praetorius, op. cit., facsimile reprint, ed. Willibald Gurlitt (Bärenreiter, Kassel 1958) p.160.

25 Ibid. p.189.

26 Praetorius, op. cit., translated by Harold Blumenfeld (St Louis 1949) p.73.

27 For a summary of information about the regal see Hugh Mountney, 'The Regal', *Galpin Society Journal*, XXII (1969) pp.3–22.

28 Francis W. Galpin, *Old English Instruments of Music*, fourth edition revised by Thurston Dart (Methuen, London 1965) p.164.

29 Mountney, op. cit. p.3.

30 See Galpin, op. cit. pp.215–22.

31 Praetorius, trans. Blumenfeld, p.62.

32 See Galpin, op. cit. pp.212–5.

33 Galpin, op. cit. p.169.

34 Sybil Marcuse, *Musical Instruments: A Comprehensive Dictionary* (New York 1964) p.53.

35 Ibid. p.442.

36 Praetorius, trans. Blumenfeld, p.74.

37 Ibid. p.75.

38 Mountney, op. cit. p.6. By this time the post must have been in the nature of a sinecure.

39 See Cecil Clutton, 'Arnault's MS.', *Galpin Society Journal*, V (1952) pp.3–8. See also chapter 4, p.24.

40 See Galpin, op. cit. p.91.

41 Willi Apel, *Masters of the Keyboard* (Harvard University Press, Cambridge, Mass. 1947) p.17.

42 Marcuse, op. cit. p.110.

43 Ibid. p.115.

44 Praetorius, trans. Blumenfeld, p.62.

45 Ibid. p.63.

46 For a complete description see Raymond Russell, *The Harpsichord and Clavichord*, second edition, revised by Howard Schott (Faber, London 1973) p.17 and plates 5 and 6.

47 Ibid. pp.42–4.

48 Ibid. pp.44–5.

49 Marcuse, op. cit. p.116.

50 For an illustration and description see James, op. cit. plate XXXIII.

51 Ibid. p.39.

52 Russell, op. cit. p.31.

53 Marin Mersenne, *Harmonie Universelle* (Paris 1635), translated by Roger E. Chapman (Martinus Nijhoff, The Hague 1957) p.165.

54 Marcuse, op. cit. p.117.

55 For an illustration and description see Russell, op. cit. plate 819.

56 Marcuse, op. cit. p.581.

57 For a contemporary account of Queen Elizabeth's playing see James, op. cit. pp.25–6.

58 *Grove's Dictionary of Music and Musicians*, fifth edition (Macmillan, London 1966) vol. IX p.3.

59 Curt Sachs, *The History of Musical Instruments* (Norton, New York 1940) p.335.

60 *Grove's Dictionary of Music and Musicians*, fifth edition (Macmillan, London 1966) vol. IX p.2.

61 Ben Jonson, *The Alchemist*, Act III Scene ii.

62 Praetorius, trans. Blumenfeld, p.67.

63 Hubbard, op. cit. p.73.

64 Ibid. pp.72–3.

65 Marcuse, op. cit. pp.489–91.

66 Praetorius, trans. Blumenfeld, p.62. Praetorius' illustrations, however, do not bear this out.

67 Ibid. pp.67–72.

68 Marcuse, op. cit. p.203.

69 For an illustration and description see Russell, op. cit. plate 103.

70 Galpin, op. cit. p.75.

Chapter 8 Brass

1 See Don L. Smithers, *The Music and History of the Baroque Trumpet before 1721* (Dent, London 1973) pp.50–2.

2 i.e. following the contour of an exponential curve.

3 See Smithers, op. cit. pp.21–3, 51.

4 Ibid. pp.64–6.

5 Sir John Hawkins, *A General History of the Science and Practice of Music* (1776), reprint of the Novello edition of 1853 (Dover, New York 1963) vol. II p.612, footnote.

6 Smithers, op. cit. p.53.

7 Marin Mersenne, *Harmonie Universelle* (Paris 1635), translated by Roger E. Chapman (Martinus Nijhoff, The Hague 1957) p.331.

8 Smithers, op. cit. p.78.

9 Stanley Applebaum (ed.), *The Triumph of Maximilian I* (Dover, New York 1964).

10 See Henry Cart de Lafontaine, *The King's Musick* (London 1909; reprinted Da Capo, New York 1973) pp.1–42.

11 Ibid. pp.12–13.

12 Smithers, op. cit. p.118.

13 Ibid. p.117.

14 Ibid. p.119.

15 Philip Bate, *The Trumpet and Trombone* (Benn, London 1966) p.105.

16 Smithers, op. cit. p.79, footnote.

17 Francis W. Galpin, *Old English Instruments of Music*, fourth edition, revised by Thurston Dart (Methuen, London 1965) p.150.

18 Michael Praetorius, *Syntagma Musicum*, II, 'De Organographia' (Wolfenbüttel 1619), translated by Harold Blumenfeld (St Louis 1949) p.32.

19 Claudio Monteverdi, *L'Orfeo*, ed. Gian Francesco Malipiero, *Tutte le Opere di Claudio Monteverdi*, XI.

20 See Robert Donington, 'Monteverdi's First Opera', *The Monteverdi Companion* (Faber, London 1968) pp.257–8.

21 Praetorius, op. cit. pp.32–3.

22 Girolamo Fantini, *Modo per Imparare a sonare di tromba* (Frankfurt 1638), facsimile edition, Blair Academy Series (The Brass Press, Nashville, Tennessee 1972).

23 R. Morley-Pegge, *The French Horn* (Benn, London 1960) p.8.

24 Mersenne, op. cit. p.318.

25 For a modern edition see Morley-Pegge, op. cit. p.80.

26 For a modern edition see Andrew C. Minor, *Music in Mediaeval and Renaissance Life* (University of Missouri Press, Columbia, Missouri 1964) pp.94–8.

27 See Horace Fitzpatrick, *The Horn and Horn-Playing* (O.U.P. London 1970) p.3.

28 Francis W. Galpin, *A Textbook of European Musical Instruments* (London 1937) p.240. See also Francis W. Galpin, 'The Sackbut, its Evolution and History', *Proceedings of the Musical Association* (London 1906) pp.1–25.

29 Curt Sachs, *The History of Musical Instruments* (Norton, New York 1940) p.326.

30 Sybil Marcuse, *Musical Instruments: A Comprehensive Dictionary* (New York 1964) p.456.

31 Francis W. Galpin, *Old English Instruments of Music*, fourth edition, revised by Thurston Dart (Methuen, London 1965) p.153.

32 Lafontaine, op. cit. pp.1–45.

33 Francis W. Galpin, *Old English Instruments of Music*, fourth edition, revised by Thurston Dart (Methuen, London 1965) p.154.

34 Gerald Hayes, 'Musical Instruments', *New Oxford History of Music*, III (O.U.P. London 1960) pp.425–6.

35 See Smithers, op. cit. p.48.

36 Anthony Baines, 'Fifteenth-century Instruments in Tinctoris's De Inventione et Usu Musicae', *Galpin Society Journal*, III (1950) p.21.

37 Praetorius, op. cit. pp.31–2.

38 Mersenne, op. cit. pp.341–3.

39 Bate, op. cit. p.76.

40 For full details see Howard Mayer Brown, *Instrumental Music printed before 1600* (Harvard University Press, Cambridge, Mass. 1965) p.414. See also Clifford Bartlett and Peter Holman, 'Giovanni Gabrieli: guide to instrumental performance', *Early Music*, vol. 3 no. 1 (1975).

41 For a modern edition see Matthew Locke, *Music for His Majesty's Sackbuts and Cornetts*, transcribed for brass and woodwind ensembles by Anthony Baines (O.U.P. London 1951). For the use of sackbuts and cornetts in the Florentine intermedii see Howard Mayer Brown, *Sixteenth-Century Instrumentation: The Music for the Florentine Intermedii* (American Institute of Musicology, 1973) pp.58–65.

42 Bate, op. cit. p.137.

43 John Wilson, *Roger North on Music* (Novello, London 1959) p.40.

44 Gerald Hayes, 'Instruments and Instrumental Notation', *New Oxford History of Music*, IV (O.U.P. London 1968) p.761.

45 Marcuse, op. cit. p.128.

46 Anthony Baines, *Woodwind Instruments and their History* (Faber, London 1957) p.260.

47 Mersenne, op. cit. p.346.

48 *The Autobiography of Benvenuto Cellini*, translated by George Bull (Penguin, London 1956) p.45.

49 Ibid. pp.45–6.

50 For a rare nineteenth-century example see Anthony Baines, *European and American Musical Instruments* (Batsford, London, 1966) number 669.

51 A mute cornett is listed twice amongst the instruments which played for the marriage banquet of Albert V of Bavaria in 1568. See chapter 7, p.59, and Frank Harrison and Joan Rimmer, *European Musical Instruments* (Studio Vista, London 1964) p.25. See also Howard Mayer Brown, *Sixteenth-Century Instrumentation: The Music for the Florentine Intermedii* (American Institute of Musicology, 1973) pp.63–5.

52 Christopher Monk, 'The Older Brass Instruments', *Musical Instruments Through The Ages* (Penguin, London 1961) p.281.

53 Praetorius, op. cit. p.36.

54 Anthony Baines, *Woodwind Instruments and their History* (Faber, London 1957) p. 261.

55 For a modern edition see Johann Walter, *Kanons*, ed. Wilhelm Ehmann, Hortus Musicus 63 (Bärenreiter, Kassel 1953).

56 Anthony Baines, *Woodwind Instruments and their History* (Faber, London 1957) p.262.

57 Mersenne, op. cit. p.348.

58 Marcuse, op. cit. p.466.

59 Mersenne, op. cit. p.352.

60 See *Grove's Dictionary of Music and Musicians* fifth edition (Macmillan, London 1966) Vol. VII, pp.712–17.

Chapter 9 Strings

1 Harvard University Press, Cambridge, Mass. 1965. See Index III: volumes described, arranged by performing medium, pp.478–80.

2 The projected series of five books by Gerald Hayes, *Musical Instruments and their Music 1500–1750*, was interrupted by the Second World War after only two volumes had appeared. Vol. II, 'The Viols, and other Bowed Instruments' (O.U.P. London 1930), remains the longest study in English of the bowed instruments of this period, although new facts have come to light since then. Much of the fruit of Gerald Hayes' research is to be found in his contributions to volumes III and IV of the *New Oxford History of Music*.

3 See Robert Spencer, 'Three English Lute manuscripts', *Early Music* vol. 3 no. 2 (1975) pp.119–24.

4 See Warwick Edwards, 'The Walsingham Consort Books', *Music and Letters*, vol. 55 no. 2 (1974) pp.209–14.

5 Sydney Beck, (ed.), *The First Book of Consort Lessons* (Peters, New York 1959).

6 See p.53.

7 Walter L. Woodfill, *Musicians in English Society* (Princeton University Press 1953, reprinted Da Capo, New York 1969) p.236.

8 See J. S. Manifold, *The Music in English Drama* (Rockliff, London 1956) pp.73–86.

9 Hamlet, Act III, sc. iii.

10 Oliver Strunk, *Source Readings in Music History* (Norton, New York 1950) p.234.

11 See Emanuel Winternitz, *Musical Instruments and their Symbolism in Western Art* (Faber, London 1967) p.95.

12 Strunk, op. cit. p. 284.

13 Ibid. pp.284–5.

14 Robert Dowland, *Varietie of Lute-Lessons* (facsimile edition, Schott 10441, London 1958). For a discussion of the problems involved see David Mitchell, 'Fretting and Tuning the Lute' in Diana Poulton, *John Dowland* (Faber, London 1972) pp. 450–59.

15 Sylvestro Ganassi, *Regola Rubertina* (Venice 1542/3; facsimile edition, Forni, Bologna 1970) *Lettione Seconda*, Ch. 20.

16 See Djilda Abbott and Ephraim Segerman, 'Strings in the 16th and 17th Centuries', *Galpin Society Journal*, XXVII (1974) pp.48–73.

17 Mentioned as early as Adrian Le Roy's cittern tutor of 1551.

18 Francesco Spinacino, *Intabulatura de Lauto Libro Primo* (Venice 1507; ed. Henry Louis Schmidt III, unpublished Ph.D thesis, 'The First Printed Lute Books . . .' 2 vols., Chapel Hill, North Carolina 1969).

19 See Rudolf Henning, 'German Lute Tablature and Conrad Paumann', *Lute Society Journal*, XV (1973) pp.7–10.

20 Gerald Hayes, 'Instruments and Instrumental Notation', *New Oxford History of Music*, IV (O.U.P. London 1968) pp.773–83.

21 Diana Poulton, *An Introduction to Lute Playing* (Schott, London 1961).

22 Michael Graubart, 'Lutes and Theorboes; their use as Continuo Instruments', *Lute Society Journal*, II (1960) p.29.

23 Ibid. p.30.

24 Ibid. p.32.

25 See pp.21–2.

26 Hayes op. cit. p.727.

27 For some examples see Roslyn Rensch, *The Harp* (Duckworth, London 1969) plates 17–20.

28 See Heinrich Glarean, *Dodecachordon* (1547; translated by Clement A. Miller, American Institute of Musicology, 1965) pp.94–97.

29 Michael Praetorius, *Syntagma Musicum* II, 'De Organographia' (Wolfenbüttel 1619; translated by Harold Blumenfeld, St Louis 1949) p.30.

30 Marin Mersenne, *Harmonie Universelle* (Paris 1635; translated by Roger E. Chapman, Martinus Nijhoff, The Hague 1957) p.217.

31 Anthony Baines, *European and American Musical Instruments* (Batsford, London 1966) p.66.

32 Praetorius, op. cit. p.56.

33 Joan Rimmer, *The Irish Harp* (Eire Cultural Relations Committee, Dublin 1969) p.47.

34 Sydney Beck, Introduction to Thomas Morley, *First Book of Consort Lessons* (Peters, London 1959) p.6.

35 Rimmer, op. cit. p.48.

36 Ibid. pp.41–3.

37 Ibid. p.43.

38 Ibid. p.43.

39 Rensch, op. cit. p.74.

40 Joan Rimmer, 'The Morphology of the Triple Harp', *Galpin Society Journal*, XVIII (1965) p.90.

41 Mersenne, op. cit. p.275.

42 See Joan Rimmer, 'Harps in the Baroque Era', *Proceedings of the Royal Musical Association*, 90 (1963) pp.59–75.

43 See Howard Mayer Brown, *Sixteenth-Century Instrumentation: The Music for the Florentine Intermedii* (American Institute of Musicology 1973) pp.107–35. See also Nigel Fortune, 'Continuo Instruments in Italian Monodies', *Galpin Society Journal*, VI (1953) pp.10–13.

44 Claudio Monteverdi, *L'Orfeo*, ed. Gian Francesco Malipiero, *Tutte le Opere di Claudio Monteverdi*, XI.

45 See Howard Mayer Brown, *Instrumental Music printed before 1600* (Harvard University Press, Cambridge, Mass. 1965) pp.87–9.

46 See Thurston Dart, 'Robert ap Huw's manuscript', *Galpin Society Journal*, XXI (1968) pp. 52–65.

47 See Joan Rimmer, *The Irish Harp* (Eire Cultural Relations Committee, Dublin 1969) p.49.

48 William Lawes, *Select Consort Music* (transcribed and edited by Murray Lefkowitz, *Musica Britannica*, XXI; second revised edition, Stainer and Bell, London 1971).

49 For more details see Joan Rimmer, 'The Morphology of the Triple Harp,' *Galpin Society Journal*, XVIII (1965) pp. 90–103.

50 See Winternitz, op. cit. pp.137–49.

51 Thomas Heywood, *A Woman killed with Kindness*, Act V, sc. iii.

52 *The Taming of the Shrew*, Act II, sc. i.

53 The sonnet is printed complete in Diana Poulton, *John Dowland* (Faber, London 1972) pp.50–51.

54 Dowland's complete lute songs are included in the series *The English School of Lutenist Song Writers*, volumes 1–2, 5–6, 10–11, 12, 14, transcribed and edited by E. H. Fellowes, revised by Thurston Dart (Stainer and Bell, London 1965–9).

55 Diana Poulton, op. cit.

56 Diana Poulton and Basil Lam (ed.), *The Collected Lute Music of John Dowland* (Faber, London 1974).

57 For a partial edition see Helmut Mönkemeyer, 'Joan Ambrosio Dalza Intabulatura, Petrucci, 1508', *Die Tabulatur* vols. 6–8 (Hofmeister, Hofheim am Taunus 1967).

58 Arthur J. Ness (ed.), *The Lute Music of Francesco Canova da Milano* (Harvard University Press, Cambridge, Mass. 1970).

59 Giovanni Antonio Terzi, *Intavolatura di Liuto Libro Primo*, facsimile edition (Monumenta Bergamensia XIV, Bergamo 1964).

60 *Grove's Dictionary of Music and Musicians*, fifth edition (Macmillan, London 1966) vol. V, p.442.

61 Facsimile edition in preparation by Minkoff Reprint, Geneva.

62 For some examples of early lutes see Baines op. cit. plates 159–98. See also Friedmann Hellwig, 'Lute-making in the late 15th and the 16th century', *Lute*

iety Journal*, XVI (1974) pp.24–38.
ove's Dictionary of Music and Musicians*, fifth edition
acmillan, London 1966) vol. v, p.438.
e foregoing information is taken from Michael
nne, 'The Lute', *Musical Instruments Through the
es* (Penguin, London 1961) pp.157–9.
na Poulton, *John Dowland* (Faber, London 1972)
388–9.
Uta Henning, 'The Lute Made Easy: A chapter
n Virdung's *Musica getutscht* (1511)', *Lute Society
rnal*, XV (1973) pp.20–36.
details of lute instruction books see H. M. Brown,
cit. p.479, and *Grove's Dictionary of Music and
sicians*, fifth edition (Macmillan, London 1966)
, v., pp.437–8.
transcription and commentary see Wilburn W.
wcomb (ed.), *Lute Music of Shakespeare's Time*
nnsylvania State University Press, University Park
6).
omas Robinson, *The Schoole of Musicke* (ed. David
nsden; Centre National de la Recherche
entifique, Paris 1971).
Robert Dowland, op. cit. p.14.
etorius, op. cit. pp.49–51.
ove's Dictionary of Music and Musicians*, fifth edition
acmillan, London 1966) vol. v, p.436.
a complete list of books of lute instruction before
o see Brown, op. cit. p.479.
is Newsidler, *Ein Newgeordent Künstlich Lautenbuch*,
36; facsimile edition, GbR-Junghänel-Päffgen-
äffer, Neuss 1974).
cenzo Galilei, *Il Fronimo* (facsimile edition, Forni,
ogna, 1969).
ald Hayes, op. cit. p.730.
toine Francisque, *Trésor d'Orphée* (facsimile edition,
nkoff Reprint, Geneva 1973).
ove's Dictionary of Music and Musicians*, fifth edition
acmillan, London 1966) vol. v., p.436.
neueröffnete Orchestre 1713. See *Grove's Dictionary
Music and Musicians*, fifth edition (Macmillan,
ndon 1966) vol. v, p.437.
omas Mace, *Musick's Monument* (London 1676;
simile reprint, Centre National de la Recherche
entifique, Paris 1966).
d. p.33.
etorius, op. cit. p. 52. But Praetorius seems to be
taken about the *viola bastarda*. See p.89.
ssandro Piccinini, *Intavolatura di Liuto, et di
tarrone* (Bologna 1623; facsimile edition [Forni],
ogna 1962).
Stanley Buetens, 'The Instructions of Alessandro
cinini', *Journal of the Lute Society of America*,
1969) pp.6–17.
nes, op. cit. p.32.
ove's Dictionary of Music and Musicians*, fifth edition
acmillan 1966) vol. VIII, p.410.
Plume's Library, Malden, Essex, pocket book
. 25. I am indebted to Robert Spencer for this
sing reference.
ove's Dictionary of Music and Musicians*, fifth edition
acmillan 1966) vol. VIII, p.411.
nes, op. cit. p.32.
nes, op. cit. plates 176 and 186.
nes, op. cit. p.31.
n indebted to James Tyler for this information.
Nigel Fortune, 'Continuo Instruments in Italian
nodies', *Galpin Society Journal*, VI (1953) pp.10–13.
also Howard Mayer Brown, *Sixteenth-Century
rumentation: The Music for the Florentine Intermedii*
merican Institute of Musicology, 1973).
udio Monteverdi, *L'Orfeo*, ed. Gian Francesco
lipiero, *Tutte le Opere di Claudio Monteverdi*, XI.
e see below p.82.
nes, op. cit. plates 180, 181.
d. p.33.
etorius, op. cit. p.27.
chael Prynne, 'James Talbot's Manuscript: IV.
cked Strings, The Lute Family', *Galpin Society
rnal*, XIV (1961) pp.52–68.
nes, op. cit.; mandora, plates 197–214; colascione,
e 220; angélique, plates 188–90.
d. p.34.
bil Marcuse, *Musical Instruments: A Comprehensive
tionary* (New York 1964) p.328.
nne, op. cit. pp.63 and 67–8.
etorius, op. cit. p.53.
Howard Mayer Brown, *Instrumental Music Printed
re 1600* (Harvard University Press, Cambridge,
ss. 1965) pp.290 and 342.
rcuse, op. cit. p.119.
nes, op. cit. p.37.
rsenne, op. cit. p.145.
nes, op. cit. p.37.
rcuse, op. cit. p.16.
nes, op. cit. p.33.
James Tyler, 'Checklist of music for the cittern',
ly Music*, Volume 2, No. 1 (1974), pp.25–9, and
orge A. Weigand, 'The cittern repertoire',
ly Music*, Vol. 1 No. 2 (1973) pp.81–3. For
ormation about English cittern music see
urston Dart, 'The Cittern and its English Music',
Galpin Society Journal, I (1948) pp.46–63.

112 See Winternitz, op. cit pp.57–65.
113 See Robert Hadaway, 'The cittern', *Early Music*, Vol. 1 No. 2 (1973) pp.77–81.
114 Praetorius, op. cit. p.55.
115 Thomas Dekker, *The Honest Whore*, Part 2, Act V, sc. ii.
116 Ben Jonson, *The Silent Woman*, Act III, sc. ii.
117 Chapter 4, pp.26–7.
118 Winternitz, op. cit. pp.57–65.
119 Praetorius, op. cit. p.28.
120 Ibid. p.28.
121 See Hadaway, op. cit. pp.78–81.
122 Translated by James Tyler from the *Dialogo della musica antica e della moderna* (1581).
123 See Thurston Dart, 'The Cittern and its English Music', *Galpin Society Journal*, I (1948) pp.46–63.
124 Masakata Kanazawa (ed.), *The Complete Works of Anthony Holborne*, Vol. II, Music for Cittern (Harvard University Press, Cambridge, Mass. 1973).
125 Strunk, op. cit. p.429.
126 Marcuse, op. cit. p.96.
127 Strunk, op. cit. p.429.
128 Vol. III, p.148.
129 Praetorius, op. cit. p.55.
130 J. Stow, *Annales, or a general Chronicle of England* (London 1631) p.869.
131 Francis W. Galpin, *Old English Instruments of Music*, fourth edition, revised by Thurston Dart (Methuen, London 1965) p.23.
132 Morrison Comegys Boyd, *Elizabethan Music and Musical Criticism* (Philadelphia 1940) p.15.
133 Donald Gill, 'The Sources of English solo Bandora Music', *Lute Society Journal*, IV (1962) pp.23–7.
134 For a discussion of the evidence see Donald Gill, 'The Orpharion and Bandora', *Galpin Society Journal*, XIII (1960) pp.14–31.
135 Ibid. p.21.
136 Marcuse, op. cit. p.34.
137 Juan Bermudo, *Declaraciòn de Instrumentos Musicales* (1555).
138 See Donald Gill, 'An Orpharion by John Rose', *Lute Society Journal*, II (1960) pp.33–9.
139 Ibid. p.33.
140 Woodfill, op. cit. appendices pp.247–96.
141 Donald Gill, 'The Orpharion and Bandora', *Galpin Society Journal*, XIII (1960) pp.15, 18.
142 Ibid. p.18.
143 Ibid. p.14.
144 Ibid. p.16. The French word *pandore* may sometimes refer to the *mandore*.
145 Ibid. p.16.
146 Praetorius, op. cit. p.54.
147 Gerald Hayes, *The Viols, and other Bowed Instruments*, Musical Instruments and their Music 1500–1750, II (O.U.P. 1930) p.127.
148 Dart, op. cit. p.61.
149 Donald Gill, 'The Orpharion and Bandora', *Galpin Society Journal*, XIII (1960) p.22.
150 Donald Gill, 'James Talbot's Manuscript: V. Plucked Strings – The Wire-strung Fretted Instruments and the Guitar', *Galpin Society Journal*, XV (1962) pp.65–6.
151 Donald Gill, 'The Orpharion and Bandora', *Galpin Society Journal*, XIII (1960) p.22.
152 Baines, op. cit. p.42.
153 Printed in Robert Johnson, *Complete Works for Solo Lute* (ed. Albert Sundermann; O.U.P. London 1972) pp.22–3.
154 Donald Gill, 'James Talbot's Manuscript: V. Plucked Strings – The Wire-strung Fretted Instruments and The Guitar', *Galpin Society Journal*, XV (1962) p.66.
155 Ibid. p.66.
156 Marcuse, op. cit. p.563.
157 James Tyler, 'The renaissance guitar 1500–1650', *Early Music*, vol. 3 no. 4 (1975) p.342.
158 Marcuse, op. cit. p.563.
159 For a description and details of modern editions, see Nigel Fortune, 'Solo Song and Cantata', *The New Oxford History of Music*, IV (O.U.P. London 1968) p.127.
160 Marcuse, op. cit. p.563.
161 In *El Maestro* 1536.
162 *Grove's Dictionary of Music and Musicians*, fifth edition (Macmillan, London 1966) vol. VIII, p.791.
163 See J. B. Trend, *Luis Milan* (O.U.P. London 1915).
164 Luis de Milán, *El Maestro* (Valencia 1536; edited and translated by Charles Jacobs, Pennsylvania State University Press, University Park 1971).
165 Ibid. p.15.
166 Ibid. p.1. Although Milán does not say so, octave stringing in the lower courses seems likely by analogy with other instruments of similar string length.
167 Michael Prynne, 'A Surviving Vihuela de Mano', *Galpin Society Journal*, XVI (1963) pp.22–7.
168 Ibid. p.22.
169 Ibid. plate VII and Baines, op. cit. plates 278–80.
170 James Tyler, 'The renaissance guitar 1500–1650', *Early Music*, vol. 3 no. 4 (1975) pp.341–7.
171 Ibid. pp.346–7.
172 Ibid. p.342.
173 Galpin, op. cit. p.218.
174 Praetorius, op. cit. p.53.
175 Marcuse, op. cit. p.431.
176 James Tyler, 'The renaissance guitar 1500–1650', *Early Music*, vol. 3 no. 4 (1975) pp.341–2.
177 Ibid. p.342.
178 Ibid. p.343.
179 Ibid. p.343.
180 Anthony Baines, 'Fifteenth-century Instruments in Tinctoris's De Inventione et Usu Musicae', *Galpin Society Journal*, III (1950) p.25.
181 James M. Osborn (ed.), *The Autobiography of Thomas Whythorne* (original spelling edition; Clarendon Press, London 1961) p.19.
182 James M. Osborn (ed.), *The Autobiography of Thomas Whythorne* (modern spelling edition; O.U.P., London 1962) pp.21–3.
183 Marcuse, op. cit. p.563.
184 James Tyler, 'The renaissance guitar 1500–1650', *Early Music*, vol. 3 no. 4 (1975) p.343.
185 Ibid. p.344.
186 Marcuse, op. cit. p.34.
187 James Tyler, 'The renaissance guitar 1500–1650', *Early Music*, vol. 3 no. 4 (1975) p.346.
188 Ibid. p.346.
189 Marcuse, op. cit. p.96.
190 James Tyler, 'The renaissance guitar 1500–1650', *Early Music*, vol. 3 no. 4 (1975) p.346.
191 See chapter 4 p.27.
192 After Curt Sachs, *The History of Musical Instruments* (Norton, New York 1941) p.347.
193 Gerald Hayes, 'The Age of Humanism 1540–1630', *The New Oxford History of Music*, IV (O.U.P. London 1968) p.710.
194 Ibid. p.713.
195 See Thurston Dart, 'The Viols', *Musical Instruments Through the Ages* (Penguin Books, London 1961) pp.184–5.
196 Marcuse, op. cit. p.568.
197 Ibid. p.568.
198 Woodfill, op. cit. p.297. Hitherto only two viol players had been listed.
199 See Ian Harwood, 'An introduction to renaissance viols', *Early Music*, Vol. 2 No. 4 (1974) pp.235–46.
200 Gerald Hayes, 'The Viols, and other Bowed Instruments', *Musical Instruments and their Music 1500–1750*, II (O.U.P. London 1930) p.252.
201 See Anthony Baines, *European and American Musical Instruments* (Batsford, London 1966) plates 76–117.
202 Ibid. p.17.
203 Martin Agricola, *Musica instrumentalis deudtsch* (Wittenberg 1528; reprint Breitkopf & Härtel, Leipzig 1896) pp.90–92.
204 Marcuse, op. cit. p.568.
205 Sylvestro Ganassi, *Regola Rubertina* (Venice 1542/3; facsimile reprint, Forni, Bologna 1970).
206 Mersenne, op. cit. p.253.
207 For translated extracts see Gerald Hayes, 'The Viols, and other Bowed Instruments', *Musical Instruments and their Music 1500–1750*, II (O.U.P. London 1930) pp.241–8.
208 Ibid. p.76.
209 Ibid. p.109.
210 Ibid. p.109.
211 Winternitz, op. cit. p.199.
212 *Twelfth Night*, Act I, sc. iii.
213 Manifold, op. cit. p.80.
214 Ibid. p.80.
215 For a good selection see Thurston Dart and William Coates (ed.), *Jacobean Consort Music* (*Musica Britannica* IX, revised edition; Stainer and Bell, London 1962).
216 Henry Purcell, *Fantazias* (Purcell Society Edition XXI, edited by Thurston Dart; Novello, London 1959).
217 Philip Brett (ed.), *Consort Songs* (Musica Britannica XXII; Stainer and Bell, London 1967).
218 Ibid. pp.10–12.
219 Philip Brett (ed.), *Consort Songs*, Collected Works of William Byrd, vol. 15 (Stainer and Bell, London 1970), pp.114–8.
220 Gerald Hayes, 'The Viols, and other Bowed Instruments', *Musical Instruments and their Music 1500–1750*, II (O.U.P. London 1930) p.96.
221 Mace, op. cit. p.245.
222 Praetorius, op. cit. p.44. He says 'a fourth or fifth lower', but from what follows this is clearly a slip and he actually means *higher*.
223 Marcuse, op. cit. p.569.
224 Michael Morrow, '16th-century ensemble viol music', *Early Music*, vol. 2 no. 3 (1974) pp.160–63.
225 Ibid. p.163.
226 Hans Gerle, *Five Pieces for four Viols*, edited by Michael Morrow and Ian Woodfield (Early Music Series, EM. 14; O.U.P. London 1974).
227 Morrow, op. cit. p.163.
228 See Anthony Baines, *European and American Musical Instruments* (Batsford, London 1966) plates 62–5.
229 Francis Baines, 'Der Brummende Violone', *Galpin Society Journal*, XXIII (1970) pp.82–5.
230 Ibid. p.82.
231 Ibid. p.82.
232 Eric Halfpenny, 'A Note on the Genealogy of the Double Bass', *Galpin Society Journal*, I (1948) pp.41–5.
233 Francis Baines, op. cit. pp.84–5.
234 Marcuse, op. cit. p.579.
235 Francis Baines, op. cit. p.85.
236 Marcuse, op. cit. p.579.
237 Francis Baines, op. cit. p.83.
238 Ibid. p.83.
239 See Ernst Hermann Meyer (ed.), *Englische Fantasien*, Hortus Musicus 14 (Bärenreiter, Kassel 1932) pp.8–17.
240 Diego Ortiz, *Tratado de Glosas* (Rome, 1553; edited and translated by Max Schneider, Bärenreiter, Kassel 1961).
241 Christopher Simpson, *The Division-Viol* (London 1665; facsimile edition, ed. Nathalie Dolmetsch, London 1955).
242 Simpson, op. cit. (edition of 1667) pp.1–2.
243 Ibid. p.28.
244 Marcuse, op. cit. p.568.
245 See Frank Traficante, 'Music for the Lyra Viol: The Printed Sources', *Lute Society Journal*, VIII (1966) pp.7–24, and 'Lyra Viol Tunings', *Acta Musicologica*, XLII (1970) pp.183–204. Some examples of lyra viol music are included in Thurston Dart and William Coates (ed.), *Jacobean Consort Music* (Musica Britannica IX; revised edition, Stainer and Bell, London 1962).
246 For an account of Hume, see Peter Warlock, *The English Ayre* (O.U.P. London 1926) pp.82–9, and Colette Harris, 'Tobias Hume – a short biography', *Journal of the Viola de Gamba Society*, vol. 3 (1971) pp.16–18.
247 Tobias Hume, *The First Part of Ayres* (1605; facsimile reprint, Scolar Press, Menston 1969).
248 See Anthony Baines, *European and American Musical Instruments* (Batsford, London 1966) plates 94–6.
249 Praetorius, op. cit. p.47.
250 Praetorius, op. cit. p.47.
251 John Playford, *Musick's Recreation on the Viol, Lyra-Way* (1661) Preface.
252 Girolamo dalla Casa, *Il Vero Modo di diminuir . . .* (Venice 1584; facsimile reprint, Forni, Bologna 1970). I am most grateful to James Tyler for this information about the *viola bastarda*.
253 Anthony Baines, *European and American Musical Instruments* (Batsford, London 1966) p.8.
254 Ibid. plate 10.
255 Marcuse, op. cit. p.311.
256 Gerald Hayes, 'The Viols, and other Bowed Instruments', *Musical Instruments and their Music*, II (O.U.P. London 1930) p.145.
257 Ibid. p.150.
258 Mersenne, op. cit. pp.263–6.
259 Howard Mayer Brown, *Sixteenth-Century Instrumentation: The Music for the Florentine Intermedii* (American Institute of Musicology, 1973) pp.97–100.
260 David Boyden, *The History of Violin Playing* (O.U.P. London 1965) p.90. For a fascinating description and discussion of Striggio's lirone and lirone playing, see Gerolamo Cardano, *De Musica* (*c.* 1546; translated by Clement A. Miller, *Writings on Music*, American Institute of Musicology, Rome 1973).
261 Ibid. pp.16 and 42–3.
262 Ibid. p.9.
263 Winternitz, op. cit. pp.86–98.
264 Ibid. p.86.
265 Ibid. p.95.
266 Ibid. pp.94–5.
267 Ibid. p.95.
268 Boyden, op. cit. p.1.
269 Ibid. p.2.
270 Ibid. p.6.
271 See Boyden, op. cit. pp.7–8, and Winternitz, op. cit. pp.17–18.
272 Boyden, op. cit. pp.15–17.
273 Ibid. p.9.
274 Ibid. pp.15–17.
275 Ibid. pp.42–3.
276 Ibid. p.42.
277 Ibid. p.31.
278 Mersenne, op. cit. pp.243–4.
279 Boyden, op. cit. pp.32–3.
280 Selected dances from Holborne's publication are available, arranged for recorder consort by various editors, and published by Schott, London: RMS 496, RMS 750, RMS 752, RMS 754, RMS 532, RMS 1330, RMS 1148. A complete edition, arranged and transposed for brass instruments, is available from Musica Rara, London.
281 Thomas Morley, *First Book of Consort Lessons* (edited by Sydney Beck; Peters, London 1959).
282 John Dowland, *Lachrimae* (edited by Peter Warlock; O.U.P. London 1927).
283 The music was published in 1582; see Boyden, op. cit. pp.51, 56.
284 Ibid. p.59.
285 Howard Mayer Brown, *Sixteenth-Century Instrumentation: The Music for the Florentine Intermedii* (American Institute of Musicology, 1973) pp.107–32.
286 Winternitz, op. cit. p.198.

Index

compiled by Sheila Borwick